Perception and Imaging

Perception and Imaging

Richard Zakia

Focal Press

Boston, Oxford, Johannesburg, Melbourne, New Delhi, Singapore

Focal Press is an imprint of Butterworth–Heinemann.

Copyright © 1997 by Richard D. Zakia

Ω A member of the Reed Elsevier group

Library of Congress Cataloging-in-Publication Data
Zakia, Richard D.
        Perception and imaging / Richard Zakia.
                p.   cm.
        Rev. ed. of: Perception and photography. 1974, c1975.
        Includes bibliographical references and index.
        ISBN 0-240-80201-2 (paperback : alk.paper)
        1. Composition (Photography) 2. Visual perception. 3. Gestalt psychology. I. Zakia, Richard D. Perception and photography.
        II. Title.
        TR179.Z34   1997
        770' . 1'1—dc20   96-31366
                                                                          CIP

British Library Cataloguing-in-Publication Data
        A catalogue record for this book is available from the British Library.

Cover photo © Barry Myers, 1996.

The publisher offers special discounts on bulk orders of this book.
For information, please contact:
Manager of Special Sales

Butterworth–Heinemann
313 Washington Street
Newton, MA 02158–1626
Tel: 617-928-2500
Fax: 617-928-2620

For information on all Focal Press publications available, contact our World Wide Web home page at: http://www.bh.com/bh/

10 9 8 7 6 5 4 3 2 1

Printed in the United States of America

To Professor Rudolf Arnheim
A dear friend, colleague, and mentor who
has kept the spirit of Gestalt perception alive
in the 20th century.

Contents

Appendix B   Answers to Selected Exercises   265

Bibliography   269

Index   273

Preface

Photography has not changed since its origin escept in its technical aspects which for me are not a major concern. — Henri Cartier-Bresson

This 1978 statement by Henri Cartier-Bresson[1] is worth considering, particularly with the increasingly sophisticated imaging technology available. Regardless of the medium used, how high-tech it might be, and with what speed images can be manipulated, it is the human factor that is important. Pictures, regardless of how they are created and recreated, are intended to be looked at. This brings to the forefront not the technology of imaging, which of course is important, but rather what we might call the "eyenology" (knowledge of the visual process—of seeing).

What is known about vision and the visual process is overwhelming; what is directly applicable to pictures is not, and this is what this book presents as an introduction. We take the eye and how we see for granted. But scientists studying the visual process and working in cognitive science recognize its complexity. Dr. Calvin Mead, a professor of computer science at the California Institute of Technology, puts it this way: "The visual system of a single human being does more image processing than do the entire world's supercomputers."[2] Our visual process is unique and how it functions is still somewhat of a mystery.

This book is a complete revision of *Perception and Photography,* which was primarily concerned with the application of Gestalt laws to photography. These same laws, introduced in the Bauhaus in the early 1900s, influenced artists such as Paul Klee, Josef Albers, and Wassily Kandinsky, who also taught there. In a review of this book Dr. Rudolf Arnheim, a lifetime advocate of the importance of visual perception for the artist and the art educator, in reference to the earlier edition, wrote, "With its treasure of ingeniously selected illustrations, Zakia's book is by far the most useful introduction to the principles of visual perception available to photographers and designers."

This new edition maintains the integrity of the earlier edition and extends it to include the other visual principles important to photographers and other imagers, regardless of the medium (including cinema, computer animation, and multimedia) used to capture, manipulate, reproduce, or display visual information.

The concepts in each chapter have been selected on the basis of the relevance to the perception of visual images and information. This book is an attempt to share with you, the imager, regardless of the technology you use, what I have over many years gleaned from a historical and contemporary parade of others having a like concern. The technology will continue to change, but the process of visual perception will remain essentially the same.

Throughout the preparation of this book, considerable attention has been directed toward having the words and pictures support each other—wordtext and picturetext as one text. As far as possible and practical, the layout of the book addresses this concern.

The quotations included along the side of each page are intended to serve as visual "sound bites" to support the information in the text. Unless otherwise noted, the quotations are from two of my earlier books now out of print (*Perceptual Quotations for Photographers* and *Quotes by Artists for Artists*).[3,4]

Notes

1. *Henri Cartier-Bresson.* A catalogue of 390 of his photographs selected by him for the Scottish Arts Council Exhibition arranged in association with the Victoria Albert Museum in 1978. The introduction is a handwritten statement by Cartier-Bresson titled, "L' Imaginaire d'aprés Nature."

2. Judith Axler Turner, "Figuring Out the Rules for How the Brain Works," *The Chronicle of Higher Education*, October 26, 1988, p. A3.

3. Richard D. Zakia, *Perceptual Quotes for Photographers*, Rochester, NY: Zimzum Press, 1994 [Out of Print].

4. Richard D. Zakia, *Quotes by Artists for Artists*, Rochester, NY: Zimzum Press, 1994 [Out of Print].

Acknowledgments

My thanks to the many people who have assisted me along the way. Dr. Leslie Stroebel, my friend, colleague, and former teacher carefully read the entire text and made many useful suggestions helping to clarify my thinking and writing. Lois Arlidge-Zakia, my wife of many years also read the entire text for grammatical correctness, and Judith Berry provided retouching service. Thanks to the students who helped me in the preparation of some of the graphics: Sunah Ahn, Suzanne Blum, Joe DiGioia, Ya-Li Hsu, Jeff Mariotti, and especially Gary LaCroix. I am also grateful to the many photographers, past and present, whose photographs serve to illuminate the text.

The staff at Focal Press were very helpful and encouraging, especially Karen Speerstra, Marie Lee, and Tammy Harvey. My thanks also to Karen Pratt and the unknown men and women who actually made this book a physical reality.

A very special thanks to all the many artists and writers whom I have quoted throughout the text. Their words add "color" to many of the perceptual ideas presented and emphasize their importance. In the words of Benjamin Disraeli,

> *The wisdom of the wise and the experience of the ages are perpetuated in quotations.*

THE SOUL NEVER THINKS
WITHOUT AN IMAGE

Aristotle

1

Selection

Many an object is not seen, though it falls within our range of visual ray, because it does not come within the range of our intellectual ray, i.e., we are not looking for it. So, in the largest sense, we find only the world we look for.

Henry Thoreau

L'URNE MYSTÉRIEUSE

French print by Pierre Crussaire, 1974 (The Metropolitan Museum of Art). How many profile faces do you find? How long did it take? What visual search strategy did you find yourself using?

GANZFELD

Imagine for a moment a visual world in which there are no visual elements. You are able to see but your visual field is completely homogeneous. The situation described rarely exists in our normal visual world, but you can imagine, for example, being in a very dense fog, looking into a large integrating sphere, or flying an airplane through a dense cloud or at a very high altitude where the sky is completely uniform in brightness. Such imaginary situations approximate a homogeneous visual field, or *Ganzfeld*.

What kind of visual experience does a Ganzfeld provide? You can discover for yourself by covering each eye with a diffusing shell such as a white plastic spoon or half of a table-tennis ball, or, easier but less effective, by just closing your eyelids in a brightly lighted area.

Experiments in which subjects were exposed to a homogeneous visual field for a prolonged length of time revealed some interesting results. The subjects typically attempted to locate something in the visual field to fixate on to provide a reference point. Failing to do so commonly resulted in a feeling of disorientation, and some subjects imagined they saw variations of tone where none existed or even experienced hallucinations or a temporary loss of vision.

Although airplane pilots, car and truck drivers, and skiers have reported disorientation when exposed to a unstructured visual field, it is an uncommon experience, but the phenomenon does emphasize the importance of having something in the visual field to fixate on for the visual system to function properly. Even when the visual field is not completely homogeneous, perception of the observed scene may not be accurate unless appropriate visual cues are also present. An illuminated spherical ball in an otherwise darkened room, for example, can be perceived as being different in size and distance by different observers, and decreasing the size of the ball by releasing air may be perceived by some observers as a ball of constant size moving away from them.

FIGURE–GROUND

The black triangle in the white square in Figure 1.1 represents a simple heterogeneous visual field. The image, like most scenes that we encounter in our daily lives, possesses a pair of distinguishable attributes identified as *figure* and *ground*. Several important observations can be made regarding figure-ground relationships:

The artist tries to wrest truth from the void.

Barnett Newman

Only feeling is real. It was no "empty square" that I had exhibited but rather the feeling of non-objectivity.

Kasimir Malevich

1. Even though the figure and ground are in the same physical plane, the figure often appears nearer to the observer.
2. Figure and ground cannot be seen simultaneously, but can be seen sequentially. (With a little effort you can see a white square with a triangular hole.)
3. Figure usually occupies an area smaller than does ground.
4. Figure is seen as having contour; ground is not.

Look at any land-scape photo-graph. You see the shape of things, the moun-tains and trees and buildings, but not the sky.

Kurt Koffka

 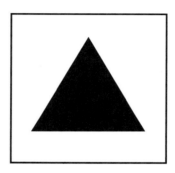

Figure 1.1   Homogeneous and heterogeneous fields

Figure is seen as having form; ground is not three-dimensional (except of course when ground is seen as figure, as in the case of a white square with a triangular hole.)

In the heterogeneous world in which we live, people are free to select what attracts their attention as figure. In a given situation different things will be seen as figure, depending upon a variety of circumstances. For example, different people walking down a main street will, at any instant and depending upon their interests, see:

In a film, video or multimedia, a good musical accompaniment will not call atten-tion to itself.

  a) a clock telling the time of day if they are hurrying to a meeting;
  b) a theater if they are looking for entertainment;
  c) a bus or taxi if they are looking for transportation (Figure 1.2).

Figure 1.2   *Figure-ground is a selective process*

Though clay may be molded into a vase, the utility of the vase lies in what is not there.

Lao Tze

Figure-ground relationships are used in many diagnostic tests. Most of us have taken tests for defective color vision in which we try to group certain color spots to see a number or design. The inability to discriminate among colors and to group some color spots as a figure identifies the presence of defective color vision. Whenever we look at a heterogeneous visual field, that which we see as an object is called *figure*, and the figure is always seen against some background. The first step in perception is distinguishing figure from ground. Sometimes it is easy to see figure against ground; sometimes it is not. What factors contribute to our perception of figure? Why do we see things as we do? A powerful and convincing demonstration of the figure-ground relationship was presented by K. Koffka in 1922 with an equivocal fence design (Figure 1.3).

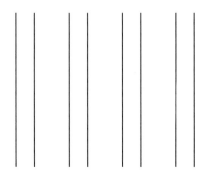

Figure 1.3   *Equivocal fence phenomenon. What do you see?*

Examine the image and describe what you see. Your first impression might well be that of black lines against a white background area. If so, the black lines are figure. A simple concept, isn't it? But let's continue. Look at it a little longer and you might see four narrow white stripes, bars, or fence slats. If you do, they are figure and the remainder of the picture is ground. But why do you see the four narrow stripes as figures? A simple answer is that it is easier to see the narrow stripes, but it explains nothing. A better answer is that the two lines that make up the narrow slat are closer together and, therefore, there is a greater tendency for the viewer to group them into some figure. Three important points can be made here:

1. One can predict that the closer together two elements are, the greater the probability that they will be grouped together and seen as figure. (This is called the law of proximity and will be discussed in more detail later.)
2. It is impossible to have figure without ground. Put differently, what we call background in a picture is very important.
3. It is nearly impossible to see the four narrow slats and the three wide slats simultaneously. You cannot have figure without ground.

Give me mud and I will make the skin of Venus out of it. If you will allow me to surround it as I please.

Eugene Delacroix

The figure-ground relationship in Figure 1.3 can be enhanced by taking a pencil and darkening the narrow stripes.

Figure–Ground Boundary

Figure 1.4 shows a single contour line that serves as a boundary for the facial profile of an old man and the head and torso profile of a woman. It is possible to see either the woman or the man. When the old man is seen it is because the opposite side of the contour line has become ground.

The border line between two adjacent shapes having double functions, the act of tracing such a line is a complicated business. On either side of it, simultaneously a recognizability takes shape.

Maurits Escher

Figure 1.4   Figure-ground boundary. Profile of an old man or head and torso profile of a woman?

The converse, of course, occurs when you see the woman. The contour line is common to both images and is called a *common contour* or a shared contour. Competition for the contour is called *contour rivalry*. The sharing of the common border creates a visual tension, a pull in one direction and then the other, that can only be resolved when the decision is made to see it belonging to one side of the contour or the other. This can readily alternate, giving a dynamic dimension to the image and even some ambiguity. (The importance of closure in resolving contour rivalry and facilitating perception will be seen in Chapter 2, "Gestalt Grouping.")

Graphic Symbols

The concept of figure-ground is used extensively by artists in the design of graphic symbols. Figure 1.5 is an example of an effective use of figure-ground. Initially one might see the black arrowheads pointing like a compass in four directions and later notice the large letter M in the white area.

Figure 1.5   Figure-ground. If you decide that the dark areas are figure, you see arrows. If you decide that the light areas contained within the dark area are figure, you see a letter. (Courtesy Mapco Inc., Tulsa, Oklahoma.)

One reason for this is that the black areas are closed and easier to see as figure than the open white area. Once the letter M is seen as figure it can alternate with the black arrows and be seen as figure or as ground. Both, however, cannot be seen as figure simultaneously. Figure needs a ground area from which to emerge.

What's in a Name?

The term figure-ground may be new to some readers but the concept is well established. Different disciplines seem to have different vocabularies for describing the same concept.

Artists and photographers often refer to it as *positive-negative space*. Such exclusiveness in terminology is further demonstrated in the field of communications engineering where the term *signal-to-noise ratio* is used to quantitatively describe figure-ground relationships. Recognizing that we may be using different words to describe the same concept can improve communications among the various disciplines.

Dynamic interaction in the field decides what becomes a unit, what is excluded from it, what is figure, and what falls back as mere ground.

Wolfgang Kohler

Discipline	Label
Psychology	*Figure-ground*
Art and Photography	*Positive-negative space*
Engineering	*Signal/noise ratio*

Figures 1.6 –1.10 show examples of figure-ground, positive-negative space, and signal/noise ratio from the point of view of a psychologist, an artist, a designer, a photographer, and a photographic and television engineer.

Figure 1.6   Figure-ground (psychologist). Goblet or profiles? Such a figure-ground reversal was first shown by the Danish psychologist Edgar Rubin in 1915.

Figure 1.7   Figure-ground: Positive-negative space (designer). (Design by Steve Chapman and Tom Morin).

Figure 1.8   Figure-ground: Positive-negative space (photographer). Some spots are selected from the complete field of spots and because of their relationship, are grouped to form the shape of a dog. (High contrast photograph by Roger Remington.)

Figure 1.9   Figure-ground: Signal/noise ratio (photographic engineer). Photograph (grainy) by Carl Franz.

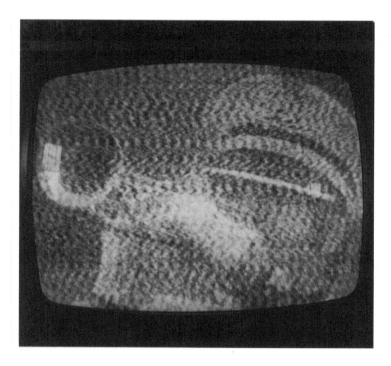

Figure 1.10   Figure-ground: Signal/noise ratio (television engineer).

Increasing the differences between figure and ground (negative and positive space, or signal and noise) increases the vividness of the corresponding perception. In Figure 1.3, for example, we could make it easier for a person to see the narrow stripes as figure by darkening them, thereby increasing the tonal contrast between figure and ground.

(Does darkening the wider stripes change your perception of figure-ground? Try it. Make a few copies of Figure 1.3, darken them differently and test them out with your friends.)

The vase gives form to the void, and music gives form to silence.

Georges Braque

Graininess and Noise

The unhomogeneity of uniformly exposed areas in photographs resulting from the microstructure and clumping of the silver or dye particles that make up the image is identified as *graininess* when viewed or judged subjectively and *granularity* when measured objectively and assigned a number.

The graininess/granularity can also be referred to as *noise* because it reduces the amount of information (signal) that the image conveys to the viewer. The grainy picture therefore has a reduced signal-to-noise ratio. Photographers can increase the signal-to-noise ratio by reducing the graininess level, for example, by selecting a fine-grain film, a fine-grain developer, or a larger-format film that does not require as much magnification as a smaller-format film.

It should be noted, however, that photographers sometimes purposely introduce graininess (or other overall texture pattern) into a photograph for any of various reasons, including to suppress fine-detail information in order to place more emphasis on areas having larger tonal masses, and to produce a desired artistic effect.

Resolution

Resolving power targets are often used in photography to determine how well a photographic system can reproduce repetitive lines that decrease in width and space (spatial frequency). If the number of black bars that can be distinguished as signal are considered, it can be seen how graininess adds to the noise level and makes the visual signal less distinguishable (Figure 1.11).

(A) Good figure-ground (high signal/noise)

(B) Fair figure-ground (moderate signal/noise)

(C) Poor figure-ground (low signal/noise)

Figure 1.11   Resolving power targets as figure-ground.
Increasing amounts of graininess lowers the
signal/noise ratio, causing a poor figure-ground
relationship. (By Carl Franz.)

A similar situation exists with video monitors and when slides
are projected onto a textured screen where the texture is visible
from the normal viewing distance.

Figure–Ground Enhancement

An interesting example of figure-ground enhancement concerns
the photographing of a sonar screen to detect the presence of
submarines during World War II. The image of a submarine on
the screen is dependent upon sound waves being reflected from the
submarine. Since there are also other things in the water reflecting
sound waves, a visual noise pattern is displayed on the screen that
obscures the image of the submarine, making the signal-to-noise
ratio too low to detect it. The following simple and ingenious
technique was used to solve the problem. A series of pictures was
made over a given time period. These pictures were then superimposed and viewed. Since the noise pattern on the sonar screen was
random, the effect of superposition of the pictures was to average
out the noise. The image of the submarine was not random and
was, therefore, enhanced. The total effect was an increase in the
signal-to-noise ratio and an image in which the distinction between
figure and ground was significantly increased.

Photographers and other image makers must continuously be
aware of the concept of figure-ground when making pictures.
Controls at the disposal of photographers to enhance the figure
include:

We can only rec-
ognize what we
know.

E.H. Gombrich

- Camera viewpoint, to select an angle that reveals the desired information about the main subject and also minimizes competition for attention between the background and the subject
- Lighting, to provide detail, form, and texture in the main subject and also to provide tonal separation between the subject and the background
- Focus and depth of field, to obtain a sharp image in the areas of interest and to allow other areas to be rendered less sharp
- Choice of film, including color, normal contrast black-and-white, high contrast, infrared, and fine grain, to provide the desired information about the main subject
- Choice of camera filter, to produce the desired tonal rendering of the subject and tonal separation between the subject and the background, and
- Printing controls, including overall contrast control and selective dodging and burning to emphasize areas of interest and subdue other areas.

One of the most common mistakes made by beginning photographers, cinematographers, and videographers is to ignore the background while concentrating on the main subject, and then discover in the two-dimensional image that the depth in the original scene has collapsed and a background object such as a pole or tree appears to be growing from the head of a person in the foreground (see Figure 2.5).

Nonvisual Figure–Ground

The concept of figure-ground is not limited to visual perception but can be applied to all sensory experiences. You can demonstrate the concept of figure-ground with sound by talking to a friend in a normal voice when there are other sounds in the background; for example, at a cocktail party, in a noisy restaurant, or when a radio is blaring in the same room. Usually it is possible to carry on a conversation. Your voices are figure (signal) and the other sounds are background (noise). In sound recording and sound mixing, minimizing background noise enhances signal quality (acoustical figure), although some background noise is often desired to provide an appropriate atmosphere.

Run your fingers over a surface of some textured object. What you feel is figure, the information that tells you the texture of the surface. The reading of Braille depends on feeling the raised dots and determining their configuration. Carefully sip from a glass of quality wine and attend to the variety of tastes and smells (one at a time) that you can distinguish, such as sweet, mild, flowery, and so on. Professional wine tasters have their own vocabulary—delicate, noble, soft, foxy, mousy, mellow, elegant, robust, simple, and complex. In a room with many different odors you will undoubtedly smell that which is strongest or, depending upon your own individual inclination, that which is least or most familiar. In so doing you are distinguishing figure from ground.

Look for what you don't see.

Rashid Elisha

Since all of our senses are tied into the same central nervous system (information processing center), it is not surprising that a concept such as figure-ground should be valid for all senses. The figure-ground relationship plays an important part in our daily lives. For example, when you purchase any item, be it a car, camera, computer, or a CD player, your choice is pretty much determined by the features that you value most. If you are looking for style when you buy a camera, that becomes figure and you choose the camera on that basis (Figure 1.12).

Figure 1.12   *Viewing system as figure. When choosing a camera in a particular price range, look for one in which the viewing system makes it easy for you to see the picture, otherwise you will miss much of the fun in making photographs. Look for a viewing system that is big and bright and makes focusing easy. Two basic types of viewing systems are shown above, a viewfinder camera (left) and a single reflex camera (right).*

A husband and wife, looking over a furnished model home, will often disagree on the home. A possible reason is that one may be looking at the quality of construction (figure) and the other at overall design as enhanced by the attractive furnishings. Florists

The more one looks, the more one sees. And the more one sees, the better one knows where to look.

Tielhard de Chardin

arranging flowers realize that the space between flowers is as important to the overall effect as the flowers themselves. Portrait photographers and cosmetologists use figure-ground techniques to accentuate the positive features in a face and eliminate the negative.

Many other examples are possible. A special field of psychology looks upon certain mental disorders as the inability of a person to distinguish figure from ground in everyday experiences. Part of the therapy is directed toward helping the patient make these distinctions. The concept of figure-ground enters into most aspects of our daily living.

NOTAN

In his book on composition published in 1919, the artist–teacher Arthur Wesley Dow wrote, "As there is no word in English to express the idea contained in the phrase 'light-dark', I have adopted the Japanese word 'Notan' (dark, light) . . . Chiaroscuro has a similar but more limited meaning . . . Darks and lights in harmonic relations—that is Notan."[1] Dow was very influential in introducing artists to the Oriental style of painting, painting that rarely represents shadows. The painter-photographer Barbara Morgan, who was strongly influenced by his work and teaching, incorporated it in her own work and introduced it into her art courses at the University of California in the early 1900s.

Related masses of dark and light can convey an impression of beauty entirely independent of meaning.

Arthur W. Dow

The importance of negative space (ground) is essential in Notan. As in music, it provides the *interval* between and among the visual elements we call figure. Criteria for one type of Notan involving simply black and white are:

1. The negative space or ground is sufficiently enclosed so that it has a potential shape.
2. Neither figure nor ground is dominant (Figure 1.13). They have a visual balance that allows the viewer to experience a reversibility where figure can become ground and ground, figure.

Figure 1.13   *The graphic symbol for Taoism, representing*
Yin/Yang, is perfectly symmetrical, either half
being seen as figure or ground. The Yin represents
the passive or feminine, and the Yang, the active
or masculine. The sigmoid line that bisects the
circle is a contour common to both the Yin and
Yang. It separates and unites, it represents the
interplay of the two forces around an unchanging
center. Depending upon the context, it represents
other dualities such as light-dark, good-evil,
earth-heaven, birth-death, pain-pleasure.

The works of the Dutch graphic artist, Maurits C. Escher, are
stunning examples of Notan (Figure 1.14).

Figure 1.14   *Sample of the type of patterns traced by M.C.*
Escher. Alhambra (Majolica), 1936.

Escher was influenced by the Moorish mosaics in the Alhambra and in the mosque, La Mezquita, at Cordola during his 1936
trip to Spain, and made detailed sketches. He noticed that the
contour lines were common to both figure and ground and served
a double function. "On either side of it, a figure takes shape
simultaneously. But, as the human mind can't be busy with two

*Every artist was
at first an amateur.*

Ralph Waldo
Emerson

things at the same moment, there must be a quick and continuous jumping from one side to the other. The desire to overcome this fascinating difficulty is perhaps the very reason for my continuing activity in this field."[2]

A properly executed silhouette can serve as Notan if attention is paid to the white background area, the interval or negative space. In 1922, Man Ray made a profile silhouette of his favorite model, Kiki, and titled it "Kiki silhouette." In 1989 the photograph sold for $66,000 at Christie's.

Mozart said at one point that he wasn't so much interested in notes as the space between them.

Harley Parker

VISUAL SEARCH

The term *visual search* implies that the viewer is purposefully looking for something specific (Figure 1.15).

It often happens that what stares us in the face is the most difficult to perceive.

Tielhard de Chardin

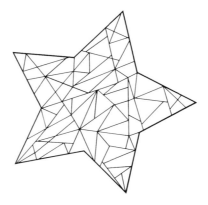

Figure 1.15   *Search the star illustration and find the small star imbedded within the larger star. Try to separate it from the interlacing lines that make up the ground, and see the small star as figure. Shared contours and continuity of line reduce the visual signal-to-noise ratio, and make the task difficult. (See Appendix B, "Answers to Selected Exercises," for the answer.)*

This is distinct from somewhat similar related activities such as selection, scanning, and attention, where the effort is generally less conscious and the objective less definite. The most satisfactory procedure for studying a person's behavior during the searching process is to tell the person exactly what is to be located. This is the procedure used by Ulric Neisser who did extensive research in this area.

Neisser presented his subjects with columns of about fifty different letter groups.[3] The subjects were instructed to look at the columns and as quickly as possible locate the specified target, which had been placed in a randomly selected position. In one experiment the visual search tasks were varied in this way:

Column A   *Find K in one of the letter groups.*

Column B   *Find a letter group that does not have a Q.*

Columns C and D   *Find Z in one of the letter groups.*

Following is a partial listing of the letter groups used by Ulric Neisser in his visual search studies.

Column A	Column B	Column C	Column D
PODC	QLHBMZ	URDGQO	XVWMEI
ZVBP	QMXBJD	GRUQDO	WXVEMI
PEVZ	RVZHSQ	DUZGRO	XMEWIV
SLRA	STFMQZ	UCGROD	MXIVEW
JCEN	RVXSQM	QUCRDO	VEWMIX
ZLRD	MQBJFT	DUCOQG	EMVXWI
XBOD	MVZXLQ	CGRDQU	IVWMEX
PHMU	RTBXQH	UDRCOQ	IEVMWX
ZHFK	BLQSZX	GQCORU	WVZMXE
PNJW	QSVFDJ	GOQUOC	XEMIWV
CQXT	FLDVZT	GDQUOC	WXIMEV
GHNR	BQHMDX	URDCGO	EMWIVX

Actual vision con-stitutes a sam-pling, as though only certain points of the per-ceived figure were fixated while others were neglected.

Jean Piaget

Neisser found that the Column A task required less time than the Column B task—it is easier to locate and identify a specified item than to note its absence, which apparently requires a more careful examination of all of the letters. Somewhat different conditions were established for the visual search task of finding the Z in Columns C and D. You may want to scan the two columns to note whether more time is required to locate the Z in one column than in the other.

Neisser discovered that subjects required less time for Column C where all of the background letters have round-like shapes than

Column D, where both the background letters and the target letter have angular shapes.

A relevant observation for photographers is that a viewer separates figure from ground more easily when their features are distinctively different. It was also found that a person can do multiple search tasks in about the same length of time required for a single task. In less than a month of practice, subjects were able to attend to five different target letters in the same time required for one. This suggests that there are perceptual strategies that can be used, analogous to combining separate small units of information into larger chunks, to make visual search more efficient.

Before tripping the shutter to capture a picture, photographers are commonly expected to perform certain visual search tasks. Such tasks can be divided into two basic categories: to locate the presence of desirable features and to confirm the absence of undesirable features. Thus, in trying to capture a fleeting expression of a person's face during a portrait sitting, a photographer will first perform a visual search to be sure the lighting and the pose are correct and that there are no distracting features such as loose hairs, wrinkled clothing, and light traps. Then, having determined the expression desired, the photographer will continuously monitor the facial features waiting for the decisive moment that stimulates the response to trip the camera shutter. Neisser's research suggests that these are perceptual skills that can be learned when the person knows the specific objective of the search.

CAMOUFLAGE

The word *camouflage* comes from the French word *camoufler*, which means disguise. It is not restricted to the visual sense as evidenced by the use of various products such as perfumes, spices, and "white noise" to disguise smells, tastes, and sounds. Tactile camouflage was reported in the Bible when Jacob stole his brother's inheritance by deceiving his blind father who depended upon touch for identification of his first-born son, Esau, who had hairy arms.

Periods in art such as anamorphosis and cubism, which dealt with the reorganization of objects in ways that contradicted everyday experiences, were involved with visual camouflage.

Anamorphic techniques, which reached their golden age in the 17th and 18th centuries, severely distorted central perspective and the observer was easily deceived by a barely recognizable image. Picasso recognized the relationship between his work and camouflage techniques when, seeing the colors of paint and geometric design used to hide artillery in World War I, he exclaimed, "We are the ones who made this—it's cubism."

There are three basic methods of concealing information. The first is by *blending* the object with the surround—by merging figure with ground. This can be done by lowering the contrast between figure and ground, and making shapes, outlines, forms, surfaces, colors, and the like common to both. In Janet Kaplan's book, *Unexpected Journeys*, she wrote of how the surrealist Mexican painter Remidios Varo embedded a sketch of herself and her lover in one of her paintings, "Embroidering Earth's Mantle."[4] Many artists, past and present, have used camouflage to add intrigue and interest, and a sense of discovery to their work. One of the most interesting is Salvador Dali. One has only to look critically at some advertisements to see how well things can be hidden in a picture to entertain and to persuade. The Sierra Club ad in the exercise section of this chapter is a playful and meaningful example. A second method of camouflage is by *hiding* the object so that it is no longer visible. In the early days of photography the "detective camera," which consisted of a camera hidden in an object such as a flask, cane, or umbrella, allowed the photographer to sneak pictures unobtrusively. Camera miniaturization now provides more subtle ways of concealment. The third way to conceal information is by *deceiving*—for example, by rearranging the figure so that it looks like something else, by dislodging old connections and introducing new configurations, by manipulating correspondences and by changing angles into crossings (Figure 1.16).

I photograph what I do not wish to paint, and I paint what I do not wish to photograph.

Man Ray

The hardest thing to see is what is in front of your eyes.

Johann W. Goethe

(A)   *Blending is the manipulation of visual elements so that figure and ground merge. Two of the rings on the ladder merge with the railings against which they rest and are seen as part of, and a continuation of, the railings. Detail from Belvedere by Escher.*

(B)   *Hiding is the covering up of an object with another. In his
       chapter on Expressionism, Rudolph Arnheim points out
       that a parabolic curve is more gentle than a circular one.[5]
       He shows how Michelangelo in the design of St. Peter's
       transforms two circular contours into a parabola by using
       a lantern to hide the intersecting points of the circles at
       the apex.*

(C)   *Deceiving is the rearranging of visual elements so that
       they form a different gestalt. Sketch of a Bull's Head by
       Picasso. The original is a bronze cast of parts of a bicycle
       in the Galerie Louise Leiris, Paris. Paul Rand wrote
       about this piece, "…to do much with little—to find a
       bull's head in a bicycle seat and handlebars—is another
       aspect of Piccaso's wizardry, his humor, his childlike
       spontaneity, his skill as a punster, and his ability to
       improvise and invent with limited, often surprising
       means."[6]*

Figure 1.16   *Blending, hiding, and deceiving*

Before taking a portrait of a person, cosmetics are often used
to *hide* blemishes on the skin, to dull its shiny surfaces and to add
color to the face. Lipstick and eye makeup are used to *deceive*—the

shape and size of the lips and eyes are altered to enhance the beauty of the face. Makeup artists in photographic studios, television studios, and stage studios are masters in the art of camouflage. Lighting can be used to change the shape, form, surface, and color of objects.

Soft lighting reduces contrast so that small irregularities on the face *blend* into the face. Other examples of camouflage are the use of color filters and soft-focus lenses when taking a photograph, and the use of texture screens and textured papers when printing. In copy work, particularly in the restoration of old photographs, filters perform wonders in optically eliminating unwanted spots, streaks, and stains and hand or electronic retouching is used to eliminate remaining imperfection.

When figures are not sufficiently different from their backgrounds, they blend in with their surroundings and no "thing" is perceived.[10]

Roy R. Behrens

Darks and lights in harmonic relations—that is Notan.

Arthur W. Dow

"Dark and Light," 1926 © Barbara Morgan. (Courtesy Willard and Barbara Morgan archives).

KEY WORDS

camouflage
common contour
contour rivalry
figure-ground
Ganzfeld
interval
Notan
positive-negative space
selection
shared contour
signal-to-noise ratio
visual search

An intention is turning of one's attention toward something. In this sense, perception is directed by intentionality. This can be illustrated by the fact that consciousness consists of a figure-ground constellation.

Rollo May

Selection Exercises

1. Notan

Many corporation logos are excellent examples of Notan. Look through magazines and start a collection of those that appeal to your visual sense. Study them and note the relationship and balance between figure and ground / positive and negative space.

Pacer Products Logo (Courtesy of Fiberboard Pacer Products)

JAL Logo (Courtesy of Japan Airlines)

Create your own personal Notan using a white and dark neutral color (black or gray), or a nonneutral color (red, green, blue, and so on).

2. The Interval

Emphasize the negative space when taking a picture. Learn to see the interval between visual elements as figure. Position your camera in such a way as to make the interval between the positive elements the integral part of your picture. (Remember a camera can move in x, y, z directions, and can also yaw and pitch.)

The anthropologist Edmund Carpenter has written, "In the West, man perceives the objects but not the spaces between. In Japan, the spaces are perceived, named and revered as the *MA*, or intervening interval." Use your camera or computer to give visual reverence to the MA, the interval.

The artist, Piet Mondrian, in his very interesting abstraction, "Flowering Apple Tree" (1912), reveals the hidden beauty in the spaces between the branches of a common tree. The photographer, Aaron Siskind, created a striking Notan by surgically cropping a large billboard sign so that the interval becomes an integral component of the image and creates a complementary duality similar, in a way, to the classic Yin /Yang.[7] (A 90-degree clockwise rotation of the image reveals the letter Siskind might have selectively photographed).

A note of music gains significance from the silence on either side.

Ann Morrow Lindberg

Sketch of Aaron Siskind's "Chicago 30" (1949)

3. Typography

Most of us, when we read the printed word, are seldom aware of the particular style of the type and its careful design. The white space (interval) within a letter form is critical to both the clarity of the letter and its aesthetic quality. No letter stands alone but must coordinate and harmonize with any of the other 26 letters in our alphabet, and the space between letters must work in unison

The artist notoriously selects his items, rejecting all tones, colors, shapes which do not harmonize with each other and with the main purpose of his work.

William James

with each other. If you have a computer, select "Font" and look at the variety of styles available.

Try designing the letters of the initials of your first and last names so that the black letter form harmonizes with the white areas. (Typographic artists work in a large size and then reduce the letter.)

4. Symmetry

You can have some fun with the ad on page 25 by considering a couple questions:

    a)   How many bottles are there in the ad?
    b)   How many drinking glasses are there?

Note the importance of the symmetry in the position of the similar glasses and bottles and the vertical layout of the type in creating a MA, a negative space or ground that can be seen as figure—as having shape. Try creating a similar ad.

5. Camouflage

Play a game of imaging hide-and-seek. Create or capture an image in which something is camouflaged (hidden, blended, rearranged) and have a friend try to find it.

6. More Camouflage

Man cannot discover new oceans unless he has courage to lose sight of the shore.

Andre Gide

Create an image in which the foreground and the background merge. Matisse and others did this by painting objects in the foreground the same color and pattern as those on the wall in the background. In the book, *Veruschka*, by Vera Lehndorff and Holger Trulzsch, a nude model is painted like the background, placed against it, and photographed.[8] The images are stunning with mythological and philosophical impact: animate and inanimate object become one. "The salt doll walks into the water."[9]

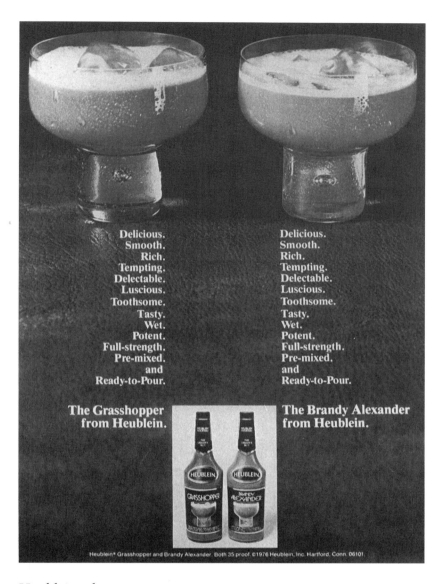

Heublein ad

7. Visual Search: Ecology

The text in the Sierra Club ad on page 26 invites one to search out the animals in the woods. Some are small and some are big, one is running and one is pecking, another with alert ears seems to be watching. Notice how easy it is to find the figures that have a clear background compared to figures that blend with the wooded background. How many "animals" can you locate? You should be able to find at least six, but there are a few more that are more difficult to find since they blend in so well with the wooded ground. How difficult was the task? (A similar task, based on geometric forms, has been used to determine "visual field dependency," which will be discussed in Chapter 8, "Personality.") Make copies of the Sierra Club ad and have friends try separating the figures from the wooded ground.

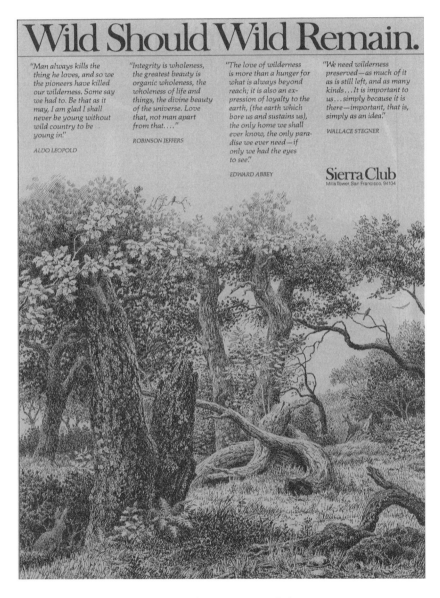

Sierra Club ad. (Courtesy of the Sierra Club.)

8. Verbal Visual Search

When you first look at the 9 × 10 letter matrix below, you see an array of letters. When you are told, however, that these letters make up words and that the words run in various directions (horizontal, vertical, and diagonal), you begin to separate figure from ground. Try it.

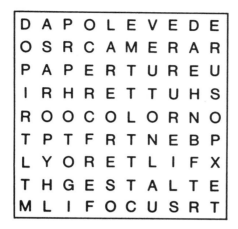

```
D A P O L E V E D E
O S R C A M E R A R
P A P E R T U R E U
I R H R E T T U H S
R O O C O L O R N O
T P T F R T N E B P
L Y O R E T L I F X
T H G E S T A L T E
M L I F O C U S R T
```

Look for these words and draw a circle around them when you find them. (Please note: Some letters are common to more than one word.)

ASA	*FOCUS*
APERTURE	*GESTALT*
CAMERA	*HYPO*
COLOR	*LENS*
DEVELOP	*PHOTO*
EXPOSURE	*SHUTTER*
FILM	*TRIPOD*
FILTER	

Notes

1. Arthur Wesley Dow, *Composition*, Garden City, NY: Doubleday, Page and Co., 1919, p. 53.

2. M.C. Escher, *Escher on Escher*, New York: Abrams, 1989, p. 32.

3. Ulric Neisser, "Visual Search," *Scientific American*, June 1964, p. 210.

4. Janet Kaplan, *Unexpected Journeys*, New York: Abbeville Press, 1988, p. 21.

5. Rudolf Arnheim, *Art and Visual Perception*, Berkeley, CA: University of California Press, 1974, p. 451.

6. Paul Rand, *Design, Form and Chaos*, New York: Yale University Press, 1993, p. 198.

7. Carl Chiarenza, *Aaron Siskind*, New York: Little, Brown, 1982, p. 128.

8. Veruschka, *Veruschka: Transformations*, Boston: Little, Brown, 1985.

9. Joseph Campbell, *The Inner Reaches of Outer Space*, New York: Harper and Row, 1988, p. 73.

10. Roy R. Behrens, *Design in the Visual Arts*, Englewood, NJ: Prentice-Hall, 1984, p. 53.

2
Gestalt Grouping

Abstract formal elements are put together like numbers and letters to make concrete beings or abstract things; in the end a formal cosmos is achieved so much like the creation that a mere breath suffices to transform religion into art.

Paul Klee

Designed by Harvey Carapella

GESTALT

The Gestalt school of psychology, which was originated in Germany about 1912 by Dr. Max Wertheimer, provides us with some simple and convincing evidence about how man organizes and groups visual elements so that they are perceived as wholes. In other words, what you experience when you look at a picture is quite different from what you would experience were you to look at each item in the picture separately.

Field Theory and Gestalt

Max Wertheimer, in carrying on his visual research, was influenced by theories being formulated in physics in the late 1800s and early 1900s. Scientists like Faraday, Helmholtz, and Hertz were studying the physical phenomena of electricity, magnetism, and gravity. They hypothesized that a type of electrical, magnetic, and gravitational "field" existed, and that elements within that field are held together by some type of sympathetic force. The field elements influence one another; they either attract or repel. Their strength is a function of such things as size, position, and nearness.

Wertheimer might have argued that physical fields have their counterpart in psychological fields—in visual fields. The main principle of Gestalt psychology supports this; the way in which an object is perceived is determined by the total context or field in which it exists. Put differently, visual elements within a person's visual field are either attracted to each other (grouped) or repelled (not grouped). The Gestalt laws of *proximity* (nearness), *similarity*, *continuity*, and *closure* describe how grouping occurs within a context or field.

The same Gestalt laws and theory, interestingly enough, were used to study human group dynamics by Kurt Lewin and by Fritz Perls to establish Gestalt Therapy.

We all work, study, play, and worship within a restricted environment or field; relationships can attract or repel. We tend to associate with people who have similar interests and values and are influenced by those closest (with most proximity) to us. We are more at ease if we can continue a task and see it to completion (closure) before undertaking another task.

Unfinished tasks (nonclosure) can cause tension and frustration. We try to keep a healthy outlook by knowing when to "bend with the wind" or "go with the flow" (*Pragnanz* in Gestalt terminology). The key element on which the Gestalt laws are based, *simplicity*, can be the key to a good life.

The whole is different from the sum of its parts.

Synergy—the behavior of whole systems is not predictable from its parts.

Every person experiencing as he does his own solitariness and aloneness longs for union with another. He yearns to participate in a relationship greater than himself.

Rollo May

Photographers out to capture a picture can succeed or fail based not only on their technical or artistic competence but also on their knowledge of and sensitivity to the field in which they are working.

In Gestalt theory, the whole is different from the sum of its parts. In Figure 2.1 a person can choose to see each visual element (the individual letters) separately or as grouped to form an image of a camera. Seeing the camera is seeing the totality of the visual elements. This single figure formed by grouping the visual elements is a gestalt.

Things should be made simple, not simpler.

Albert Einstein

In a gestalt, components interact to such an extent that changes in the whole influence the nature of the parts and vice versa.

Rudolf Arnheim

Figure 2.1   An example of Gestalt—the camera as a whole is different from the sum of the visual elements.

Figure 2.2 is an early example of how an artist grouped a variety of powerful symbols to create a gestalt that serves as a visual metaphor for the suffering caused by the exploits of Napoleon.

GESTALT LAWS

The Gestalt psychologists were especially interested in figure-ground relationships and in the things that help a person to see objects as patterns or "good figure." They suggested a number of principles, but we shall concern ourselves with only four:

1. Proximity
2. Similarity
3. Continuity
4. Closure

These four Gestalt principles or laws are important to conceptualize, for if a photographer knows how a person most probably organizes or groups visual elements when looking at picture, the elements can be arranged to favor or disfavor certain groupings.

It is curious that I always want to group things: a series of sonnets, a series of photographs: whatever rationalizations appear, they originate in urges that are rarely satisfied with single images.

Minor White

Figure 2.2   *"Triump des Jahres 1813" by Johann M. Voltz
(John Hay Library, Brown University). The hat
represents the Prussian eagle digging its claws into
Napoleon. The visual elements that make up the
face are some of the countless dead caused by
Napoleon's lust for fame and power.*

Proximity

*The closer two or more visual elements are, the greater is the
probability that they will be seen as a group or pattern.* Look at
the black dots in Figure 2.3.

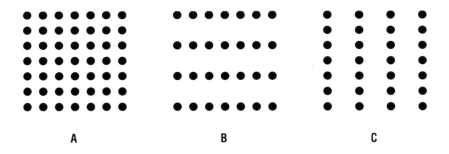

Figure 2.3   *Organization of visual elements according to
proximity.*

Each configuration of dots A, B, and C can be seen as forming a square. Within the square in B, the dots are closer together horizontally than vertically and, therefore, are seen as groups of horizontal rows or as a horizontal movement. It is difficult to see them otherwise. The effect can be enhanced by moving the horizontal dots closer together. Move the dots to a position where they are physically or psychologically (visual resolution) touching and you would see a line.

The dots in C are seen as vertical columns or movements since they are closer together in the vertical direction. Because the dots in A are at equal distances, they are not easily seen as vertical or horizontal.

The dots in A, B, and C in Figure 2.3 demonstrate that using the same visual elements and by simply changing their proximity, a viewer will group them in different ways. As an exercise you might try rearranging the space between the dots so that a person sees groupings of dots in a slant direction. Try some other arrangements. To test your success have your friends look at the arrangements.

Moving the dots in Figure 2.3 closer to each other horizontally facilitated a horizontal grouping of dots; closer vertical proximity facilitated a vertical grouping. If the dots were in a three-dimensional array one could move into greater proximity in the third dimension and facilitate grouping in terms of depth. This is exactly what happens, for example, when photographs are taken of people with no consideration for the background. Since a photograph is a two-dimensional representation, objects in three-dimensional space are brought into closer proximity and tend to be seen as one group. The problem increases as the focal length of the lens and the camera distance increase.

Proximity of objects in space, then, influences the way in which we group visual elements. Since space is three-dimensional, *think* three-dimensionally when preparing to take a picture. Look at Figures 2.4 and 2.5, which illustrate the ways in which objects arrange themselves side by side or front to back.

Spacing between letters or numbers plays an important role in what is seen. Read the words shown here:

    FAT   HER
    HAT   RED
    PEN   TAX

Did you read the letters as six separate words or as three?

Some time ago while browsing in a bookstore I noticed a book with the title *Super-vision.* I was delighted and excited to have found a new book dealing with extraordinary visual phenomena. A scanning of the text was disappointing, however, for it proved

The coherent way of investigating any field is to examine its possible relatedness to other things.

  Frederick Sommer

Proximity is the simplest condition of organization. We hear words in verbal coherency, primarily because of the temporal proximity of their sound elements.

  Gyorgy Kepes

Figure 2.4   Proximity facilitates grouping side by side.

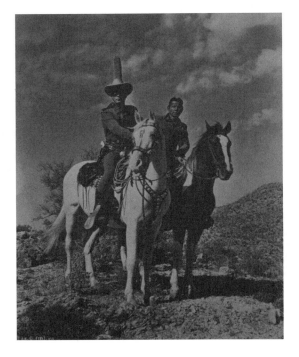

Figure 2.5   Proximity facilitates grouping front to back.

to be a business book on supervision (supervising people). I wondered whether the publisher realized how this particular division of the title on the cover might be perceived by viewers.

Consider the critical nature of horizontal space between the visual elements "1" and "3" shown in Figure 2.6.

| 1 and 3 | 13 | 13 or B? | 13013 or BOB? |

Figure 2.6   Although the visual elements are the same (1 and 3), their changing proximity can cause different perceptions and perhaps even uncertainty and ambiguity.

Proximity and Learning

Information presented side by side or in the same time frame facilitates learning. Not only do we tend to group events that occur close together; we also tend to associate them and make comparisons. This has always been used effectively in advertising and, occasionally, in teaching. Figure 2.7 shows examples of proximity in learning and in advertising.

The proximity of optical units is the simplest condition for a crystallization of unified visual wholes.

Gyorgy Kepes

It is important to note that the eye can make the most critical judgments of whether two visual stimuli are the same or different when the stimuli occur side by side in space. Visual instruments such as densitometers and calorimeters operate on this principle. When you are trying to make a better photographic print you usually compare it side by side with your previous print or some reference print.

One of the most difficult tasks for a photofinisher is to print your color negative so that the print matches a print you have received earlier. When you get the new print and compare it with the previous one you will invariably find differences. One of the first things students learn in color printing is that it is easier to get acceptance of a color print when it is not compared with another print.

In imaging, the more bits, the more tones that can be displayed in a digitized image. A 7-bit image (2^7) can display 128 tones.

Many students are not clear about the relationships that exist among some familiar terms used in photography: *stops, factors, neutral density (ND) filter,* and *exponents*—photographers usually talk about changing camera exposure by stops, realizing that a one-stop change means an increase or decrease by a factor of two.

(A)

(B)

Figure 2.7   (A) Proximity facilitates learning by comparison.
Note how the white shadows in the negative and
the black shadows in the positive affect the design
imprint. In one case the imprint looks raised and in
the other depressed. Rotate the book 180 degrees
and observe what happens. Make comparisons at
different angles. At what angle does the imprint
reverse itself? (B) Proximity facilitates comparisons
in advertising. Photography by James Katzel.
(Courtesy Honeywell Photographic Products.)

How is this related to exponents to the base 2 and to ND filters
in 0.30-density increments? Making a table in which exponents,
factors, stops, and ND filters are in close proximity helps one to
see and remember the relationships.

Relationships

Factors	Exponents (Base 2)	Stops	Natural Density Filter
1	2^0	0	0.00
2	2^1	1	0.30
4	2^2	2	0.60
8	2^3	3	0.90
16	2^4	4	1.20

Note that stops are exponents to the base 2. Factors are the numbers that result from raising base 2 to a power (exponent). The factor doubles each time the exponent increases by 1. The relationships among exponents (base 2), factors, and stops seem logical, but the increments for ND filters do not. The reason is that density values are based on exponents to base 10. It can be somewhat confusing, but all you need to remember is that a density change of 0.30 is 1 stop (0.15 is a 1/2 stop change). Mathematically, $2^1 = 2$. Density values for all filters are log 10 values, and logarithms are exponents $10^{0.30} = 2$.

Whatever favors organization and comparison will also favor learning, retention, and recall. Thus the law of proximity is equivalent to what educators call "association by contiguity." In terms of information processing, pictures presented side by side and in proximity require less memory storage and retrieval. Pictures presented in a *time* sequence rely more on memory, and the longer the time delay the more probable the loss of information or distortion of information in memory.

Proximity and Area

The smaller an area or space, the greater the probability that it will be seen as figure. This statement is similar to the one made about proximity. Every area is bounded by an edge or line. The greater the proximity of these edges or lines the greater the probability that the area within the lines will be seen as figure. This was demonstrated in Chapter 1 in the equivocal fence diagram (Figure 1.3).

Figure 2.8 shows how proximity of lines determines the size of the enclosed area and how proximity facilitates the selective segregation of the smaller visual segments from the larger so that the smaller segments are seen as figure.

.30 neutral density filters gives you half the light

.30 neutral density filters gives you half the light. An average outdoor scene has a brightness ratio of 128:1 (seven stops, seven zones, 2^7).

Figure 2.8   *The closer the radial lines, the smaller the enclosed*
             area and therefore the greater the probability it
             will be seen as figure. It is easier to see the smaller
             segments as figure against the larger segments as
             ground, even when the image is rotated so that the
             larger areas are vertical and horizontal.

Notice also that it is much easier to see the smaller segments
as figure in the middle illustration than in the other two. This
demonstrates the importance of contrast and how it can be used
along with area to increase or decrease the ease with which certain
visual patterns are seen as figure. An example of the effective use
of area and contrast in the design of graphics is shown in Figure
2.9.

Figure 2.9   *Area and contrast play an important role in the*
             design of graphics.

Temporal Proximity

Proximity is not limited to the spatial arrangement of things. It also applies to the temporal arrangement of events. Things that occur close together in time will tend to be grouped together. Tell someone that you are going to spell a word aloud and that you want them to identify the word. The person will think it an easy task and indeed it is unless you pause between certain letters. If the word CHO PHO USE is spelled aloud in groups of three letters, it will be difficult to identify the word unless the listener repeats the letters so that the pauses between all letters are equal. This experiment has been tried with a number of people and few were able to identify the word without repeating the letters or writing them down without the pauses.

Music provides yet another example of the importance of proximity to perception. The sound of middle C on a piano represents a frequency of 262 cycles per second. If the frequency is increased, the sound vibrations occur closer together in time and the acoustical experience is an increase in pitch.

Motion picture and television editing require careful place-ment of frames so that their projection in time will favor grouping. One of the major reasons for editing is to facilitate the perceptual grouping of elements that occur in time and space. Events that occur close together in time and space tend to be grouped together.

Apply the Gestalt law of proximity to the arrangements of things you photograph and design and you can encourage people to see the relationships you want them to see. For the most part they will be unaware of how you arrange the visual elements since spatial and temporal proximity are natural ways for us to group things. When things are experienced as grouped, we see the whole and not the individual elements that make up the whole.

Black on white provides a good level of visual contrast. The result is a high signal-to-noise ratio—a strong figure-ground rela-tionship. What is seen as figure, however, depends not only on contrast but also on area. In Figure 2.10A, the areas of the black bars and white bars are the same and it is equally probably that either will be seen as figure. In Figure 2.10B, reading from top to bottom, figure evolves from a black line to a white line as area changes. Note, however, that about midway both the black and white bars are of equal area and there is a perceptual situation similar to Figure 2.10A.

In Hopi, there is no word which is equivalent to "time" in English. Because both time and space are in-extricably bound up in each other, elimination of the time dimension alters the spatial one as well.

Edward Hall

(A)   (B)

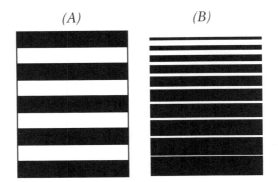

Figure 2.10   What is seen as figure is determined by area and influenced by contrast.

Another example of the visual relationship between area and contrast is the halftone graphic-arts screen shown in Figure 2.11. Reading from left to right, the figure changes from a black dot to a white dot.

Figure 2.11   A halftone screen in which small dot areas, whether black or white, are seen as figure.

Area and contrast influence what is first seen as figure.

Many other factors, of course, will influence what a person sees as figure—things such as shape, texture, color, closed areas versus open areas, pattern, expectancy, and so on. Figures 2.10 and 2.11 emphasize two important variables in design and perception—area and contrast. Add other variables to these illustrations such as color, and what is seen as figure can change.

Similarity

Visual elements that are similar (in shape, size, color, movement, and so on) tend to be seen as related. When we see things that are related we naturally group them and therefore see them as patterns. This is readily observable in Figure 2.12.

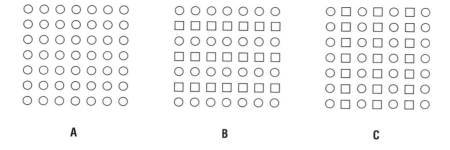

A   B   C

*Figure 2.12   Organization of visual elements according to the
                law of similarity (shape).*

The overall configuration for A, B, and C remains square, but
B is now seen as having horizontal rows of alternating circles and
squares and C is seen as having vertical columns of alternating
circles and squares. Since all the visual elements in Figure 2.12A
are similar and have the same proximity, no patterns are seen
within the array. Note that the proximity of the visual elements in
B and C remains constant but that the grouping of these elements
in alternating vertical and horizontal directions is based on the
similarity of circles or squares. This demonstrates the influence of
similar elements in the way we see and group things. It also
suggests that similarity can be a stronger force than proximity in
perceptual grouping. Additional examples are presented in Figure
2.13.

*Similarity is a pre-
requisite for notic-
ing difference.*

Rudolf Arnheim

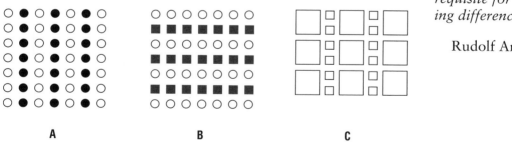

A   B   C

*Figure 2.13   Additional examples of the ease with which
                similar visual elements are grouped.*

Refer to Figure 2.8 and note how natural it is to group the four
small (or large) pie-shaped segments together and how extremely
difficult it is to group dissimilar segments such as a small segment
and two large segments. There are many different patterns that
one could abstract from Figure 2.8 by various groupings of small

and large pie-shaped segments. It is relatively easy to do this by using pencil and paper but extremely difficult to do just by looking. Try it!

Similarity of Shape

Visual elements that have similar shapes such as those shown in the skeleton of a leaf tend to be grouped together. Because of the similarity and proximity of the curved lines they are easily seen together to form a pattern. Such repetition of similar lines can be thought of as a visual "beat"—a visual counterpart of the rhythm that is associated with motion and sound.

Figure 2.14A shows how a particular camera angle and lens serve to record a picture in which three objects group to make an interesting composition.

All three objects are similar in form but different in size, which gives perspective and depth to the image. The interval between the first and second objects (proximity) helps to keep the composition from losing its interest. One can find many images in which three persons standing side by side are grouped in a similar manner—Figure 2.14B is one example.

In Figure 2.14B, three young German farmers, dressed alike in their dark suits and white shirts, stand posed, looking directly at the camera. They are positioned in a way similar to that in Figure 2.14A. The proximity between the man on the left and the two on the right is critical and adds interest to the arrangement. It is integral to the composition—to the visual syntax. The play and counterpoint between the similarity and dissimilarity provides additional interest. All three men have similar suits, hats, canes, and look directly at the viewer.

The farmer on the left, however, strikes a dissimilar pose. His hat and cane are tilted, a cigarette dangles from his mouth, and he seems to have a different expression on his face, but his body posture is similar to that of the other two men. Note also the left hand of the man in the middle. It is a powerful working man's hand and it stands out prominently as a figure-ground element giving the composition further interest. Was August Sander aware of all this? I doubt it, but I do believe he may have been unconsciously "aware" of it. He has captured a decisive and historical moment in time that we now share.

Henri Cartier-Bresson's 1945 photograph of two prominent scientists who are husband and wife titled "Irene and Frederick Joliot-Curie" is a tender visual display of how a loving married couple grow more alike as their marriage matures.[1] Bresson reveals this by capturing their similar facial expressions, hand and body gestures, and their similarity of dress.

(A)

(B)

Figure 2.14   *(A) Eroded Sandstones, Monument Park,
Colorado, by William H. Jackson. George Eastman
House; (B) Jungbauern Westerwald (Young
Farmers), 1914, August Sander, George Eastman
House.*

Similarity and Repetition

The familiar painting "American Gothic" by Grant Wood provides some interesting observations on similarity (Figure 2.15).

Figure 2.15   *"American Gothic," by Grant Wood (The Art Institute of Chicago).*

How many times do you think a person should see a movie to catch everything in it?...Three times, at least, to pick out all the details and the intentions behind them.

Alfred Hitchcock

Perhaps the most obvious is the shape of the three-pronged pitchfork and the "three-pronged" design in the man's overalls just to the right of the pitchfork.

One can also find the shape elements of the pitchfork rhythmically repeated in several places—the upper part of the woman's apron and the white collars and chin lines of the wife and husband. Other "tridents" can also be found in the painting:

1. The three vertical stripes in the man's shirt group with the three-pronged design in the overalls;
2. Both faces are shaded in such a way that it is easy to group the nose and the area below it into the center prong of a trident (the outer prongs being the outer facial contour);
3. The three parallel roof lines on the extreme left and right; and
4. The three parallel fingers on the man's hand.

If one assumes that the pitchfork could be symbolic of Satan, then the expressions on the faces of the people in the picture take on new meanings and one can understand why this classic portrait of rural Americans precipitated an uproar among Midwesterners when it was first exhibited at the Art Institute of Chicago in 1930.

In Figure 2.16 the positions of the hands, fingers, and pens are similar, as are the size and shape of the pens and the angles at which they are held. The photographer has been careful to show the same side of both pens. Even the shadows from the pen points are similar. In addition, the pens are in close proximity. Similarity of visual elements and proximity facilitate grouping.

Merely copying the object is not art. What counts is to express the emotion called forth in you, the feeling awakened....

Henri Matisse

Figure 2.16   Similarity of size, position, and shape, and dissimilarity of hands. (Courtesy Parker Pen Company.)

Similarity and Proximity

Photographers sometimes use symbolic associations to provide similarity and grouping. Figure 2.17 shows how an advertiser used a photograph of a cat sleeping curled up alongside an air conditioner that has a unit similar in shape to that of the cat. The similarity of shapes facilitates grouping, which in turn enhances association between the familiar quietness of the sleeping cat and the implied quietness of the air conditioner.

Figure 2.17   Similarity of shape and projected similarity of meaning. (Courtesy York Division Borg-Warner Corporation.)

> *Metaphor joins dissimilar experiences by finding the image or the symbol that united them at some deeper emotional level of meaning.*
>
> Jerome Bruner

In his book "East 100th Street," Bruce Davidson* has a photograph of a child partially naked with straggly hair and head tilted standing limp on a fire escape against a steel bar railing that takes the form of a cross (Figure 2.17A).[2] It serves as a reminder (for many) of the paintings of the crucifixion of Jesus, hanging partially naked and limp on a cross. By using similar design elements the photographer facilitates our grouping of these two

---

* In a conversation with Bruce Davidson on September 5, 1996 he provided this additional information regarding his photograph.

The photograph should be seen in context of the others in the book. It is a statement about the space in which the people of East 100th Street lived, their rooms, vacant lots, alley ways, as well as the relation of shadows and shapes. Symbolically, yes, the photograph can be seen as a Christ figure. Beyond that it is a child playing on a fire escape. The face is in deep shadow with little to no detail, the half light, half dark of her environment.

The time context is also a factor. The photographs were made in the 1960s, a time in which man was exploring outer space. The photograph is about inner space.

separate events (the photograph and what is in memory). When this occurs the photograph takes on a much deeper meaning and feeling. If one sees the child as representing innocence, then the question might be asked, "Who is responsible for the child's 'crucifixion'?" A nonreligious interpretation might be that the child, representing innocence and humanity, is being imprisoned by the "bars" of the fire escape. Who is responsible for this imprisonment? Powerful images such as this are layered, have archetypal reference, and, therefore, live on and on.

Some elements are seen together because they are close to each other; others are bound together because they are similar in size, direction, shape.

Gyorgy Kepes

Figure 2.17A   *"Untitled" by Bruce Davidson. One of a series of photographs for his book, "East 100th Street," taken by Bruce Davidson in the Harlem area in New York City in 1966.*

Symmetry and Asymmetry

Split an apple down the center and you have two very similar halves. This is an example of bilateral symmetry. It occurs frequently in nature—man being a prime example with symmetrical features such as the face, arms, hands, legs, and the not-so-familiar bilateral brain.

There are various types of symmetry, which can be described in terms of design elements such as letters and symbols. Place a mirror on one side of and at a right angle to the letter A and the reflection is unchanged, while the reflection of the letter D remains unchanged only if the mirror is placed above or below the letter.

In both cases, *reflection* is used to describe this type of symmetry. Letters such as N, H, and X can be rotated 180 degrees (upside down) and appear the same. This is called *two-fold symmetry*, while a symbol such as a plus sign (+) possesses *four-fold symmetry*, appearing identical in four different rotations.

A circle remains the same regardless of rotation or reflection and therefore represents complete symmetry.

Symmetry can be considered a special case of similarity. Visual elements that are symmetrical provide for visual balance—for a "good gestalt." The more symmetrical an area is, the greater the tendency is to group it and see it as figure. Figure 2.18 shows how one readily groups symmetrical shapes to see the vertical areas 1, 3, and 5 as figure.

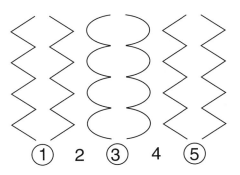

Figure 2.18   Symmetry facilitates grouping.

Photograph by Charlotte Marine.

It is extremely difficult to see vertical areas 2 and 4 as figure since their vertical boundaries are not symmetrical. The more symmetrical an area is, the more readily it is seen as figure. Figure 2.18 represents a simple situation to illustrate the importance of symmetry to grouping and asymmetry to nongrouping. Much of what we encounter in life is in some way symmetrical, including our bodies. In the visual world, symmetry of line or shape is also accompanied by other attributes such as color, tone, texture, and form.

Symmetry also has an effect on our perception of depth. Generally speaking, the more symmetrical a design the more it is seen as two-dimensional.

In printing a photograph or showing slides, a problem can occur if the emulsion side of the image is positioned away from the enlarger or projector lens rather than toward it. Surprisingly enough, this is a problem only with pictures that include man-made objects, for in nature it is difficult to identify left and right sides.

When making montages of nature scenes, however, care must be taken that the sun angles and shadows are alike in the component images if the combination picture is to appear balanced and realistic.

Complete or perfect symmetry in photography is often undesirable since it tends to portray a static or monotonous situation. Some asymmetry is necessary to establish interest and tension. In portrait photography, lighting is normally adjusted to break up the symmetrical form of the face, and the subject is rarely photographed straight on.

Similarity and Symmetry

Visual elements do not need to be symmetrical to be similar in shape, form, color, and so on. However, when they are both similar and somewhat symmetrical they can provide a visual rhythm—a balanced, repetitive grouping. In terms of communications theory there is a desirable redundancy. In the terms in which Henri Cartier-Bresson[3] talks about photographs, one might say that there is a relationship of form and geometric pattern.

Symmetry and Graphic Symbols

Symmetry plays an important part in the graphic identifications used by many corporations. Note in Figure 2.19 the visual balance provided by the symmetry of the visual elements. Note also the proximity of the visual elements and how proximity and symmetry work together to facilitate the grouping of the visual elements into a whole visual unit—into a gestalt.

You have probably also observed the strong figure-ground relationships present in these logos as well as a fine example of Notan.

A vertical axis produces more compelling visual symmetry than a horizontal axis.

Rudolf Arnheim

In art there are perceptions, opinions, speculations, and interpretations, but no proof. This is both its mystery and its magic.

Paul Rand

Figure 2.19　Examples of symmetry in the design of graphics: (A) Weyerhauser Company; (B) Chrysler Corporation; (C) Chase Manhattan; (D) Rockwell International.

Continuity

Visual elements that require the fewest number of interruptions will be grouped to form continuous straight or curved lines. If you refer back to the array of small circles in Figure 2.12A and consider all the possible lines or shapes that could be generated from such a 7×7 array of circles, it becomes apparent that man's visual process seeks simple lines and shapes—those that require the least change or interruption in the visual experience.

If the circles in Figure 2.12A were electric lights and if each light was wired to go on and off independently, we would have a system for generating just about any line, shape, or picture we might desire. There are such signs located in Times Square, Picadilly Circus, and the Ginza. (When all the lights are on or off we have, however, a situation similar to Figure 2.12A.) A television screen is, in a way, similar to such signs, for it has thousands of little phosphor lights (pixels).

Analogies could be made to other display systems such as the halftone dot matrix in graphic arts (refer to Figure 2.11). Such an array is the basis for a video screen and dot matrix printers.

Now look at Figure 2.20 and notice the first thing that you see.

Figure 2.20   Organization of visual elements according to the law of continuity.

In working with multimedia, it is imperative that sound and sight be experienced holistically. Continuity in design is essential, including any interactive development.

Was it a pair of Xs? Seeing a pair of Xs would require the fewest interruptions or changes. Seeing a diamond is also relatively simple. Both the Xs and the diamond are familiar and require few visual changes. The diamond, in addition, is a closed figure and this facilitates its perception. We will be discussing this later when we talk about closure. If you look hard enough you can see other familiar figures, perhaps a W, an M, or a V. The letters W, M, and V are harder to see because they require more visual changes. Put differently, it is easier to see the slanting lines as continuous than discontinuous. To see them as discontinuous one has to visually tear the gestalt apart. This requires great effort and concentration.

The Union Flag or Jack shown in Figure 2.21 provides an interesting example of continuity. It is easy to see a cross and an X.

Figure 2.21   The Union Flag of the United Kingdom.

The cross is continuous and it would be extremely difficult to see it otherwise. The X, however, is discontinuous, but because of the arrangement of visual line elements it is relatively easy to see as continuous. It is interesting to note that this Union Flag is a combination of national emblems of England, Scotland, and Northern Ireland.

Figure 2.22A is a detail of a pencil drawing by William Blake. It shows an old man seated with a book between his knees arguing with two men in monkish habits. Note the careful placement of the monk's extended finger, which groups easily with the curved cowl of the monk. Note also that the tips of the extended fingers continue on to group with the cowl of the other monk.

A photograph that serves as an excellent example of the importance of continuity is Edward Weston's "Nude 1936" (Figure 2.22B). The model for the photography was Weston's wife Charis. The photograph is also titled, "Charis, Santa Monica." Charis described her modeling experience thus:

> *. . . I sat in the bedroom doorway [to the sunroof] with the room in shadow behind me. Even then the light was almost overpoweringly bright. When I ducked my head to avoid looking into it, Edward said, "Just keep it that way." He was never happy with the shadow on the right arm, and I was never happy with the crooked hair part and the bobby pins. But when I see the picture unexpectedly, I remember most vividly Edward examining the print with a magnifying glass to decide if the few visible pubic hairs would prevent him from shipping it through the mails.*[4]

I never hear Bach without deep enrichment—I almost feel he has been my "influence."

Edward Weston

A nude figure sits with one leg tucked under her body and the other upright with the model's tilted head resting on it. Both arms embrace the legs in an oval shape with hands joined together at one knee. The model's face is not visible, just the top of her tilted head, with the hair clearly parted. If one were to put a piece of tracing paper over the photograph and then trace the contours of the body, they would discover a magnificent continuation of line. Of all the photographs Weston made, this, according to his son Cole, was his favorite. On photographic nudes, Weston wrote "...without any instructions to the models (I never use professionals, just friends) as to what they should do, I would say, 'move around, all you wish to, the more the better.' Then something happened. I would say, 'Hold it.' And things did happen all the time."[5]

(A)

(B)

Figure 2.22   (A) Detail of unidentified historical scene by
William Blake. (National Gallery of Art,
Washington, D.C., Lessing J. Rosenwald
Collection); (B) "Nude, 1936," Edward Weston
© 1981 Center for Creative Photography,
Arizona Board of Regents.

Continuity and Typography

Type comes in many different styles (Figure 2.23). One style that has dominated printing for many years is the serif type style. The upper word WINE (Figure 2.23A) is an example of serif type style, while the lower word WINE shows the same word in a sans serif style.

One possible reason for the dominance of serif letters in text type styling might be that they provide a "good" gestalt. Serif letters group together more naturally than sans serif letters, as you can see by looking again at Figure 2.23A. The terminal strokes (serifs) on serif letters provide better visual continuity. Figure 2.23B shows a novel example of the use of continuity in typography. One could think of it as a visual onomatopoeia—the word looks like what it says.

Figure 2.23   Different type styles give different effects. The letters in the popular serif style in the upper word WINE (A) group easier than they do in the lower sans serif style). Continuation can be used to provide some interesting effects with printed words (B). (C) shows the Caustic Biomorph type design by Barry Beck.

An example of a novel and contemporary type design is shown in Figure 2.23C. Notice the number of changes the shape of each letter takes on. Change demands attention. A number of perceptual studies have shown that the eye is attracted by change: change in contrast, color, texture, shape, line, position—change in direction.

Continuity and Sequences

Moving images (whether the medium is film, disc, videotape, or computer generated) can be thought of as a sequence of visual images that vary in their spatial as well as temporal arrangement. The same can be said for still pictures that are sequenced in a spatial array, for a person viewing each picture in sequence does so in a time frame (Figure 2.24).

Figure 2.24   Sequence still photography. "Women Jumping over Chairs—20 Lateral Views" Eadweard Muybridge, George Eastman House.

One difference between motion pictures and still pictures that have been arranged in sequence is that with the latter far fewer pictures per event are represented.

Jumping abruptly from one scene to the next, or from one train of thought to another, reduces the strength of the relationship between adjacent pictures. What precedes or follows a frame or a picture influences the perception of it. There are situations, of course, when creating just such an experience—a disruption, a dissonance—is desired. But for the most part, the attempt is to provide a smooth and continuous (both in space and time) transition. Dissolves, fades in or out of focus, wipes, and similar techniques are designed to enhance this transition.

When we try to represent visual and auditory experiences through the use of sight-and-sound media and multimedia it is imperative that a good continuity of events be established. This is the main purpose of script writing, storyboarding, and editing film, videotape, audio tape, and written texts. One of the major

In putting images together I become active, and excitement is of another order—synthesis overshadows analysis.

Minor White

problems in television programming is how to introduce commercials without interrupting the integrity and continuity of the program.

Closure

Nearly complete familiar lines and shapes are more readily seen as complete (closed) than incomplete lines and shapes. In Figure 2.25 the viewer groups the visual elements to see a triangle, not three unrelated lines—a circle, not a series of dots.

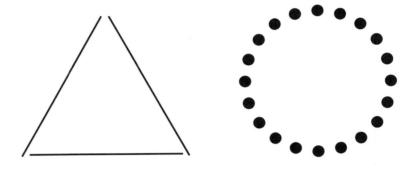

Figure 2.25   Organization of visual elements according to the law of closure.

Forces of organization driving toward spatial order, toward stability, tend to shape optical units into closed compact wholes.

Gyorgy Kepes

The proximity and similarity of the visual elements are important in order to facilitate this perception of a triangle and a circle as one seeks to establish a visual equilibrium—a balance, a closure. The design of the five-star flag for a general of the United States Army provides an effective example of closure (Figure 2.26).

Figure 2.26   General of the Army Flag. A pentagon shape can be seen when closure within the star is made.

A careful look at the area within the five stars causes one to see a pentagon shape. The physical shape formed by the edges of the stars is not continuous, but is perceived as continuous because the Gestalt law of closure is operating. Other Gestalt laws are also operating to facilitate this perception:

    a) proximity—the closeness of the stars,

    b) similarity—all the stars are of the same size, shape, and color (white), and

    c) continuity—the orientation of the stars is such that straight continuous lines are formed from each of the five pentagon apexes.

Closure and Nonclosure

U.S. presidential flags further illustrate the interdependence of the Gestalt laws (Figure 2.27). Both the presidential and vice-presidential flag symbols have visual elements (stars) that can be grouped together to form a circle. With the presidential flag symbols, however, the stars are more easily seen as forming a continuous line describing a circle. Closure to form a circle of stars provides a good gestalt.

An object in possession seldom contains the same charm that it had in pursuit.

Pliny the Younger

(A)   *(B)*

Figure 2.27   *(A) Symbol of the flag of the Vice President of the United States. Although the thirteen stars are the same, they are not in proper proximity to allow easy closure of the visual elements. It is difficult to see a circle even though the stars are laid out in the form of a circle. (B) Symbol of the flag of the President of the United States. The proximity of the stars and the similarity of their orientations and shapes provide for continuation and closure.*

Several years ago a friend from Queensland, Australia sent a cartoon showing a person standing in front of a psychotherapist's office, about to enter but pausing with a puzzled look. The name plate on the door read PSYCHO THE RAPIST. Humor here highlights the importance of the interval to perception.

This is true regardless of the sensory modality but especially true for sight and sound. Change the interval between tones in music and you change the music. In Michelangelo's painting of "The Creation of Adam" (Figure 2.28), changing the distance between the finger of the Creator and the finger of man changes the event—closure is denied.

If we listen to a continuous note on the fringe of audibility, the sound seems to stop at regular intervals and then start again. Such oscillations are due to a periodic decrease and increase in one's attention, not to any [physical] change in the note.

Carl Jung

Figure 2.28   *The critical space between the fingers of God and Adam provides a decisive distance that invites closure. From "The Creation of Adam" by Michelangelo.*

The interval allows the viewer to complete the action; it is a critical distance, it is an invitation to participate in the event—in contemporary jargon, it is interactive. The same can be said for the painting "La Danse" by Henri Matisse in which five nude women are dancing in a circle and in a clockwise movement, their hands all joined together except for the two women in front. Between their outstretched hands is a gap, a narrow separation, an interval that invites the viewer to complete the action, to join in.

Henri Cartier-Bresson's famous photograph "Place de l'Europe, 1932" shows a man leaping over a large pool of water in a flooded street and his reflection in the water.[6] One of the things that makes

this photograph memorable is that the man appears to be sus-
pended in air. As he leaps, his forward motion is captured on film
just before the heel of his outstretched right foot touches its
reflection in the water. The *decisive moment* becomes the decisive
distance—the critical interval that invites the viewer to participate
in the photograph by completing the jump.

REM EMB ERTH ISIFYO UPU TTH EINT ERV ALINTH
EWRO NGPLA CEITC ANCA USEP ROB LE MS.*

*Whoever listens
to the drum hears
silence.*

Georges Braque

Closed Areas

*Areas with closed contours are more readily seen than areas with
open contours.* In Figure 2.29A the closed areas 2 and 5 are easier
to see than the open areas 1, 3, 4, and 6, even though the jagged
lines are all similar and are in the same proximity to each other. In
Figure 2.29B, the closed black bars are also easily identified as figure.

Figure 2.29   (A) Closed areas are more easily seen as figures.
(B) The closed black bars on a resolving-power
target are easily seen as figure.

---

* Remember this if you put the interval in the wrong place it can cause problems.

One of the reasons the letter M shown in Chapter 1 (Figure 1.5) is so difficult to see is because the area is open rather than closed. The arrows, being closed, are readily seen as figure.

The widths of the black bars in a resolving power target are exactly the same as the widths of the white spaces between them (Figure 2.29B). The lengths of the black bars are definite because they are closed areas, whereas the white spaces are not even seen as bars because they are open areas. To see the white spaces as white bars, one has to provide for closure. You can do this by simply drawing a line around the three black bars to form a square.

Also in Chapter 1 (Figure 1.4), a single contour line was used to show a figure-ground boundary. This line, with some effort, could be seen as belonging to the face of an old man or to part of the face and body of a woman. The perception of one over the other can be controlled by enclosing the single contour line (Figure 2.30).

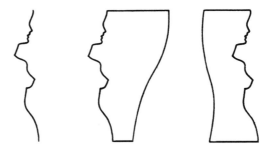

A closed area appears more formed, more stable, than one which is open and without boundaries.

Gyorgy Kepes

Figure 2.30   *Profile of an elderly man or head and torso of a woman? Closed areas are more readily seen as figures. Contrasting the enclosed areas by darkening them would make them even easier to see as figures.*

In this way one can manipulate visual elements so that perception of what is to be communicated is more certain.

The Zeigarnik Effect

The incomplete image and the unexpected image set the mind a puzzle.

E.H. Gombrich

In 1927 a Russian psychologist, Bluma Zeigarnik, conducted a series of experiments in which she showed that tasks that are interrupted before completion are more likely to be remembered than similar tasks completed without interruption.[7] Subjects were asked to perform simple tasks such as recalling favorite quotations from memory, solving a riddle, or doing mental arithmetic problems. Some of the subjects were given sufficient time to solve the problems and others were not. Upon questioning a few hours later, it was discovered that the subjects who were not allowed sufficient time for completion had better recall. This superiority of memory recall for uncompleted tasks, however, is short, and seems to disappear within twenty-four hours.

The experience is not an uncommon one, as evidenced by the fact that after a test or similar event one tends to give more attention to the questions that could not be answered. A similar situation exists when one is puzzled about something they have read or seen that did not make sense so they decided to sleep on it. During the night the unsolved puzzle keeps the mind active and sometimes makes sleep difficult. Until the puzzle is solved, or frustration takes over and it is dismissed, it remains active in the mind.

Unresolved, complex personal problems and worry are even more persistent in refusing to be dismissed from the mind. Television soap operas and the old movie serials such as "The Perils of Pauline," are examples of the Zeigarnik effect.

The Zeigarnik effect is a variant of the Gestalt principle of closure. Research suggests that personality plays an important role. People who are highly anxious recall completed tasks better, while those who are achievement-oriented recall uncompleted tasks better. A task that is not completed can cause tension. People have different tolerances and strategies for coping with tension—for some, tension can provide motivation; for others it can encourage withdrawal.

A certain amount of visual tension in a picture—an ambiguity, an illusion, a confusion, a novelty, an unexpected situation—can result in a pictorial Zeigarnik effect. The picture becomes a visual riddle that may remain unsolved during viewing. This unanswered riddle remains in memory and is recalled and thought about until it is solved and a closure is formed. Many pictures have such riddle characteristics. The most common, perhaps, are those used in advertising. Often, picture and copy go together to produce a puzzle that is not solvable in the short time typically devoted to viewing the advertisement. Rebuses (riddles composed of word syllables depicted by pictures or symbols) can be found in some advertisements.

I propose that many authors are influenced more by writers they only partly understand than by those they fully comprehend, for the former leave unfinished business in one's mind.

Rollo May

GESTALT CRITIQUE

A photograph that shows excellent geometric form and nicely demonstrates various Gestalt laws is Henry Jackson's photograph of three American Indian women and a child (Figure 2.31). The positions of the faces of the three women are such that they are

"Golfer's Dream"

David Spindel

easily grouped to form a symmetrical triangle. A similar but inverted triangle could also be formed by grouping the faces of the two seated women and the young child. Other groupings are also possible, such as the diamond shape as the foot position of the child is grouped with the faces of the three women. The light area around the child is also triangular in shape.

Figure 2.31   Three North American Indian women photographed by Henry Jackson. (Smithsonian Institution National Anthropological Archives, Bureau of American Ethnology Collection.)

The grouping of the various visual elements into triangular shapes might be analyzed in this way:

- *Proximity.* The faces of the three women are in position to form a symmetrical triangle. The two who are seated are at eye level with each other. They form a base line for the standing woman's head as one apex, or the baby's face or toes as another.
- *Similarity.* Grouping into a series of triangular shapes is facilitated by the similarity of the shapes of the faces, the facial features, hair style, and expression.
- *Continuity.* The outer shape of the women provides visual line elements that are close enough and in proper position to be grouped as continuous. Another example of continuity can be seen in the striped blanket of the standing woman. Jackson must have arranged the blanket carefully so that there would be continuity of stripes and so that they would form inverted triangular shapes.
- *Closure.* One example of closure, of course, is the grouping of faces to form stable shapes such as triangles. Other examples are the ease with which one sees closed areas such as the black-and-white stripes that do not blend in with the background.
- *Figure-ground.* You may have noticed that Jackson was careful to position one of the hanging light-colored dress pieces behind the head of the standing woman so as to provide a good figure-ground relationship in a critical picture area.

The recognition, in real life, of a rhythm of surfaces, lines, and values is for me the essence of photography; composition should be a constant of preoccupation, being a simultaneous coalition, an organic coordination of visual elements.

Henri
Cartier-Bresson

Man as Participant

Man derives satisfaction from being able to form a closure that allows him to become an active participant in the visual experience. The concept of closure is not restricted to vision. It is basic to our humanity—to the way we experience things. A variety of examples can be cited to illustrate this. The art of teaching, in part, consists of providing learners with enough information organized in such a way that they can put it together, add the missing elements, and discover for themselves (closure) what the teacher wants them to experience. If someone recited "Mary had a little lamb whose fleece was white as _ _ _ _ _ _ _," it could be predicted that most people would finish the nursery rhyme (closure) with the word *snow*.

Years ago when cake mixes were first marketed they were a dismal economic failure even though the product was of good quality and convenient to use. Research studies determined that

Forming is more important than form.

Paul Klee

the failure was due, ironically, to the fact that manufacturers had done everything but bake the cake. They had, in fact, made the product too convenient to use. By changing the cake-mix ingredients and making it necessary for the user to increase active participation by cracking, adding, and mixing in an egg, cake mixes became an almost instant success.

Every artist who successfully paints or photographs nudes knows that, in part, what is excluded is as important as what is included. The viewer is allowed the freedom to participate to form closure. The lesson is simple. In any planned experience, never deprive the participant of the opportunity to participate—to become involved. Raising questions throughout this book and providing exercises are ways of attempting to apply this rule.

Gestalt Laws as a Means

Knowledge of language, by itself, does not make one a great writer or poet. Knowledge of the Gestalt laws, in and by itself, does not assure a good picture any more than does knowledge of imaging processes or of sophisticated equipment and materials. Some of the excellent photographs made in the early days of photography attest to this. It is not sufficient merely to know about something. One must be able to apply that knowledge skillfully. A good picture is a result of knowledge and ability—of knowing and doing. Both can be achieved with rigorous discipline and practice.

The Gestalt laws, therefore, are not an end in themselves, but merely a means to an end—a means of improving the effectiveness of pictures. The laws, which might better be thought of as guiding principles, attempt to describe in a simple way how man segregates and groups visual information. These principles, then, can guide a photographer in creating pictures that facilitate visual communications.

A Word of Caution

The Gestalt laws of perceptual organization have been separated in this book for convenience—convenience in presentation and convenience in learning. You must not, however, think of them as separate, for they are related and work together to facilitate seeing. Visual elements that are close together, that are similar, that form a smooth contour, and allow for closure can produce an effective composition.

Keep in mind, however, that there are many excellent pictures that do not conform to the Gestalt laws of perceptual organization.

Examples of such pictures are those with strong emotional appeal and those that delve into the unconscious.

There is also a flip side to the Gestalt laws. If you know how to arrange visual elements so that they are easy to group visually, you also know how to arrange them so that they are difficult to group. You may choose to do the latter in order to create a feeling of tension or dissonance in your photograph, to camouflage, or merely to force the viewer to look harder.

The classic concept of the [Freudian] primary process (which forms unconscious phantasy) denies it any structure.

Anton Ehrenzweig

PRAGNANZ

The Gestalt laws of organization are one attempt to formulate a set of principles that seem to describe the way we segregate and group visual elements into patterns or units. The overall rationale for why people organize and group information the way they do is explained in part by the law of Pragnanz, which was introduced by the founder of the Gestalt movement, Dr. Max Wertheimer. In the words of Koffka, the law of Pragnanz can be formulated like this:

"Psychological organization will always be as 'good' as the prevailing conditions allow."

Although the term good is not defined, it is associated with such properties as regularity, symmetry, simplicity, uniformity, and closure—in short, properties that minimize stress and maximize stability. Prevailing conditions refer to the stimulus pattern (see Figure 2.32). More broadly, it refers to the perceptual environment.

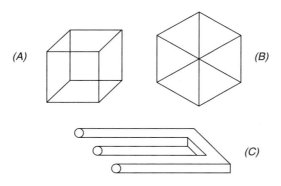

Figure 2.32   Prevailing conditions influence psychological organization: (A) Stable as a three-dimensional pattern; (B) Stable as a two-dimensional pattern; (C) Unstable.

Ideally I want every piece analyzed, technically, structurally, formally. And I want it to come out shatteringly integrated, like a crystal, totally whole, defying analysis.

Michael Tilson

Seeing

Seeing, however, involves more than just the stimulus pattern (picture) and environment. Much of what we see depends upon our past experiences (memory), our own personalities, and what we are looking for. This is why the same picture often gets a variety of responses from viewers. What people experience depends upon external and internal factors—what they are looking at and what they are looking for.

Figure 2.33 provides some insight into the complexity of what appears to be the simple process of seeing.

Figure 2.33   Seeing and saying are not the same. Saying is a verbal attempt to describe a visual percept.

What a person sees and experiences is called a percept (the product of perception, which is a process). What a person reports seeing is a verbal attempt to describe a nonverbal experience. It is an attempt to verbalize a percept and often falls short. *Saying is not seeing.*

Psychologists and others still have no way of positively knowing a given person's percept and probably they never will. The percept is a result of interactions between the physical stimulus pattern and the unique psychological makeup of a person. No two people are completely alike, not even identical twins. To further complicate things, a person's psychological makeup varies from time to time and from place to place. The same cup of coffee will taste different in the morning than later in the day. Hot dogs taste different at a football game than they do at home.

Many factors, therefore, influence what we experience, and people will respond differently to what is looked at. In spite of the differences among us there are some basic similarities, and these influence how we organize things.

This, it is thought, is the meaning of the law of Pragnanz. We tend to organize our world so that we can cope with it. We search for stability, meaning, balance, security, and so on. We feel more comfortable when what we are looking at can be comprehended or experienced. If there is too much information presented at one time, we either filter out some of it or simplify it by grouping or "chunking" it. If there is insufficient information we add to it to form a closure and maintain meaning. We strive to reduce tension and stress to obtain stability and equilibrium.

The visual art of mentally disturbed patients often reflects the chaotic conditions created by their illness or their inner struggle to achieve some sense of balance and stability. The Prinzhorn Collection of the art of the mentally ill is a moving example of this.[8]

Order and Complexity

We defined Pragnanz law as an overriding principle under which the Gestalt laws of perceptual organization operate. According to this principle, psychological organization or grouping of information is facilitated by such things as regularity, symmetry, and simplicity. The organization of information by a person is dependent upon the amount of information presented, which, in turn depends on the redundancy and predictability of the various individual elements present within an array of information. In other words, if visual elements are well ordered, there is a high degree of redundancy and, therefore, predictability.

Man, actively though unconsciously, structures his visual world. Few people realize that vision is not passive but active…in fact, a transaction between man and his environment in which both participate.

Edward Hall

The artist does not draw what he sees, but what he must make others see.

Edgar Degas

The sole difference between myself and a madman is the fact that I am not mad.

Salvador Dali

It took years to become spontaneous and simple. Nijinsky took thousands of leaps before the memorable one.

Martha Graham

To define is to destroy, to suggest is to create.

Stephane Mallarme

You have to know how to preserve that freshness and innocence a child has when it approaches things.

Henri Matisse

In order to be able to understand the great complexity of life and to understand what the universe is doing, the first word to learn is synergy.

Buckminster Fuller

Psychological organization of the visual elements will be facilitated, but what is experienced (percept) could be quite boring.

The point is this: The Gestalt laws, if mechanically applied in the practice of photography, filmmaking, art, design, multimedia presentations, or any other means of communications, might be technically correct but the product could be monotonous and mundane. There may be no challenge for the person viewing what has been designed, no sense of excitement or of curiosity, no motivation to become involved. Too much has been done by the designer and there is little left for the viewer to add. Psychological organization is an active process from which a person derives pleasure and satisfaction.

Too much order in a picture or presentation or design deprives a person of the creative act of participation. Some variation is needed to engage a person—to add a little spice.

Rudolf Arnheim, who was a student of Max Wertheimer in the 1920s, eloquently describes the importance of variation in the design of things. He talks about order and complexity, defining order as "the degree and kind of lawfulness governing the relations among the parts of an entity" and complexity as "the multiplicity of the relationships among the parts of an entity." He then goes on to say:

> *Order and complexity are antagonistic, in that order tends to reduce complexity while complexity tends to reduce order. To create order requires not only rearrangement but in most cases also the elimination of what does not fit the principles determining the order. On the other hand, when one increases the complexity of an object, order will be harder to achieve.*
>
> *Order and complexity, however, cannot exist without each other. Complexity without order produces confusion—order without complexity produces boredom. Although order is needed to cope with both the inner and outer world, man cannot reduce his experience to a network of neatly predictable connections without losing the stimulating riches and surprises of life. Being complexly designed, man must function complexly if he is to be fully himself—and to this end the setting in which he operates must be complex also. It has long been recognized that the great works of man combine high order with high complexity.*[9]

INFORMATION THEORY

There are alternate ways to describe a given visual experience. The Gestalt laws were formulated in the early 1900s to provide some principles of how man tends to group visual elements. In the mid 1900s visual elements were identified as informational elements, and the ways in which such elements were grouped could be described in terms of information or communication theory. The principal concepts are uncertainty and redundancy.

The amount of information conveyed by what we see (percept), for example, depends upon the number of different ways in which visual elements can be grouped (uncertainty or alternatives). The more redundant the visual elements, the fewer the alternatives and the easier the grouping. One of the reasons why things that are symmetrical are so easy to see is that there is great redundancy of information. Information on any one side of the symmetrical figure is readily predictable from information on the opposite side. Symmetry is one of the things that provides for a "good" gestalt or Pragnanz.

The graphic symbols used by many corporations and businesses are often symmetrical (Figure 2.34).

Many of the Gestalt principles pertain to the distribution of information in the pictures. For example, "good" figure is a figure with a high degree of internal redundancy.

Ralph Norman
Haber

PURE WOOL ®

Figure 2.34   The Pure Wool mark provides a good gestalt. There is good figure-ground relationship, regularity, symmetry, proximity, continuity, simplicity, balance, closure, and stability. It has a high redundancy of visual elements, many of which can be eliminated without loss of recognition but with severe loss of the aesthetic experience.

The eye appears to act according to the principle of least effort and do no more than is imposed on it.

Floyd Ratliff

Such redundancy means that there is little uncertainty in the probability that the symbols will be identified, even when some of the redundant information is missing. *The experience itself, however, would be different.*

The Gestalt laws operate to reduce uncertainty by facilitating the grouping of visual elements—by redundancy of information. Information that is easily grouped is said to have properties for Pragnanz (Gestalt theory) or redundancy (information theory). Roughly speaking then, the Gestalt laws of perceptual organization describe various types of redundancy. The Gestalt laws are easy to comprehend but are not easily quantifiable. Information theory, although quantifiable, is more difficult to grasp and leads to error when one tries to use it to quantify human perception.

This thou must always bear in mind, what is the nature of the whole, and what is thy nature, and how this is related to that, and what kind of a part it is of what kind of a whole; and that there is no one who hinders thee from always doing and saying the things which are according to the nature of which thou art a part.

Marcus Aurelius

Figure 2.35 gives a visual summary of the Gestalt principles covered in this chapter, and Figure 2.36 shows graphic examples.

The designs of many of the international graphic symbols presently in use and being proposed provide excellent examples of the Gestalt laws. The few shown in Figure 2.36 were selected from the several thousand categorized by H. Dreyfuss.[10] Two symbols, the Star of David and that for Yin/Yang, remind us that graphic symbols go far back into history and that their design is ageless.

All four Gestalt laws are readily identified in the Olympic graphics (Figure 2.26H). The dark wavy lines are similar in contour, but vary in thickness. The closed dark wavy lines are narrower than the white lines and are, therefore, more readily seen as figure. In certain areas the dark wavy lines become thicker (greater *proximity*) and facilitate a grouping of visual elements in that area.

Similarity, proximity, and continuation work together to facilitate the closure of a person in action. This closure provides meaning and psychological balance (Pragnanz).

All things are connected. Whatever befalls the earth befalls the children of the earth.

Chief Seattle

For me expression…is located in the entirety of my painting: the position the figures are in, the empty spaces around them, the proportions—all of it contributes. Anything that is not necessary to the painting damages it. A work must establish an overall harmony.

Henri Matisse

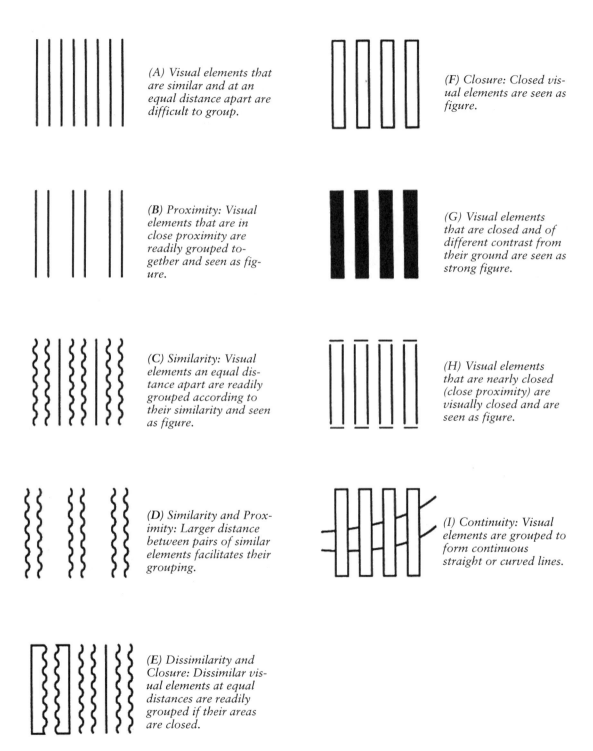

(A) Visual elements that are similar and at an equal distance apart are difficult to group.

(F) Closure: Closed visual elements are seen as figure.

(B) Proximity: Visual elements that are in close proximity are readily grouped together and seen as figure.

(G) Visual elements that are closed and of different contrast from their ground are seen as strong figure.

(C) Similarity: Visual elements an equal distance apart are readily grouped according to their similarity and seen as figure.

(H) Visual elements that are nearly closed (close proximity) are visually closed and are seen as figure.

(D) Similarity and Proximity: Larger distance between pairs of similar elements facilitates their grouping.

(I) Continuity: Visual elements are grouped to form continuous straight or curved lines.

(E) Dissimilarity and Closure: Dissimilar visual elements at equal distances are readily grouped if their areas are closed.

Figure 2.35   Gestalt summary.

(A) Gestalt: The graphic symbol for Judaism is seen as a total configuration of a star, not as six separate triangles surrounding a hexagon. The whole is different from the sum of its parts.

(B) Figure-ground: The graphic symbol for Taoism, representing Yin/Yang, is perfectly symmetrical, either half being seen as figure or ground.

(C) Proximity: The closeness of the small bars allows easy grouping into a clockwise movement.

(D) Similarity: (1) Bright or hazy sun; sand; snow; (2) Cloudy bright, no shadows.

(E) Symmetry: (1) Water sports area; (2) Shooting. The wavy lines are similar and therefore are grouped together.

(F) Continuation: The wavy line is easier seen as one continuous line than not.

(G) Closure: Radioactive sign. The three dark segments are easily seen since they represent closed segments. The similar unenclosed (white) segments are difficult to see.

(H) Similarity, Proximity, Continuation, and Closure: Ice hockey (1) and cross-country skiing (2).

Figure 2.36   Graphic examples of Gestalt principles.

KEY WORDS

asymmetry
closure
continuity
field theory
Gestalt
information theory
interval
Pragnanz
proximity
similarity
simplicity
symmetry
Zeigarnik effect

"Minor White" by David Spindell

Gestalt Grouping Exercises

1. Tandem Gestalts

Expose a roll of film in such a way that pairs of frames serve as one through some kind of connection or association. The Gestalt principles of similarity, continuation, closure, proximity, symmetry, and common fate can serve as connectors. (Cut the roll of film into appropriate strips and make a contact print of each strip.)

2. Cut-and-Paste Gestalt

Take some of your old photographs or those printed in magazines and cut them into smaller pieces. Lay the pieces on a table as you would a jigsaw puzzle. Now select pieces and arrange them in a way so that they create an interesting gestalt. As a variation try grouping visual elements that do not normally belong together, elements that when combined provide humor or puzzlement (Zeigarnik effect).

Photo by Jose Henrique Lorca.

3. TV Screen

Consider your TV screen as a source of moving and changing pictures in which each frame is on for 1/30th of a second. In one second you have an opportunity to photograph thirty different pictures—in one minute up to 1,800 different pictures.

Place your camera so that you can focus on the entire TV screen and set the shutter speed at 1/30th of a second (1/15th with a focal-plane shutter). If you are using film with an ISO speed of 160/23°, set the aperture at about f/2.8.

Sit close to your camera with your finger on the shutter release. Think of the Gestalt laws and watch the changing TV pictures

Art is not an object but an experience.

Josef Albers

until you see an image that has a Gestalt design. Quickly take a photograph of it.

Expose a few rolls of film in this way and then study the results. It is an excellent way to develop your perception and timing so that you can capture pictures that exist for only a fleeting second.

4. Chance Video Gestalts

There is no "must" in art, because art is free.

Wassily Kandinsky

The surrealist artists used techniques of *free-association* and *automatic writing* to tap their unconscious from which creative ideas spring. Had they been living during our electronic age they might have used *electronic writing*.

Robert Heinecken used the unpredictable spontaneity of video imagery combined with a photographic transparency taped to the screen to create new images. The creative mind of man blends photography and videography into new gestalts. Try the Heinecken approach.

5. Chance Camera Gestalts

There is an old standard saying about the arts, "You need to learn all the rules and then forget them."

Joseph Campbell

Images can be superimposed in a camera with double exposures. Double-expose a roll of film one frame at a time, half of the roll by careful choice and the other half by chance. Compare the images. If your camera does not allow double exposures to be made, expose an entire roll of film, rewind it and then expose it again. (Take precautions to prevent the film leader from being completely rewound into the cassette.) Make prints and study them.

Photograph of Dr. Rudolf Arnheim (right) and author. Happy accident (chance).

6. Chance Enlarger Gestalts

Images can be superimposed by choice or chance in the darkroom to create other images.

Superimpose any two negatives in a negative carrier and print them. Do it two different ways:

a) By choice
b) By chance

Try these variations:

a) Rotate one of the negatives 180 degrees and print the sandwich. Compare.
b) Instead of superimposing the negatives in the carrier, project and expose each separately on the same sheet of photographic paper.
c) Project and print one negative with the paper in a flat position and then project and print the second negative with the paper tilted.
d) Project and print one negative in focus and then the other slightly out of focus.

7. Similarity: Dissimilarity

Photograph two people in such a way as to accentuate their similarities. Think in terms of facial features and expressions, hands, gestures, gender, and so on.

Photo by Scott Calder. (Courtesy Ilford, Inc.)

There is nothing new in art except talent.

Anton Chekhov

To think is to differ.

Clarence Darrow

8. Cropping and Closure

The Gestalt laws can help you while you are framing a picture in a camera viewfinder or cropping a picture that is being printed. Notice in the photograph below how careful the photographer was in framing the scene. She wanted to show the similarity of shapes between natural terrain and animals. Her tight framing of the upper section of the white and black horses does this dramatically. She was also mindful of the white area on which her photograph was to be mounted so that the lower black area is closed by the white mountboard, and the white area is closed by the dark area of the photograph itself.

Photo by Lisa Jones.

Lisa Jones wrote of her photograph, "I like the look of fields that have hills and slopes in them... I like the body shapes to animals and their textures. There are some field hill contours that feature animal shapes... And when there is harmony between the field forms and the animal shapes, then it really resounds nicely."

9. Treasure Hunt

Take another look at some of your contact prints and see if cropping can improve the photograph. You might also look around and see if some photographs or parts of photographs might work well together in pairs. The same can be done with film or video footage not used. Play around, you may discover treasures.

10. Typography

Search out different styles of typeface being used in advertisements, posters, film or video titles, and identify the Gestalt laws that are operating.

Try styling your own type. Check your library for books on typography.

11. Gestalt Scrap Book

Start a scrap book of various examples of the Gestalt laws that you can identify in magazines. Cut out pictures and illustrations and paste them in your scrapbook with proper identification. You may want to lay out your book in this sequence:

a) Figure-ground
b) Proximity
c) Similarity
d) Continuity
e) Closure
f) Pragnanz

Start looking for stamps that have incorporated in their design some of the Gestalt laws of perceptual organization. You will be surprised at how many you can find once you begin looking for them. Do not limit yourself to any one country. Stop at a stamp-collector's store and look around. Start a collection.

12. Tangrams

A tangram is a seven-piece Chinese puzzle similar to our jigsaw puzzle in that the object of the game is to fit pieces together. It is quite different from a jigsaw puzzle, however, since it contains only seven geometric pieces that can be fitted together in different ways to form a variety of greater shapes.

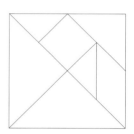

It is a good example of Gestalt because the figures that result from the various possible combinations of the same seven pieces are different from the sum of the pieces or parts.

The seven pieces that make up a tangram can be traced and cut from the square shown: The object of the game is to group these seven pieces to form figures other than squares, such as a cat.

The task is difficult because there are many different ways in which the seven pieces can be positioned and you must group them to make a whole figure. Note that even when the seven parts are clearly shown, the initial tendency is not to see seven individual parts but to see the totality of these parts grouped into the form of a cat.

Paul Rand in his book *Paul Rand—A Designer's Art,* writes about the importance of tangram exercises:

Many design problems can be posed with these games in mind; the main principle to be learned is that of economy of means—making the most of the least. Further, the game helps to sharpen the powers of observation through the discovery of resemblances between geometric and natural forms. It helps the student to abstract—to see a triangle, for example, as a face, a tree, an eye, or a nose, depending on the context in which the pieces are arranged. Such observation is essential in the study of visual symbols.[11]

Here are some forms for you to try. (The answers are in Appendix B, "Answers to Selected Exercises.")

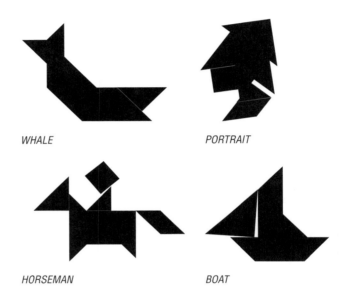

WHALE   PORTRAIT

HORSEMAN   BOAT

It takes formidable energy and discipline to evoke the subjective from the literal, to convert the specific into the universal.

Barbara Morgan

If you are interested in more information on tangrams, books on the subject are available in some museum bookstores and from Dover Publications, 31 East 2nd Street, Mineola, NY 11501.

13. Don't Be a Square

Try solving this visual-tactile problem if you have not seen it before. If you have seen it, try it on friends and observe how they attempt to solve it.

Given the array of nine dots shown below, connect them all together with only four straight lines. You are not allowed to lift the pencil from the paper. Try solving the sixteen-dot problem using the same technique. (The answers are in Appendix B.)

9 Dots: Connect the dots with only four straight lines.
16 Dots: Connect the dots with only six straight lines.

Notes

1. *Henri Cartier-Bresson,* New York: Aperture, 1976, p. 43.

2. Bruce Davidson, *East 100th Street,* Cambridge, MA: Harvard University Press, 1970.

3. Henri Cartier-Bresson, *The World of Henri Cartier-Bresson,* New York: Viking Press, 1968.

4. Amy Conger, *Edward Weston Photographs,* Tuscon, AZ: Center for Creative Photography, University of Arizona, 1992, (Figure 968).

5. Nancy Newhall (ed.), *Edward Weston,* New York: Aperture, 1971, p. 84.

6.   *Henri Cartier-Bresson,* op. cit., p. 39.

7. Leslie Stroebel, Hollis Todd, Richard Zakia, *Visual Concepts for Photographers,* New York: Focal Press, 1980, pp 166, 167.

8. Hans Prinzorn, *Artistry of the Mentally Ill,* Springer-Verlag, 1922, 1923, 1968; English edition, 1992.

9. Rudolf Arnheim, *Psychology of Art,* Berkeley: University of California Press, 1972, p. 124.

10. H. Dreyfuss, *Symbol Sourcebook,* New York: McGraw-Hill, 1972.

11. Paul Rand, *Paul Rand: A Designers Art,* New Haven, CT: Yale University Press, 1985, p. 192.

3
Memory and Association

*The more facts a fact is associated with in the mind, the better
possession of it our memory retains.*

William James

"Cherill Horse, Wiltshire, England" © Marilyn Bridges, 1985. This decorative chalk marking of
a horse embedded in a hillside was created in 1780 and photographed from a very low-flying
airplane. Its length is 123 feet—over a third the length of a football field.

81

When photography first came into existence with the daguerreotype in 1839, it was referred to as "a mirror with a memory." A person could hold a photograph and recall past events. Photo albums, school yearbooks and the like, serve as visual diaries of past experiences, memories of times past.

Memory is an integral part of perception. It is much easier to see what we know, what is stored in memory, than to see what we do not know, what is not in memory. In fact, one of the familiar problems in teaching students how to draw is to convince them to draw what they *see* and not what they know. The same can be said in photographing—photograph what you see and not what you know and project onto the object. "Let the object come to you, don't go to the object," Henry Thoreau reminds us. This is a difficult task since memory and perception are so closely tied together. Minor White in photographing landscapes recognized this connective problem and prayed for "pristine vision," vision that can avoid memory, vision with the innocence of a child.

SHORT-TERM MEMORY/LONG-TERM MEMORY

All of our senses are connected in memory. We have memories not only of visual experiences but also of experiences involving sound, smell, taste, touch, movement, and balance. The memories we remember for a long time are called *long-term memories* (LTM) and are contrasted with *short-term memories* (STM) that we remember just long enough to use and then forget. One example of STM is a telephone number that we look up, dial, and then forget. A number in LTM that we don't forget, for example, may be our social security number.

There is a limit to the amount of unrelated information a person can hold in STM, from five to nine items, averaging seven. One researcher[1] referred to this limitation as "The magic number 7, plus or minus 2." To experience this limitation, have someone read to you a set of unrelated numbers such as 7932586 or letters such as RFGLMPQ. Then try to recall them in proper sequence by saying them or writing them. Sound easy? Try it with five to nine unrelated numbers, letters, or words.

Since we are limited in the amount of information we can retain correctly in STM, one should be cautious with the amount of information included in the design of a photograph, poster, advertisement, or multimedia program if it is going to have some memorable impact.

From STM to LTM

There are a number of strategies one can use to transfer information from STM to LTM such as rehearsal, association, attention, and mnemonics—common procedures we use to learn things and remember them. Some 50 years ago, as a navy radio operator I learned Morse code so well that I can still easily recall it. Practice, practice, practice shifts things from STM to LTM.

One does not become a great athlete, dancer, musician, or photographer without practice. Students of Minor White recall his taking hundreds of pictures without film in his camera, just for practice.

The human brain is a 3 pound universe having 100,000,000,000 cells.

Body as Memory

Our entire body is a memory system. I am, for example, writing this manuscript by hand, even though I have a computer to which I will transfer the text later. Why do I do this? Somehow, perhaps like an artist-painter, my hand movements help coordinate my thinking and tickle my memory. Athletes and dancers use their entire body as a memory system and practice with it. (A typical square inch of skin has about 19,000 sensory cells.)

Deaf people who use finger spelling and sign language use their fingers to recall how to spell a word and their hands to recall other things.

I see again in memory my dear.

Francis Picabia

Mnemonics

Another technique for fixing things in memory so they can be recalled later is through the use of a mnemonic. The familiar mnemonic used to remember whether to set a clock one hour ahead in the spring of the year and one hour behind in the fall is, "Spring forward, fall back." Mnemonics I have used to help students avoid common misspellings of words such as visible (visable) and aperture (aperature) is that the word visible has two "eyes" ("i"s) to see with, and that there is no "rat" in aperture. I also remind them that the correct spelling for the word gray in *America* is with an "a" and that in *England* it is with an "e," grey.

Zone System photographers use Roman numerals from 0 to X as a mnemonic for visualizing the different colors in a scene in terms of their tonalities or lightnesses. A maximum black is Zone 0, pure white Zone X, and a middle gray Zone V.

There are more cells in the human brain than there are stars in the universe.

VISUAL MEMORY/COLOR MEMORY

My way is to seize an image that moment it is formed in my mind, to trap it as a bird and to pin it at once to canvas.

Joan Miro

Visual memory is as important in all phases of photography as is taste memory for a chef or wine taster, smell memory for a fragrance designer, kinesthetic memory for a dancer.

Photographers, in printing a negative, try to recall the experience they had when exposing the film and what their intentions were; how they visualized the scene initially. In making a color print it is necessary to realize that colors in the scene photographed are not remembered as they are seen; light colors are remembered as being lighter, dark colors as darker, and hues as being more saturated. Film manufacturers are aware of this and design their products so that the color reproduction coincides with remembered colors.

Color memory is vital in post-production work such as editing color film or video, in film to videotape transfer, and in multimedia work. In editing film or video, for example, an outdoor scene shot in daylight in which a woman is wearing a red dress has to look similar to one that might have been shot with the same red dress at another time, indoors at a cocktail party.

It is a poor sort of memory that only worked backwards, the Queen remarked.

Alice in Wonderland

In a film-to-videotape transfer, a person sits in front of a video screen as film passes, frame by frame. Some of the film may have been shot in different cameras, under different lighting conditions, and sometimes with different color films. The person has to make color corrections so that there is a continuity of colors as well as tonalities and levels of brightness. This is a difficult task requiring excellent visual memory as well as color memory. It is a highly sought-after talent.

Sequencing

To engage a sequence we keep in mind the photographs on either side of the one in our eye.

Minor White

Visual memory is essential in any work requiring sequencing—preparing large exhibits of photographs, editing pictures for a book, film or video, slide presentation, multimedia, computer animation, storyboarding.

The task becomes increasingly difficult when one moves from working strictly in a visual mode such as with photographs to a film/video mode, and to a multimedia mode. Computer imaging, manipulation, and integration using CD-ROM opens a range of opportunities and challenges to image makers.

ASSOCIATION

We remember things through association. When I was first introduced to a gentleman named Lothar, I could not remember his name on later occasions, since it was strange to me. He advised me to remember it as "*Low tar*, more taste," a slogan for a cigarette at that time. I have never forgotten it. Whenever I *hear* opera, I am transported to Verona, Italy where I once sat in the coliseum listening to the grandeur of live Italian opera. When I am in my car behind a stopped bus, the *smell* of diesel reminds me of my Navy days aboard the diesel-burning destroyer, the *USS Duncan*.

When I *look* at the photograph by Bruce Davidson of a child standing on a fire escape (see Chapter 2), I see the Christian image of a crucified Christ and experience the emotions associated with that image.

When Minor White was teaching at the Rochester Institute of Technology (RIT), he would, during his critique sessions, make remarks such as, "Yes, this is a photograph of a tree (or rock), but what else is it?" The "What else is it?" is significant. It is what the image is *about*. Seeing the tree or rock as only a tree or a rock is a literal interpretation. What the tree or rock may signify, the associative meaning, the connotation, is what makes a photograph a good or great photograph, a memorable one. Edward Weston's photograph of a rock cluster, "Eroded Rock No. 51, 1930"[2] is more than a literal eroded rock, and the assocation one can make is one of the things that makes it a great photograph-—it is a visual metaphor, a poetic statement (Figure 3.1).

The graphic solution of the problems of perspective and space by their [Japanese] art incited me to find something analogous in music.

Igor Stravinsky

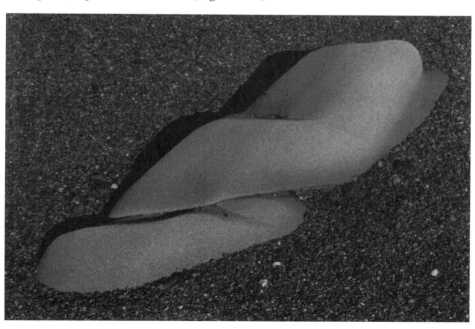

*Figure 3.1   Edward Weston, "Eroded Rock No. 51, 1930."
Center for Creative Photography, Arizona Board
of Regents.*

Weston titled this photograph quite literally. What makes this rock more significant than the many others he must have photographed? Literally it is a rock formation resting on small pebbles of stone, but what else is it? In Weston's own words, it is more than just a rock. The aim is "...to photograph a rock, have it look like a rock, but be *more* than a rock."[3] Visually and poetically it is more than a rock or rock cluster. The shape, form, and lying position of the rock suggest that of a reclining nude model or a sculpture of one.

In a similar way the photograph in Figure 3.2 can be seen as a visual metaphor; as such, it becomes a more interesting picture. Men are in various positions of dress in a primary grade school room. Four are seen putting on their white robes, one has a black robe. Who are they, and what is their purpose? One might easily mistake them for Klansmen but they are not; they are Trappist monks away from their monastery dressing for a special ceremony in which one of the monks (not shown) will be consecrated as their Abbot. This is a literal description of the photograph. At another level it is interesting to contrast the monks in white against the monk in black. White signifies innocence and purity, black darkness and death. The monk in black appears ghost-like, in profile, walking out of the picture.

Every concept in our conscious mind, in short, has its own psychic associations.

Carl Jung

Figure 3.2   "Trappist Monks," Richard Zakia.

The contrast of white against black also suggests *Notan*, a Japanese word meaning dark-light, the interaction between two opposing forces (see Chapter 1). In the ancient Chinese symbol of Yin/Yang these opposing forces are seen in perfect harmony. (Niels Bohr, a Danish theoretical physicist who died in 1962, would remind us that opposites are complementary.)

Advertisements

Advertisements are based on associations (see Figure 2.17), and the associations made are your very own. Advertising operates on the basis of visual suggestion. Popular figures in sports are shown in ads for related products to suggest success, winning; the archetypal hero image.

In like manner, the cowboy in cigarette ads can project the same rugged hero archetype. Women's products suggesting beauty, slimness, playfulness, and so on, are always in the context of appropriate signifiers such as an admiring handsome male figure, a beautiful female celebrity, flowers, diamonds, and the like.

Many ads are based on familiar works of art, directly or indirectly by style (Figure 3.3).

The copy in a romantic ad for Perrier reads:
Kiss
Love
Joy
Desire
Man
Woman
Perrier

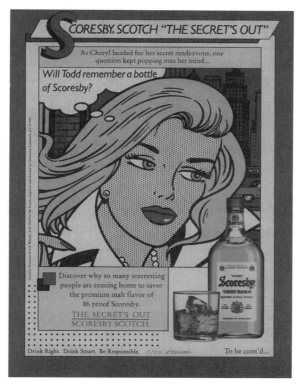

Figure 3.3   Art in ads. (Courtesy of Scoresby Scotch.)

Associating a product with a work of art gives it significance and value. It "...suggests a cultural authority, a form of dignity, even wisdom...." The association, according to John Berger in his book, *Ways of Seeing*, is that, "Art is a sign of affluence; it belongs to the good life; it is part of the furnishing which the world gives to the rich and beautiful ... art also suggests a cultural authority, a form of dignity, even wisdom, which is superior to any vulgar material interests...."[4]

Works of art have intrinsic formal qualities and are easily recognized by a large public; they become a sort of Gestalt. "Art expresses some of the most intense testimony to who the members of a society are, what they do, what they think and feel. Once acknowledged as art and valued as such, works created by artists acquire a special status ... they become symbolic expressions ... successive interpretations of the same work accumulate in a shared way of seeing and understanding ..."[5]

Props (Signifiers)

The props used in creating a photograph are intended to have associative value. They can be thought of as *signifiers*. A snake or serpent, for example, can signify temptation, danger, sexiness, or rebirth as it sheds its skin, depending on the context in which it is used. A serpent can also take the form of a *ouroborus,* coiled in a circle and biting its own tail. It represents a primitive idea of a self-sufficient Nature, a Nature that always returns in a cyclic pattern to its own beginnings. In its broadest sense it is symbolic of time and of the continuity of life. The circular form of the ouroborus symbol can often be seen in advertisements of women's bracelets.

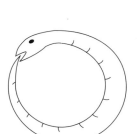

In selecting a particular prop, think of what you want it to *signify* or suggest in the context in which it will be used. What association do you want the viewer/reader to have? An apple with a bite in it by a sensual-looking woman signifies one thing; an apple in a bowl of fruit as part of a photo still life signifies something else.

In designing a photograph, poster, advertisement, or any visual message decide first on what you would like the message to convey, how you would like it to be read, and then select the props, including models, and arrange them to create a good gestalt.

Props as signifiers can take many forms and what they signify or connote is context-dependent. Props serve to foster associations and, for convenience, here is a list of props by categories:

Animals: Bat, bear, bull, cat, cow, coyote, crocodile, deer, dog, dolphin, elephant, fish, fox, frog, goat, horse, lamb, lion, monkey, mouse, pig, serpent, turtle, whale, wolf.
Birds: Dove, eagle, falcon, goose, magpie, owl, peacock, pelican, phoenix, raven, robin, stork, swallow, swan, wren.
Flowers: Bluebell, columbine, dandelion, hyacinth, iris, lily, lily of the valley, lotus, orchid, pansy, poinsettia, poppy, rose, sunflower.
Fruit: Apple, apricot, banana, cherry, fig, grape, kiwi, mango, orange, peach, pomegranate, quince.
Insects: Ant, bee, butterfly, fly, grasshopper, mantis, scorpion, spider.
Nature: Cave, cloud, lightning, moon, mountain, night, ocean, rain, rainbow, rivers, sea, sun, water, wind, trees.

(Information on these signifiers and others including categories such as motifs, sacred objects, rituals, deities, supernaturals, zodiac, body parts, plants, and minerals, can be found in *The Woman's Dictionary of Symbols and Sacred Objects* by Barbara G. Walker, Harper and Row, 1988.)

Colors

Colors also serve as signifiers and are culture- as well as context-dependent. The following is a list of some colors and the various meanings they can take on, realizing that for each named color there are hundreds of variations in hue, chroma, and lightness.

Black: Glossy black suggests formal wear and class while dull black suggests mourning and death.
Blue: Propriety, truth, masculinity, businesslike, timeless, inner peace.
Brown: Earth, security, comfort.
Gold: Wealth, generosity, expensive, upper class.
Green: Environment, health, self-esteem, fertility.
Yellow: Happiness, success, intellect, sunlight, warmth.
Orange: Assertiveness, endurance, pride.
Purple: Sorrow, penitence, spiritual mastery.
Red: Passion, vitality, creativity, warmth.
Silver: Intuition, dreams.
White: Purity, honesty, cleanliness.

Color is symbolic and in its millions of hues, chromas, and lightnesses, feeds our emotions with various connotations that are culturally agreed upon. The listing here given is for western culture. In other cultures the color associations are different. For

When a painting is said to represent nothing but significant form— to carry no meaning, associative connections—the speaker does not know what he is talking about.

Arthur Koestler

Analogy is the only language understood by the unconscious.

Carl Jung

Feeling blue; green with envy; seeing red.

example, in many Asian countries, white symbolizes mourning; in Mexico blue does.

Equivalents

Another way to think of association is in terms of what Alfred Stieglitz and his followers called *equivalents*. In simple terms it is the ability of one thing to bring to mind something else. A photograph can serve as an equivalent that triggers memory and elicits certain feelings and experiences. Stieglitz in the early 1920s photographed clouds that, for him, evoked feelings similar to those derived from listening intently to classical music; visual and auditory became equivalent. Edward Weston in his diaries refers to some of his photographs of peppers, rocks, and sea shells in terms of visual metaphors or equivalents of the human torso. Minor White wrote about different levels of equivalence. At a graphic level one can establish equivalents of shape, form, color, texture, direction, and movement.

At a higher level, symbols, personal imagery, and inner experiences come into play. "Any photograph, regardless of its source, might function as an Equivalent to someone, sometime, someplace. If the individual viewer realizes that for him what he sees in a picture corresponds to something within himself—that is, the photograph mirrors something in himself—then his experience is some degree of Equivalence."[6]

An equivalent can be represented as a triad as shown in Figure 3.4.

Things have always found their expression through a system of reciprocal analogy.

Charles
Baudelaire

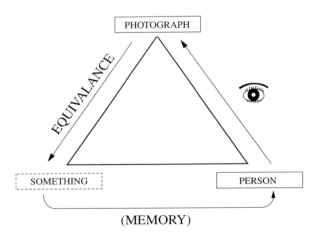

Figure 3.4   Equivalence. A photograph serves to trigger an experience held in long-term memory. Memory and photograph resonate. What is in memory and what is seen in the photograph become equivalent.

The scientist Wolfgang Pauli wrote, "...the conscious realization of new knowledge...seems...to be based on a correspondence, a 'matching' of inner images pre-existent in the human psyche with external objects and their behavior."[7]

People look at photographs and are reminded of something held in memory. The photograph therefore serves as an equivalent for something latent in memory. The process can also work in reverse: something brought forth from memory and pondered can recall a photograph. On the day Edward Weston died, Minor White photographed a waterfall near Rochester, New York at a fast shutter speed so as to stop the action —the flow of water over the falls. For Minor the photograph served as an equivalent for the death of his friend and mentor, and the memory of his death calls forth the photograph he made.

Synesthesia

Associations can also be brought forth by what is called *synesthesia*; the ability of one sensory input to trigger another. As an example, a person can be so moved by music that he or she actually experiences colors. A powerful photograph for a food advertisement is one that will make a person looking at it begin to salivate; here the visual triggers the taste sense. Objects in photographs having visual texture can be experienced as tactile. In some way all of our senses are interconnected and interactive. Sight can and does set off other senses: sound, smell, taste, touch, movement and balance. A photograph with a tilted horizon line, or tilted person or object can elicit a sense of imbalance.

I want a red to be sonorous, to sound like a bell.

Pierre Renoir

A painting by Mondrian titled, "Broadway Boogie-Woogie," is a visual invitation to experience the bouncing movements of an earlier dance craze. It consists of a "bouncing" pattern of hundreds of bright little red, yellow, and blue squares against a light gray background.[8]

Our eyes...work in constant cooperation with the other senses.

Rudolf Arnheim

Onomatopoeia

Another way to think of association is in terms of *onomatopoeia*, the formation of a word that sounds like what it represents: bang, crash, buzz, cuckoo, tick-tock, choo-choo. Traditionally, onomatopoeia refers to words that *sound like* their referent, but we can extend the definition to include more than just the sound of words but also their meaning, as in the use of *simile:*

*Everything is con-
nected to every-
thing else.*

      Lenin

(Seeing) It looks like ...
(Hearing) It sounds like ...
(Touching) It feels like ...
(Tasting) It tastes like ...
(Smelling) It smells like ...

I recall seeing a photograph that was poorly printed and messy, and being puzzled by it until I realized that the photographer was making a statement about the slums in a major city pictured in the photograph. One could think of this as a visual onomato-poeia—the messy, poorly printed photograph itself *looks like* the city slums shown in the photograph. Presentation and content work together to underscore the visual statement.

In his book, *Mirrors, Messages and Manifestations*, Minor White, who extends equivalence to a metaphysical level, makes this statement:[9]

*Everything is
shared by every-
thing else; there
are no disconti-
nuities.*

Frederick Sommer

Not equal to   equivalent to
Not metaphor   equivalence
Not standing for   but being also
Not sign   but direct connection to invisible
Resonance.

KEY WORDS

association
color memory
equivalents
long-term memory (LTM)
metaphor
mnemonic
Notan
onomatopoeia
ouroboros
short-term memory (STM)
signified
signifiers (props)
simile
synesthesia
visual memory

"Rag" © Ruth Bernhard

Memory and Association Exercises

1.   The Magic Number 7, Plus or Minus 2

Discover how many numbers or letters you and your friends can recall correctly after looking at or hearing each of the following sequences once.

(3 items) 852	RLZ
(4 items) 9352	WKNS
(5 items) 58401	RSYWQ
(6 items) 693195	KGDPRM
(7 items) 8251743	HXSWRNW
(8 items) 03756419	ZWUNVRVC
(9 items) 480651975	YTRWSXMKJ
(10 items) 9128374653	RVSXWJHNMK

Variations:
Try recalling the letters or numbers after 5 or 10 minutes with no interruptions and with interruptions (interference). Try the same with these numbers and letters: 246813579 and AEIOUABCDEFG. Although there are nine number and twelve letters, if one sees the relationships in the numbers and letters, they are no longer inde-

It was a cleaning rag hanging on the line to dry. But when I saw it, I didn't see a rag. I saw a crucifixion. And I loved the way the light was touching it.

Ruth Bernhard

Winning at cards requires luck and good short-term memory.

pendent and can be grouped so that there are only two unrelated number sets and letter sets. Grouping reduces the amount of information that has to be remembered.

2. Visual Memory

Select a photograph or advertisement from a magazine and study it for a few minutes with the intention of remembering all the details. Now close the magazine, and after a time try to *draw* a sketch of it and write in the colors as you remember them. Compare your sketch and colors with those of the picture in the magazine.

3. Tonal Memory/Color Memory

Make a good print of one of your black-and-white negatives photographically or electronically. Study the print and remember it. At a later date, without referring to the print, make another print so that it will match tones in the first print. Now compare the two prints. Try the same by making a color print from a color negative or transparency.

4. Visualization

The heart of the Zone System is the ability to visualize a color scene as not having hue or chroma (chrominance) but only lightness. Black-and-white photography records only lightness or brightness. This is a difficult task that takes much practice and a good visual memory. Expose a roll of film to different objects that you see and believe will reproduce as a middle 18% gray (Zone V) in the print.

Process the film as you normally do and print each frame for the same time. Study your results and try again. Ansel Adams has remarked, "Without visualization, the Zone System is just a 5-finger exercise." Visualization requires practice, practice, practice!

5. Coupling

Expose a roll of film so that the two images in each pair of adjacent frames (1 and 2, 3 and 4, 5 and 6, and so on) will couple to form a single image. To be successful you have to remember the content and position of the first image that is to be coupled to the second image.

6. Doodle Memory

A good way to gain practice in visual memory is to draw a doodle, cover it, and then try to duplicate it immediately afterward, and a short and long time afterward.

7. Picture Association

Words can trigger images stored in LTM of which we may not be aware. What picture first comes to mind when you think of:

a) a sports hero	e) an advertisement
b) the moon landing	f) Olympics
c) a male or female vocalist	g) MTV
d) a humorous event	h) terrorism

(In deciding whether or not to caption a photograph, ask yourself whether you want to direct, and perhaps limit, the interpretation, or leave it open to "free association.")

8. Potential Signifiers/Props

What association do you make for the following signifiers:

a) moon
b) dog
c) lotus
d) dove
e) peach
f) butterfly
g) rainbow
h) orchid

9. Clouds as Equivalents

The photographer/cinematographer Ralph Steiner exhibited some of his cloud pictures at Dartmouth College some years ago and invited the attendees to title his photographs. The associations they made were interesting and playful and can be found in his book *In Pursuit of Clouds* (Albuquerque, NM: University of New

Life rhythms felt in no matter what become symbols of the whole.

Edward Weston

Mexico Press, 1985). Here are some examples: The devil's spear, Riding the surf, Night comes creeping, Inflated ego, Primeval swamp, Skeleton in a ballet class, The wind bird, Hysterical pinwheel, Divine grace, Shroud of darkness, Goya's "Chronos Devouring His Children," Dazzling chaos, Eggdrop soup, Marshmallow lava, and many others.

Take some photographs of clouds that you see as equivalents and have friends independently title them, and then compare their titles with titles you may have given the photographs.

10. Visual Metaphors

Look over some of your photographs and write a sentence or two describing them metaphorically. Example: A photograph of a scenic view of hills and valleys with a highway rambling through it might be described in this way; "The highway is a serpent sliding over and around the landscape," or simply, "The highway carpets the land." As a variation, find a poetic sentence or a metaphor that speaks to you and try to find its photographic equivalent.

Notes

1. George Miller, "Information and Memory," *Scientific American*, August, 1965, p.195.

2. Nancy Newhall (ed.), *Edward Weston*, New York: Aperture, 1971, pp. 40, 41.

3. Ibid., p. 41.

4. John Berger, *Ways of Seeing*, New York: Penguin Books, 1988.

5. Mihai Nadin and Richard Zakia, *Creating Effective Advertising Using Semiotics*, New York: Consultant Press, Ltd., 1994, p. 119.

6. Nathan Lyons (ed.), *Photographers on Photography*, New York: Prentice Hall, 1966, p. 169.

7. Harry Robin, *The Scientific Image*, San Francisco, CA: W. H. Freeman, 1993, p. 146.

8. Robert Hughes, *The Shock of the New*, New York: Alfred A. Knopf, 1981, pp. 206, 207.

9. Minor White, *Mirrors, Messages and Manifestations*, New York: Aperture, 1969.

4

Space, Time, and Color

It is through the magic of photography that light becomes the
subject matter with colors, forms, space, and time relationships
that express my deepest feelings and beliefs.

Wynn Bullock

"College Basketball," © Andrew Davidhazy

The wonderful variety of visual experiences available within our visual field can be grouped into three areas; space, time, and color as shown in Table 4.1.

Table 4.1 Three Visual Attributes (Adapted from R. W. Burnham, et al., *Color: A Guide to Basic Facts*)[1]

Visual Experiences		
Space	*Time*	*Color*
depth	movement	hue
transparency	flicker	saturation (chroma)
size	sparkle	brightness (value)
shape/form	fluctuation	
texture	glitter	

SPACE

Capturing pictures with a camera involves the transformation of objects located in a three-dimensional field to that of a photographic two-dimensional field.

In a 3-D field the ability to see depth—to judge distance—involves a number of visual cues, two of which directly involve the eyes: *disparity* and *convergence*. In looking at objects at varying distances in space, the eyes converge; the closer the object the more the convergence (Figure 4.1).

Perspective: From medieval Latin perspectiva, optics; from late Latin, perspectivus, of a view; from Latin perspicere to see through or into.

American
Heritage
Dictionary

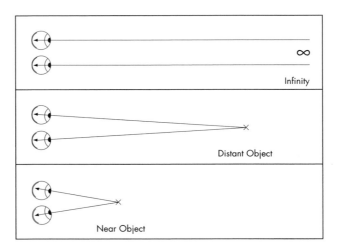

Figure 4.1   Convergence is a 3-D depth cue. At infinity the eyes point straight ahead. For various distances the eyes converge; the nearer the object the more the convergence.

Whereas convergence involves the movement of the eyes, disparity, the basis for stereoscopic depth perception, involves the position of the images formed on the retina from each eye. The two images locate in slightly different positions, and in order for the person to make sense out of this disparity, or incomplete fusion of the two images, the disparity is perceived as representing depth.

When looking at a picture in a 2-D field there are a number of depth cues in the image that provide the perception of depth, and we respond to them automatically. Figure 4.2 provides examples of several types of two-dimensional depth clues:

- *Relative size*—The same object at a far distance appears smaller than at a close distance.
- *Linear perspective*—Railroad tracks (parallel lines) appear to come closer together as distance increases.
- *Texture gradient*—Imagine a plowed field photographed from a perpendicular position; as distance increases the rows appear closer and closer in the photograph.

It is striking to note how few straight lines, parallel or not, appear in a landscape not yet touched by human hands.

Maurits Escher

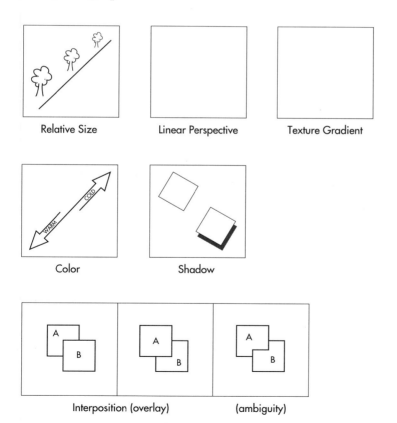

Figure 4.2   *Two-dimensional depth clues. When looking at a 2-D picture there is no physical depth.*

Vertical columns, such as those found in Greek and Roman temples, look parallel from the ground level because they are wider on the top than on the bottom.

- *Color*—There is a tendency for warm colors such as reds to be seen as advancing and cold colors such as blues, receding.
- *Shadow*—An object casting a shadow appears to have more depth (separation) than one that does not.
- *Interposition (overlap)*—A person standing in front of a car overlaps or blocks out part of the car.

Figure 4.2A illustrates another type of depth perception, aerial perspective. Objects at far distances are less clearly seen than near objects due to aerial haze.

Figure 4.2A   Aerial perspective, Kerry S. Coppin, photographer.

To see an object in space means to see it in context.

Rudolf Arnheim

For a moving image, two additional depth cues come into play; *motion perspective* and *motion parallax*. With motion perspective we experience depth because the image of an approaching object increases in size. With images moving across our visual field, near objects appear to move faster than far objects (Figure 4.2B).

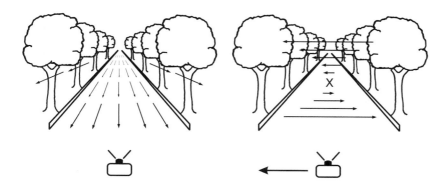

Figure 4.2B   Motion perspective. Left: Near objects appear to move faster when looked at or photographed than far objects. Right: If a person fixates at the (x) position and moves from right to left, objects beyond (x) move in the same direction while those forward of (x) move in the opposite direction. Movement appears least near the fixation (x) point. The same condition exists when a photographer, moving from right to left, fixates his video camera or movie camera on the (x) position.

With motion parallax a lateral change in camera position reveals objects in the background that were blocked from view by objects in the foreground. To experience this, imagine a window as a viewfinder on a camera; moving your head (camera) from side-to-side causes parts of the objects previously covered by the window frame to be seen. Color also plays a role as a depth cue; warm colors such as reds appear to advance while cool colors such as blues seem to recede.

Camera as a Space Vehicle

A camera in space can be moved in three different directions: up or down, left or right, forward or backward, plus three rotational movements, as with a plane or space vehicle: pitch, yaw, and roll, as shown in Figure 4.3.

Our sense of motion as we experience it in changes of balance, in muscular tensions and compensations, in exhilaration is probably an evolutionary experience earlier than vision.

Barbara Morgan

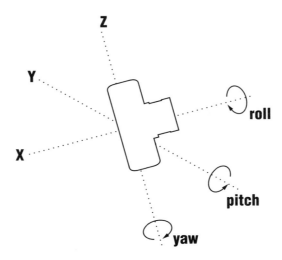

Figure 4.3   The camera as a space ship. Maneuver your camera up, down, and around, and take some unusual pictures. Play around, experiment.

Since one has to look through a viewfinder of a camera when composing a picture, photographs are usually made at eye level. This, however, should not restrict photographers to their height—the distance from ground level to eye level. Imagine the camera as a space vehicle and not restricted by the person holding it. Move it about as if it were a space vehicle in three different directions and three different rotations (pitch, yaw, and roll) to arrive at the best composition and unusual perspective. Ansel Adams photographed landscapes standing on the top of his van using a platform to hold his tripod and view camera.

Anisotropicity

When something is identical in all directions it is called *isotropic*. Adapting this word to a visual field suggests that the visual weight of an object would be the same regardless of its position within the field. This, of course, is not the case, and the word *anisotropic* defines the fact that the same object will have a different visual weight depending upon its position within the picture. Imagine the visual field bisected horizontally and vertically as shown. An object positioned in the upper half of a picture, or the right half, will have more weight than the same object at the bottom half or left half of the picture.

The color of the object also carries weight. Dark colors will appear heavier than light ones. In composing a picture to establish a visual balance one must take into account size, color, and position of the objects within the field, their relationship to each

A circle is isotropic, a square is anisotropic.

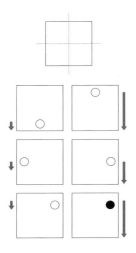

Objects within a picture frame, depending on their size, position, tonality, and color have different visual weights.

other as well as the negative space that surrounds the objects. Creating balance and harmony within a picture is strictly a subjective visual task.

The importance of the anisotropic nature of our visual field can readily be seen in typographic design—the design of letters. Not only must each letter form be balanced top to bottom and left to right but it must also balance when the various twenty-six letters are combined to make the millions of words at our disposal. The letter S, for example, looks visually balanced top to bottom because the top half, which carries more weight, is made smaller than the bottom half. Turning the letter form upside-down emphasizes the difference.

Convexity/Concavity

As shown in the margin, a curved surface can be seen as having two sides, an inner side and an outer side. If the outer side is seen as figure, the shape is seen as convex, and it is experienced as pushing out. When the inner side is seen as figure, the shape then appears to be concave and it is experienced as collecting, as being receptive.

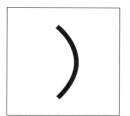

The sail on a sailboat demonstrates this nicely; the concave side of the sail is receptive and as it collects the wind; the convex side pushes out and pulls the boat along with it. A similar situation exists with a hot air balloon; as the inner concave part of the balloon collects hot air, the outer convex side pushes up. An open hand raised in prayer is receptive, while a closed fist is convex and aggressive. Generally speaking, concavity is seen as receptive, nurturing, and feminine, while convexity is seen as masculine and aggressive. Concave seating arrangements in theaters, classrooms, and houses of worship tend to give the gathering a sense of participation and togetherness.

Transparency

A material that is completely *transparent*, such as glass, is nearly invisible, and any object behind it can be seen clearly. A partially transparent (*translucent*) material allows an object to be seen in a veiled or muted way, which is often more interesting. Translucency in a picture is associated with a loss of contrast of an object, as represented in Figure 4.4.

*Figure 4.4   "Nok Kettavong," Samantha Powell. A partially
transparent material will reduce the contrast of
what is behind it.*

Translucency in a photograph can be simulated during printing
by dodging and burning-in techniques and by using various filters
that alter contrast. With electronic imaging, the manipulation to
alter contrast is more direct and simpler.

Photographs of moving objects taken during a long exposure
time of seconds to minutes result in the moving objects appearing
somewhat transparent. The reason for this is that, as the objects
move they receive less exposure, and the edges of the objects are
not sharp. The result is a loss of contrast that gives the moving
object an appearance of transparency. The technique was used in
the early days of photograph in what was called "Ghost Photography." The ghost-like images were used to deceive the gullible
into thinking the photographs were the ghosts of their deceased
loved ones.

TIME (MOVEMENT)

Photography, the ability to stop time and capture an image using
light, had its beginnings in the 1820s with the heliographic work
of Joseph Nicéphore Niépce, and in the 1830s with the photogenic
drawings of Fox Talbot and the daguerreotypes of Louis Jacque
Mandé Daguerre. Motion pictures, the ability to recreate time and

movement using a series of projected photographs, had their beginnings in the late 1800s. "Beginning in 1872, the analysis of motion by the camera was carried on for some 20 years by Eadweard Muybridge and Thomas Eakins in the United States, by Etienne Jules Marey in France, and Ottomar Anschütz in Germany."[2]

Photographers and cinematographers have this in common: Both use cameras and film, and both take still pictures. The primary difference is that with a movie camera the cinematographer can take still pictures in a continuous mode at a rate of 24 pictures a second, while the photographer, with a shoot-and-advance camera, takes pictures one at a time.

And when the still pictures are projected, the photographer's images are shown one at a time, while the cinematographer's images are shown in continuous time. The photographer wishing to create the impression of motion in a picture must do it with a single photograph or two or more adjacent photographs.

Each successive frame of a movie is projected on exactly the same space—the screen—while each frame of comics must occupy a different space. Space does for comics what time does for film.

Scott McCloud, *Understanding Comics*, 1994.

Implied Motion

In simulating the feeling of movement in a still photograph, photographers use techniques such as a slow shutter speed or focus to slightly blur the image, or panning a moving object to cause the background to blur. Multiple exposures have also been used to suggest movement in a still photograph. The American painter Thomas Eakins, in his photographic studies for his painting, photographed on a single plate successive stages of a man jumping, which he titled, "History of a Jump." The famous, "Nude Descending a Staircase" by the French artist Marcel Duchamp (1912), transforms a "posed female nude—into a supremely energetic statement..."[3]

The development of electronic stroboscopic flash by Dr. Harold Edgerton of MIT in the 1940s made the task of recording multiple images on a single sheet of film, to suggest motion, a routine matter.

Motion can also be implied in a single still photograph by capturing the action at the precise moment the gesture and position of the entire articulated body lie between stillness and mobility (see Figure 4.5). This figure shows a photograph from Barbara Morgan's book, *Summer's Children*. Her ability to suggest motion in her still photographs of dancers in the early 1940s was referred to as "Stillness and Mobility" by Professor Rudolf Arnheim.

A basic problem in art is how to project action upon an immobile, flat surface.

Rudolf Arnheim

Figure 4.5   *"Children Dancing by the Lake," 1940. © Barbara
Morgan (Williard and Barbara Morgan Archives,
Dobbs Ferry, New York). Implied motion is
suggested in this joyful photograph of spirited
children.*

Disappearance

In the early days of photography slow film speeds required long
exposure times, which resulted in moving vehicles and people
being underexposed and a bit blurry. The longer the exposure time,
the more the blur and the fainter the image of a moving object.
And, if the exposure was sufficiently long, the moving object
would be underexposed so badly that no detectable image would
be formed. By controlling exposure time, therefore, one can make
moving objects "disappear." Such control is most useful when, for
example, one is trying to photograph a store front on a busy street.
Using a small aperture and neutral density filters in front of the
lens allows for long exposure times. A scene requiring an exposure
of 1/125th of a second at f/8 would receive the same exposure at
1/30th of a second at f/22. Adding a 3.0 neutral density filter in
front of the lens increases the required exposure time by 10 stops
to 32 seconds at f/22. Each additional 0.30 of neutral density (ND)
corresponds to one full stop (a 0.10 ND filter is 1/3rd of a stop)
as shown in Table 4.2.

Table 4.2 Using Neutral Density Filters to Increase Exposure Times

0.30	1 stop	2X
0.60	2 stops	4X
0.90	3 stops	8X
1.00	3 1/3 stops	10X
2.00	6 2/3 stops	100X
3.00	10 stops	1000X
4.00	13 1/3 stops	10,000X

An alternative method for the disappearance of moving objects is to repeat a series of very short intermittent exposures, exposures too short to record moving objects. For example, if a scene requires an exposure of 1/50th of a second at f/22, a summation of 20 intermittent exposures of 1/1000 of a second at f/22 would be equivalent (20/1000 = 1/50). (This assumes no intermittency effect.)

COLOR

Just as space is three-dimensional, so is color in the sense that it has three dimensions or attributes: hue, saturation (chroma), and brightness or lightness (value). Color is a visual experience dependent on light—if there is no light, then there is no color. The often-read and repeated statement that black is the absence of color is incorrect: *Black is a color.* More correctly, black is a color that has no hue. Blacks, grays, and whites are all colors having different lightnesses. They are neutral colors—achromatic colors—colors without hue. Black-and-white photography records only the lightness dimension of color—the tones or values.

The Zone System is based on the ability to visualize and photographically control the lightness dimension of color in tones of blacks, grays, and whites.

Color Is a Chameleon

Color is not only dependent upon light, and of course an observer, but also on its context or *surround.* Change the surround of a color and the color, which is strictly a visual experience, changes. A red apple against a green background will look more saturated (reddish) than against a maroon background or a neutral background.

I have an infamously low capacity for visualizing relationships which made the study of geometry and all subjects derived from it impossible for me.

Sigmund Freud

Black is the queen of all colours.

Henri Matisse.

The zone system is based on the ability to visualize and photographically control the lightness dimension of color in tones of blacks, grays, and whites

A color cannot exist without an environment.

Edwin Land

Every time the background of a color changes the color changes; it is an interdependent and interactive figure-ground relationship.

Artist and Yale professor Josef Albers in his classic book, *Interaction of Color,* wrote that, "…with color—'we do not see what we see.' Because color, as the most relative medium in art, has innumerable faces or appearances."[4]

Simultaneous Contrast and Assimilation

A dark surround makes white areas (highlights) in a picture appear lighter.

A light surround makes dark areas (shadows) in a picture appear darker.

Physical and psychophysical measurements made to specify color do not account for the effect that different backgrounds can have on the appearance color. The importance of this can be seen in Figure 4.6A in which the lightness dimension of a gray color changes as a function of the changing background. To make a color appear darker, choose a lighter background and vice versa. The greater the difference between a color and its background—between figure and ground—the more the change. The lightness of a color can also be changed by simply adding lines across the color as shown in Figure 4.6B.

(A)

(B)

Figure 4.6   (A) Simultaneous contrast. A light surround
                  darkens the small area. (B) Assimilation. A light
                  surround lightens the small area. (Assimilation is
                  the opposite of simultaneous contrast.)

Notice in Figure 4.6B, however, that adding dark lines across the color darkens the color and that light lines lighten the color. The level of lightness change can be controlled by increasing or decreasing number and width of the lines. The closer the lines are together the greater the change. This visual effect of *assimilation* is opposite that of *simultaneous contrast*.

Color Modality

"The contexts in which colors are experienced are called the *modes of appearance of color*; they are aspects of a total visual experience *apart from color*."[5] In practical terms, a fashion model will not look the same in a color reflection print, a transparency, or a video screen having the same measurable colorimetric characteristics. The reason is that the "modes of appearance of color" are different. Color is not only unique to its surround but also to its mode of presentation.

There are five different modes of appearance of color, and it is important to distinguish these whenever color reproduction and comparisons are being made:

- *Object color* is the color of the surface of an object such as a blue spruce tree, blue blouse, or sweater. Color reflection prints are surface colors.
- *Volume color* is the color seen when looking into a transparent medium such as water, glass, or plastic. It is the color of a blue lake or swimming pool, a glass of red wine. Liquid filter colors are volume color.
- *Aperture color* refers to color seen in space but not recognizable as belonging to an object, such as the bluish color of the sky. Color measurements made with densitometers and colorimeters using small apertures are aperture color measurements.
- *Illumination color* is the color of light, other than white light, falling on an object, such as a bluish light reflected from a white dress or shirt for dramatic effect. The blue shadows on snow seen in photographs are a result of illumination from the blue sky on a sunny day. A color slide projected on a screen is illumination color.
- *Illuminant color* is the color of the light source itself such as a red, yellow, and green traffic light, Christmas tree lights, and fire.

The color seen on a video screen is illuminant color consisting of red, green and blue phosphor lights. A color transparency

Strong form and space inhibits colour interaction while strong colour interaction obliterates form and space.

Anton Ehrenzweig

Viewing of a color in a particular situation is, at best, a peculiar mixture of attention, intention, and memory.

Ralph Evans

Primary colors. Subtractive Primaries: *cyan, magenta, and yellow (dyes, inks);* Additive Primaries: *red, green, and blue lights (phosphors);* Psychological Primaries: *red, green, blue, and yellow.*

*Color is a means
of expressing light.*

Henri Matisse

viewed on an illuminator is a combination of illuminant color and surface color.

Recognizing that the appearance of color is dependent not only on its surround but also on the different modalities of object, volume, aperture, illuminant, and illuminance should caution one when making direct comparisons between different color modalities. Appearances of the same image in a print, in a transparency on an illuminator, or projected, or on a video screen, will not be the same.

Back in the 1960s Marshall McLuhan coined the phrase, "The medium is the message." To paraphrase this slightly one might say that the medium changes the message or, in terms of color appearance, the medium changes the color appearance.

Complementary Colors

When a neutral color is formed by the mixture of only two colors, those colors are said to be *complementary*. Imagine the beams of light from two slide projectors superimposed on a screen. Over one projector lens is placed a blue filter and over the other, a yellow filter. If adjustment of the intensities of the beams can produce the appearance of a neutral white, the two colors are complementary. By such an *additive* mixing of lights, a very large number of complementary colors can be found.

Subtractive complementary colors are of interest since they can make many near-neutrals and, thus, desaturated colors. In photography, it is usual to examine a test color print through a variety of CC filters, changing the filters until a "neutral" appears neutral. Such a procedure aids in distinguishing a cyan color-balance error requiring a red complementary filter from a blue error requiring a yellow filter.

Complementary
colors:
*Red + Cyan
Green + Magenta
Blue + Yellow.*

The term complementary is also used with pigment mixtures. Two paints are complementary if, when they are mixed in correct proportions, a visual neutral gray or black results. Not all pairs of pigments that appear to be complementary are capable of producing a truly neutral mixture due to the complex light-absorbing characteristics of most pigments.

In most color imaging systems three primary colors are used to produce color images since variable mixtures of three colors provide maximum control over hue, saturation, and lightness—red, green, blue (r, g, b) with the additive system and cyan, magenta, and yellow with the subtractive system.

Because of afterimages, complementary colors can also be seen using only one color. If one looks steadily at a vivid blue patch for a minute or so and then looks at a white surface, a complementary yellow afterimage is seen.

Such perceptual complements are significant in color composition. When complements are made part of the design, each has the effect of making the other appear more saturated, and thus making the composition more dramatic than otherwise. On the other hand, an effect of delicacy and softness results from a design in which complements are avoided.

Color Temperature

A candle is said to give off light having a color temperature of 1800 degrees Kelvin (1800K); a 100-watt tungsten lamp has a color temperature of 2900K. Any source of light may be given a color temperature rating if it visually matches the light produced by a blackbody at the same temperature. The reddish color of light given off by a candle matches that of a *blackbody* at a temperature of 1800K. A blackbody is an ideal object capable of absorbing all light falling on it and then reflecting it.

Color temperatures of some other sources of light are:

250-watt photographic lamp	3200K
250-watt studio flood lamp	3400K
Direct sunlight	500K
Photographic daylight	5500K
Electronic flash	6000K
Overcast sky light	8000K
North sky light	15,000K

As color temperature increases the color of the light source goes from reddish, to bluish, to white. Color film can be balanced for only one color temperature. The most accurate color is obtained when the film is exposed at that color temperature.

Daylight film is best when it is exposed at a color temperature of 5500K; a mixture of sunlight and daylight from about 10 am to 3 pm. Color temperature is also important in establishing standard viewing conditions for printing, judging, and displaying color images.

Mireds

Because the significance of a given change in color-temperature values varies with the magnitude of the values themselves, a conversion of the numbers into *mireds* is useful. The number of mireds is found by dividing the color temperature value into 1,000,000 (for example, 2500K = 400 mireds).

A given change expressed in mireds has about the same significance at any level of color temperature. Color conversion filters are often identified with the change in mireds they produce with any blackbody source operated at any temperature level.

Don't confuse the spelling of the word complement with compliment. A mnemonic for remembering this is that the latter word has an "i" in it. "I" pay someone a compliment.

Different video screens have correlated color temperatures that range from about 6500K to 10,000K.

Filter Conversions: *An orange 85B converts daylight to tungsten. A bluish 80A filter converts tungsten to daylight.*

Photographic daylight is 5500K or 182 mireds.

Correlated Color Temperature

Light sources that do not approximate blackbody sources in their spectral emissions cannot be given true color temperature values. Fluorescent lights are such an example. They are, however, assigned a designation of *correlated or equivalent* color temperature.

Color Names

Considering that one can, under controlled conditions, distinguish between a million or so different colors (including variations in hue, chroma, and value) in *side-by-side comparisons*, it is inconceivable that any system of color names could be devised that would provide accurate identification of such a large number of different colors.

Color names, however, are the most commonly used means of identifying colors in nontechnical communication. When greater precision is not required, the basic hue names serve their purpose well—as when referring to red, white, and blue flag colors. Other hue names can be added by identifying intermediate hues such as a reddish-blue. Also, value (lightness) variations can be identified as light or dark, and chroma (saturation) variations as strong or weak.

Although there are size limitations to any system that identifies colors by names, the Inter-Society Color Council (ISCC) and the National Bureau of Standards (NBS) produced *The ISCC-NBS Method of Designating Colors and a Dictionary of Color Names* in 1955 that included 267 different colors, identified by Munsell notations, and 7,500 color names. Table 4.3 shows a sample of some color names and their Munsell values.

(These Munsell notations can also be converted to the scientific CIE (1931) system of color notations. For example, strong red with a Munsell value of 5R 4/12 has a CIE value of x=.54, y=.31 and Y=12.)

Table 4.3 Color Names, Munsell Notation, and ISCC-NBS Names

Color Names	Munsell Notation		ISCC-NBS Names
	Hue	*Value/Chroma*	
Red	5R	4/12	Strong red
Orange	5YR	6/11	Strong orange

Color Names	Munsell Notation		ISCC-NBS Names
	Hue	*Value/Chroma*	
Yellow	5Y	8/11	Vivid yellow
Foliage	6.7 GY	4.2/4.1	Moderate olive green
Blue sky	4.3 PB	5/5.5	Moderate blue
Dark skin	3 YR	3.7/3.2	Moderate brown
Light skin	2.2 YR	6.5/4.1	Light reddish brown
White	N	9.5/0	White
Gray	N	5/0	Medium gray
Black	N	2/0	Black

Imagine a piano having seventy-five thousand different sounds. This is the situation of painters.

Salvador Dali

Hooray for Hue!!

Advertisement, 1994

In the field of advertising, color names seem to be created primarily for emotional impact. It has been found, for example, that changing the name of the color of a product from a common name, such as pink, to a name that has a contemporary, exotic association, such as Oriental pink, without actually changing the color, can increase the sales of that product dramatically.

Cosmetic manufacturers marketing products such as lipstick commonly use sensually charged words such as

Strawberry Red	Dreamy Red
Lilac Champagne	Little Red-Red
Rose Crush	Darling Pink
Wild Wine	French Pink
Whispering Wine	Spicy Pink

The words *spicy pink* and *whispering wine*, for example, tend to stimulate the palate in addition to the eye, or ear, a phenomenon known as *synesthesia*.

The painter of the
future will be a
colorist such as
had yet never
existed.

Vincent Van Gogh

The Munsell color tree has a vertical trunk that represents a scale of values, *branches that represent different* hues, *and leaves extending along the branches that represent* chromas. *The hues change as you walk around the tree, the values increase as you climb up the tree, and chromas increase as you move out along the branches.* (From Munsell, A Grammar of Color *edited by Faber Birren,* © 1969 *by Litton Educational Publishing Inc. Reprinted by permission of Van Nostrand Reinhold.*)

KEY WORDS

afterimage

anisotropic

aperture color

assimilation

blackbody

chroma

color modality

color temperature

complementary colors

convexity/concavity

correlated color temperature
hue
illuminant color
illumination color
isotropic
lightness
mired
modes of color appearance
motion parallax
motion perspective
neutral
neutral density (ND) filter
object color
saturation
simultaneous contrast
surface color
volume color

Space, Time, and Color Exercises

1. Space Vehicle

Make several photographs of the same scene using your camera as a space vehicle. Observe the scene as you move your camera up and down, left to right, forward and backward, and as you pitch, yaw, and roll it.

2. Cubistic Space

Take a series of photographs of the same subject from different positions—front, side, back, top, and at different distances from the subject. Make prints and mount the prints in such a way as to create an interesting and visually challenging mosaic. Look at some of the cubistic images of artists such as David Hockney, Robert Heinecken, and Joyce Neimanas for ideas.

3. Anisotropicism

Rudolf Arnheim writes, "The dominant pull of gravity makes the space we live in asymmetrical. Geometrically, there is no difference between up and down; dynamically, the difference is fundamental."[6]

Arrange a setup so that the objects are balanced top to bottom, left to right, and then take a photograph. Now add another object or two to the setup without disturbing the balance. Make a photograph and compare it to the first photograph.

All works of art are created on a certain scale. Altering the size alters everything.

Edward Hall

4. Convexity/Concavity

Look around for architectural structures, building interiors, outdoor and indoor sculptures that have convex and concave shapes. Study them and then photograph them to emphasize their shapes.

5. Transparency/Translucency

Photograph someone moving their hands up and down or head to the left and right using an exposure time of about 1/2 second. Repeat this using longer or shorter exposure times. (Look at some of the photographs by Man Ray and by Richard Avedon that display this type of transparency.)

6. Ghosts

Using an exposure time of about 1/2 second, photograph a person moving left or right out of the picture area as the shutter is tripped. (Review some of Duane Michals' photographs.)

7. Implied Motion

Take a series of photographs to capture the gesture of a person that suggests movement. Study them and select the one that best captures the implied movement.

8. Levitating

Using a fast shutter speed, photograph a person jumping up and down. Try to capture them in midair so as to make it appear they are levitating.

9. Panning

Create the appearance of movement in a still photograph by "locking" your camera on a moving object, and then moving the camera smoothly with the object as it passes your field of view.

10. Disappearance

Photograph an outdoor sculpture (or other stationary subject) on a busy street and record only the sculpture, and not the people or vehicle traffic in the area.

11. Disappearing/Reappearing

People and objects can be made to appear from nowhere and disappear simply by stopping the film or video camera during a shoot and having an object or person inserted into a scene or taken out, and then continuing the shoot.

12. Creeping Shadows

Photograph a stationary object on a bright day, at different times of the day, to capture its "moving" shadow.

Does a pictorial work come into being at one stroke? No, it is constructed bit by bit just like a house.

Paul Klee

Habit diminishes the conscious attention with which our acts are performed.

William James

The shadows are full of play. What resourcefulness in their relationship with each other.

Edgar Degas

13. Flip Photo Animation

Set up a tabletop scene and place your camera on a tripod to photograph it. Make a series of photographs moving one or more of the objects slightly between each exposure. Make small prints, about 4×5 inches, and place them in a stack so that you can flip through them and create a "moving" image.

14. Color, Colour, Couleur

Using the same outdoor lighting, take color photographs of a person dressed in colorful clothes against a red brick wall, green foliage, and a neutral or near neutral background. Make color prints and compare the person's skin tones and other colors.

It was when everything was covered with snow that I perceived that the doors and the windows were blue.

Albert Camus

15. Lightness Matching

Obtain samples of papers having different solid colors (paint-sample chips, construction paper, and the like) and a photographic gray-scale. Place a small square of each color on the gray-scale tone that appears to match the *lightness* of the color. If the color appears to be between two tones in lightness, place it on the dividing line.

16. Color Temperature

Using color film in light having the wrong color temperature can sometimes result in some interesting slides. Daylight film shot at early morning or early evening will have a warming effect. Try moonlight, street lights, car headlights, gallery lights, mixed lights. Experiment, play around with different films and light sources.

Solid materials such as tungsten emit a continuous spectrum of light. Gases and vapors such as mercury found in fluorescent lights emit a discontinuous spectrum.

17. Reciprocity

Extended exposure times will cause reciprocity failure, which can result in a color imbalance. Try a normal exposure time of about 1/125th or 1/60th of a second and then exposure times of 1/2 second, 1 second, 2 seconds, and so on. Adjust the camera f-stop as needed to maintain equal exposures each time. You may need to add neutral density filters for long times. Remember, adding a 0.30 neutral density filter is the equivalent of one stop; a 0.60, two stops; a 0.90 (0.30 + 0.60), three stops, and so on. Compare the results. Look for both a loss in exposure effectiveness (a darker-looking slide) and a shift in color balance.

18. Complementary Afterimage

Stare at the dot in the snowflake pattern in the following figure for about 30 seconds and then shift your gaze to the dot in the white area. You should experience a reverse image. If the snowflake were the color blue, you would see a yellow afterimage; if red, a cyan image; if green, a magenta image. You may want to color the character and test this out.

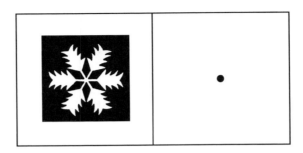

Complementary afterimages. Afterimages can be either positive or negative with respect to lightness and hue.

Notes

1.   R.W. Burnham, R.M. Hanes, and C. James Bartleson, *Color: A Guide to Basic Facts*, New York: John Wiley, 1963, p. 12.

2.   Naomi Rosenblum, *A World History of Photography*, New York: Abbeville Press, 1984, p. 249.

3.   Ibid, p. 255.

4.   Josef Albers, *Interaction of Color*, New Haven, CT: Yale University Press, 1972, p. x.

5.   Burnham, et al., *Color: A Guide to Basic Facts*, p. 11.

6.   Rudolf Arnheim, *The Power of the Center*, Berkeley, CA: University of California Press, 1982, p. 11.

5
Contours

The borderline between two adjacent shapes having double functions, the act of tracing such a line is a complicated business. On either side of it, simultaneously, a recognizability takes shape.

Maurits Escher

Mosaic patterns, Alhambra.

119

The Alhambra, located in southern Spain, was visited by Escher in 1936. "For whole days at a time he and his wife made copies of the Moorish tessellations [mosaic patterns], and on his return home he set to work to study them closely."[1] The repeated cloning of the shape that makes up the mosaic varies in orientation and tonality but all share a common contour. "These patterns represent a high point of the Arab exploration of the subtleties and symmetry of space...."[2] Seen from the outside, the Alhambra takes the form of a fortress. From the inside it is a palace of honeycomb courts and chambers. "The Alhambra is the last and most exquisite monument of Arab culture."[3]

Contrast (density differences) between adjacent areas in an image allows us to see *contours* or edges. The sharper the edge the higher the contrast appears; the higher the contrast the sharper the edge appears. Sharp or "hard" edges appear to advance while soft edges appear to recede. Controlling the sharpness of an edge by selective focus controls, to some extent, contrast and depth. The more abrupt the tonal change at an edge the sharper it appears. The judgment of sharpness is strictly visual. A physical measure of sharpness is called *acutance*. Some films are rated in acutance as well as speed, resolution, and graininess. Some slow-working developers enhance the acutance of an edge in a photograph by increasing the density difference at the very edge. This result is called an *adjacency effect*.

Whereas sharpness is a visual effect, adjacency effects are physical effects within the photographic image; there is an actual increase and decrease in density at the edges (contours, boundaries) of an image.

> *Most tribal art is hard-edge. It is art of sharp contrasts, sudden juxtapositions, and superimpositions. So is children's art.*
>
> Edmund Carpenter

COMMON CONTOUR

In his book, *Art and Visual Perception*, Dr. Rudolf Arnheim asks this question, "What happens when two similarly qualified competing surfaces both claim the same contour?"[4] The illustration in the margin shows that there is a competition between the two shapes sharing the same or common contour. Arnheim refers to this as *contour rivalry*. "Perceived as a whole, the figures look stable enough, but when we concentrate on the common central vertical we notice a tug-of-war. The sharing of borders is uncomfortable, and the two hexagons exhibit an urge to pull apart since each figure has a simple independent shape of its own."[5]

Examples of common or shared contours abound in the work of the Dutch artist Maurits Escher (1898–1972). Escher was keenly aware that shapes have a "double function," and he used this brilliantly in his drawings.

The Danish psychologist, Edgar Rubin, in the early 1900s called attention to the ambiguity and playfulness of common contours in his writing and exemplified in his figure-ground vase/face illustration seen previously in Chapter 1, Figure 1.6.

But even much earlier than this, artists used common contours to embed shapes in a visual hide-and-seek game to make a variety of statements, some dangerously political. The 1794 print by Pierre Crussaire titled, "The Mysterious Urn," shown at the beginning of Chapter 1, is loaded with symbols and a number of embedded profile faces, the most prominent being the two that share contours with the urn.

In the photograph "Dunes, Colorado" seen in Figure 5.1, a common contour is shared by the very edge (contour) of the white and black areas.

Edgar Rubin's double profiles, 1921. The two profiles share a common contour but are unable to share a kiss.

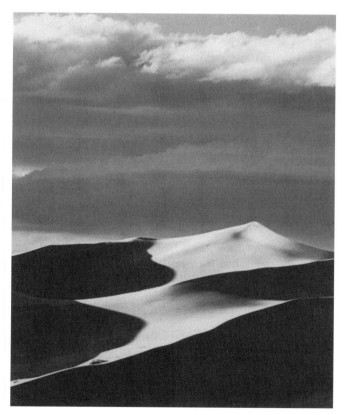

Figure 5.1   *"Dunes, Colorado" © Thomas L. McCartney. At the very edge where the black and white areas meet, a common contour is shared. Rivalry for possession of the edge serves to shift the figure-ground relationship.*

Where the edges are sharp (hard edge), a competition takes place between the black and white shapes. Where the edges are not as sharp (soft edge), the competition is less noticeable. This photograph by Dr. McCartney is also a wonderful example of Notan; dark/light, opposites in harmony, opposites as complementary, figure and ground as one.

An example of the use of common contour in typography can be seen in the design of letter combinations such as Æ or æ. This tying together or binding of letters is called *ligature*—something that unites as seen in the text in Figure 5.2. Gutenberg's movable type consisted of a large assortment of ligatures so that he could create a printed page that was similar to that of a manuscript page.

A ligature is a character that contains two or more letters. Ligatures were employed by the medieval scribes since they could be easily constructed with a pen and enabled them to write at a more rapid rate. Gutenberg's movable type included an extensive assortment of ligatures because he wanted to create a printed page that was undistinguishable from the hand drawn manuscript. The number of ligatures decreased as time went on for economic rather than esthetic reasons.

Figure 5.2   Common contour is the basis for ligatures in typography.

To perceive an image is to participate in a forming process; it is a creative act.

Gyorgy Kepes

Photographers can have fun with common contours by photographing objects located at different distances in space from a point of view that results in shared contours (Figure 5.3). This results in an ambiguous situation in which the perception of depth in the photograph is lost only in the contour area where the two disparate objects share a common contour. This illusionistic ambiguity can add interest and intrigue to a photograph.

Figure 5.3   *"A Playful Common Contour," Scott Johnson.*
When near and far objects share the same contour,
there is no overlap. The perception of depth is lost.
Overlap is an important depth cue.

A rather interesting color photograph made some years ago by Pete Turner shows a trash can on a sandy beach photographed from a set perspective that positions the edge of the red top of a yellow trash can so that it coincides with the blue horizon line. The shared contour of the top of the trash can and the horizon line not only collapses depth in the photograph but according to the British psychiatrist Anton Ehrenzweig, and others, such a juxtaposition causes an enhancement in the colors at the very edge of the shared contours. Ehrenzweig calls attention to the experimental work of Josef Albers' nesting of squares and points out, "…how much color interaction depends on a comparative weakness of form…."[6] The simplicity of form in Turner's photograph makes it subservient to the colors that are set free to interact. At the very edge, the blue horizon line becomes bluer and the red top of the trash can, redder.

Line drawing of Pete Turner's color photograph, "Push."

SUBJECTIVE CONTOUR

The two triangles shown to the side provide a powerful example of how our visual system, given incomplete information, fills in to form a closure on a familiar shape. The incomplete triangle with the disrupted lines is readily seen as a complete triangle due to the Gestalt laws of continuation and closure. The other, far less complete triangle, having no lines but only short edges where the three black discs are located, is also seen as a complete triangle. It is difficult not to experience it as a triangle, even with the minimum amount of information provided. Notice also that the white area enclosed by this triangle is whiter than the white of the surround. This is strictly a subjective visual experience.

Subjective contour.

The contour lines are *virtual lines* and the triangle is a *virtual triangle*—existing as a visual effect and not as an actual physical form. A famous photograph by Dr. Harold Edgerton of a golfer swinging his club shows a similar effect (Figure 5.4). Between the repeated ends of the golfer's club and his body, there appears to be a curved contour and the enclosed area appears to be blacker than the black surround. Density measurements would reveal no physical difference. (This photograph also serves as an example of the Gestalt laws in action. A shell-like pattern emerges as the visual elements (white golf clubs) are visually connected, as in a moving image. The similarity of the repetitive golf clubs and their proximity to each other provides for easy continuity, implied movement, and closure.)

Perception is a process of construction, of participation, of creativity, and the need to form closure is a basic perceptual need.

*Figure 5.4   "Densmore Shute Bends the Shaft," Harold
Edgerton, © The Harold E. Edgerton 1992 Trust.
(Courtesy of Palm Press, Inc.) Notice how the
enclosed "crescent" between the repeated ends of
the golfer's club handle and his body appears
darker than the surround; an example of subjective
contour in a photograph.*

MACH BANDS

In a completely homogeneous visual field—a Ganzfeld—there is
no vision, as mentioned in Chapter 1. Vision is dependent upon
change as is all perception—hearing, touching, smelling, tasting.
Perception is a dynamic, interactive process.

The familiar gray scale in Figure 5.5 shows that at the very
edge of the areas where there is a change in lightness, there appears
to be an edge or contour.

*In the fields of
observations,
chance favors
only the mind
that is prepared.*

Louis Pasteur

Figure 5.5   *The Mach effect. At the very edge of each gray area in the gray scale, there appears to be a very narrow dark and light band. This is strictly a visual effect. Without it there would be a loss in contrast. It is the way our eyes process edge information and shows why edges are so critical to perception.*

The edge is a virtual edge and exists as a result of the tonal change—the contrast—between adjacent areas. If one looks closely at the edge, an increase in contrast at the very edge is noticed. This increase, consisting of a very narrow darker band in the dark area and a lighter band in the light area, is a visual effect known as a *Mach band*, named after the Austrian scientist, Ernst Mach (1838–1916) who first described it. It is important to realize that Mach bands have their existence in the way we see and not in the actual image. And, since it is a visual phenomenon, it is independent of the particular medium used.

The photograph of the Colorado dunes shown earlier in Figure 5.1 provides an excellent example of how the Mach effect enhances the contrast of the very edge of two adjacent areas. An attentive look at the edge separating the white and black areas will reveal the Mach phenomenon operating to enhance contrast and therefore sharpness. Contrast and sharpness go hand in hand. With a camera, the sharpness of an edge can be controlled by selective focus, depth of field, and special filters. This in turn will have an effect on the contrast of the image. In short, the contrast of an image can be manipulated by controlling the sharpness of the edges in the image. Software such as Adobe Photoshop increases sharpness and contrast of an image by electronically enhancing its edges.

Artists have known and used this contrast enhancement effect for centuries. "Artists of the 19th-century Neo-Impressionist school were unusually meticulous in their observations ... A good example is Paul Signac's 'Le petit déjeuner.' In this painting there are numerous contrast effects in and around the shadows and half-shadows."[7] Similar effects can be seen in Edward Weston's photograph "Nude 1936" (Chapter 2, Figure 2.22B). Observe how some shadows have a soft edge and some a hard edge, and how this affects the local contrast.

The observer is part of the observed.

Thomas Merton

VISUAL VIBRATIONS

Contours, boundaries, and edges are very important to the process of visual perception. The eyes continuously search them out for information. Under certain conditions, a shimmering movement can occur at a boundary of an area. With color images, boundaries of color areas having similar lightness and complementary hues, such as red and cyan, tend to appear to vibrate or shimmer.

The more saturated the colors, the stronger the effect. An early movement called OpArt was based on this phenomenon, most notably perhaps in the paintings by Victor Vasarely.

Vincent Van Gogh was aware of the effect and used it in subtle ways. In a letter to his brother Theo in 1888, he wrote of trying "...to express the feeling of two lovers by a marriage of two complementary colors, their mixtures and their oppositions, the mysterious vibrations of tones in each other's proximity."[8] Josef Albers, who did extensive experimentation with color interactions in his "Homage to a Square" series, wrote in his chapter on "Vibrating Boundaries," "The conditions for these [vibrating boundary] effects occur between colors which are contrasting in their hues but also close or similar in light intensity."[9]

Vibrations can also be seen with certain repetitive patterns of black-and-white lines, as in Figure 5.6. Although visual vibrations are not as evident in conventional photographs, they are easily created photographically by making high contrast photographs of moiré patterns or by playing off images using various darkroom techniques such as relief images and masking, or simply digitizing a photographic image and manipulating it on a computer.

The reason that edges seem to vibrate under certain conditions is complex but appears to be related to physiological factors such as the inhibitory process in the retina and the tremors of the eye called *nystagmus*, and to perceptual phenomena such as simultaneous contrast.

Without contraries there is no progression.

William Blake

Optical art (OpArt) was based on repetitive patterns that vibrate.

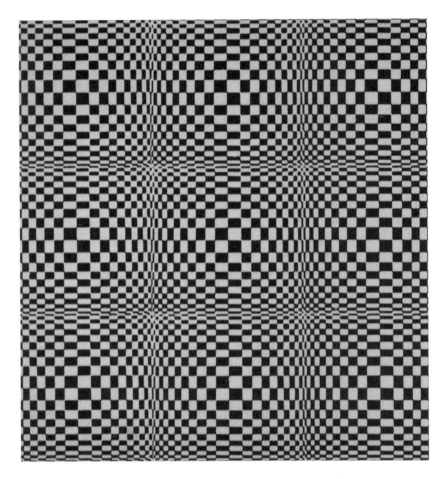

*Figure 5.6   Visual vibrations. Various patterns of edges restrict
                the ability of the eye to fixate, thereby frustrating
                the eye and causing a shimmering sensation.*

PHOTOGRAPHIC EDGE EFFECTS

*1mm = 1000
microns*

A *physical* phenomenon similar to the *perceptual* Mach effect of
an increase in contrast at the edges in an image occurs in photography, xerography, and in video and computer monitor displays.
In photography these effects exhibit a physical increase and decrease in density at the very edges of the image. Figure 5.7 is a
graphical representation showing this density enhancement. It
occurs over a very small distance on the order of a fraction of a
millimeter—about 50 microns.

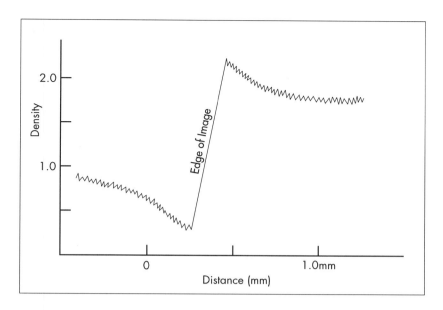

Figure 5.7 Photographic edge effect. The decrease and increase in density at the very edge of an image increases the density difference (amplitude) and therefore the sharpness of the image.

This increase in contrast as a result of an increase in edge density, in addition to being called an edge effect, is also referred to as an adjacency effect, neighborhood effect, border effect, fringe effect and, depending upon the size and shape of the image, the Eberhard effect and the Kostinsky effect.

Acutance

Photographic edge effects serve to increase the sharpness of an image. How much that sharpness is increased is a subjective judgment. If a quantitative measure of sharpness is required, microdensity measurements of the edges are made with a scanning microdensitometer. The density numbers are then put into a mathematical formula, fed into a computer, and a measure of sharpness in terms of acutance values is arrived at. There is a positive correlation between acutance values and the subjective judgment of sharpness. Some technical and scientific films are rated in terms of acutance values.

Acutance is a physical measure of sharpness.

Development

Some developers can increase sharpness.

Acutance and sharpness are dependent on not just the film characteristics but also the type of development the film receives. "Development factors that alter edge effects, and therefore image sharpness, include developer strength, developing time, and agitation. Diluting the developer and developing for a longer time with no agitation enhances edge contrast and sharpness. Unfortunately, this procedure can also cause uneven development with some film-developer combinations...One developer specifically formulated to enhance image sharpness with normal-contrast film is the Beutler High Acutance Developer,"[10] named after the man who pioneered developers of this type.

The formula is:

Sodium sulfite (Na_2SO_3)	5.0 grams
Metol	0.5 grams
Sodium carbonate (Na_2CO_3)	5.0 grams
Water	1 liter

As you can see, it is a rather simple formula, having only a few ingredients that are readily available. You may want to give this formula a try with the film you are using. As a starting point, increase your development time to 50 percent more than your usual development time. If your normal development time is eight minutes, try twelve minutes.

"Elizabeth," © John Fergus-Jean. This photograph was taken by a former student of mine, John Fergus-Jean. The photograph is of his then-girlfriend, now wife/mother/artist. I know the narrow long leaf is in the front of Elizabeth's face, but why does it appear to embed itself in her nose and forehead?

KEY WORDS

acutance
adjacency effects
boundary
closure
common contour
continuation
contour
edge
ligature
Mach band
nystagmus
shared contour
subjective contour
virtual contour
virtual lines
visual vibrations

You can observe a lot by just looking around.

Yogi Berra

Contour Exercises

1. Common Contour

Photograph two objects located at different distance so that their contours or edges,
    a) coincide (are shared)
    b) do not coincide.

2. Homage to Alber's Square

Create a photographic "Homage to a Square" by making four overlapping multiple exposures of a uniform square target and enlarging the square each time. This can be done on a computer or with a camera or enlarger. Remember that every photographic exposure increases the previous exposure and builds up density after processing. The opposite is true for reversal films.

3. Typography

Design a word so that the letters share a common contour, and with an alternating figure-ground as in this Eaton logo created by the firm of Lippincott and Margulies Inc. (Courtesy of the Eaton Corporation.)

4. Subjective Contour

Arrange some toothpicks or similar objects on a plain background so that they form a pattern that creates a virtual or subjective contour, and then photograph that pattern. Alternatively, create the patterns on a computer screen and observe the effects. Photograph them if you wish, and remember to use an exposure time longer than 1/30th of a second, or simply print them on a laser printer.

5. Sunlight, Shadow, and Mach Bands

Photograph an object in full sunlight and include the shadow. Observe closely the *borderline* area between sunlight and shadow. Notice a narrow half-shadow (penumbra) that exhibits a thin dark band at the shadow edge and a thin light band at the bright sunlit edge. Edward Weston's "Nude 1936," Figure 2.2B, photographed in bright sunlight, exhibits this Mach band phenomenon.

Josef Alber's color studies in his "Homage to a Square" series were precursors to the OpArt movement in the 1960s.

6. Contours and Vibrations

Visit museums, galleries, libraries and study the paintings of Josef Albers, Victor Vasarely, Paul Signac, Georgia O'Keeffe, and others to discover how they represented edges and contours. Do the same with photographs by photographers such as Ralph Gibson, Eikoh Hosoe, and Barbara Kasten.

7. Contours and Computers

Select an image to scan that emphasizes contours. Make certain the image is cleaned well before scanning. After scanning the image, move it to a computer program such as Adobe Photoshop. Use either brightness/contrast control, levels control, or curves control and you will be able to significantly enhance the contours within your scanned image. Apply changes slowly, however, so that the visual effects of the contour enhancement can be studied.

8. Computer-generated Contours

Create your own Mach band contours without a photograph by using Adobe Photoshop, Aldus Freehand, or Adobe Illustrator. Use one of the programs to draw shapes that vary in brightness and color, and fit them so that they share a common contour. In retouching programs such as Photoshop you will have to fill in selected areas with your paint bucket or paint brush. If you use a draw program such as Illustrator or Freehand you can actually draw the shapes and fill them with color afterward. No matter which route you follow you will be able to explore the vivid effects of contouring.

The color of a spot changes if its size is enlarged or reduced.

Anton Ehrenzweig

Notes

1. Bruno Ernst, *The Magic Mirror of M.C. Escher*, New York: Ballantine Books, 1976, p. 36.

2. J. Bronowski, *The Ascent of Man*, New York: Little, Brown, 1973, p.172.

3. Ibid., p.169.

4. Rudolf Arnheim, *Art and Visual Perception*, Berkeley, CA: University of California Press, 1974, p. 223.

5. Ibid., p. 223.

6. Anton Ehrenzweig, *The Hidden Order of Art*, Berkeley, CA: University of California Press, 1967, p. 155.

7. Floyd Ratliff, "Contour and Contrast," *Scientific American*, June 1972, p. 90.

8. *The Complete Letters of Vincent Van Gogh,* Greenwich, CT: New York Graphic Society, 1958, p. 277.

9. Josef Albers, *Interaction of Color*, New Haven, CT: Yale University Press, 1972, p. 62.

10. Les Stroebel, John Compton, Ira Current, and Richard Zakia, *Basic Materials and Processes*, Boston: Focal Press, 1990, pp. 265, 266.

6
Illusion and Ambiguity

Those things which are most real are the illusions I create in my paintings.

Eugene Delacroix

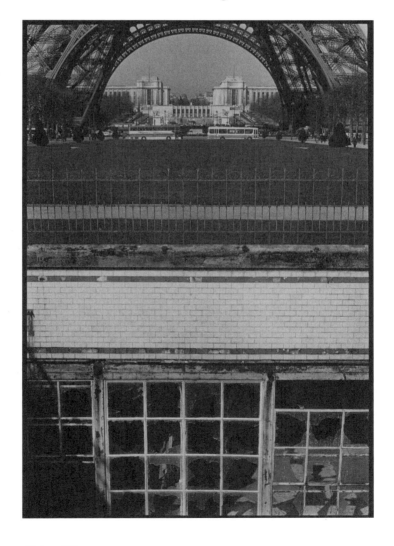

"Paris," © Aaron Usher III

Even the clearest water appears opaque at great depths.

Anonymous

What we see is not identical with what is imprinted upon the eye.

Rudolf Arnheim

Illusions have been studied extensively by perceptual psychologists in an effort to understand the process of vision and to create robotic vision or machine vision. Knowledge of illusions can be useful to photographers, graphic designers, and animators in creating images that defy physical constraints.

People in theatre and movie special effects technologists have done this for years with sight and sound. Illusions can also be used to create visual tension. Knowledge of perceptual illusions provides explanations as to why contradictions between our physical reality and our perceptual reality are part of our experience.

Illusions are real. They are real in the sense that they are *perceived* as being real. We deny this reality when we insist that the visual reality agree with the physical reality. There can be a difference between what we know to be and what we see.

Illusions are defined as experiences that are not in accord with physical reality. Usually when we think of illusions we think of *visual* illusions since vision is our dominant sense. The artist, René Magritte, in his painting of a large eye titled "False Mirror," calls attention to the fact that the eye mirrors our world just as photography, the "mirror with a memory" does. The eye with its lens and iris diaphragm is but a camera. The image on the retina is not what we see. What we see is the result of millions of neurons exchanging information in the cerebral cortex of the brain. The retinal image is just the first step in the process.

All of our senses, sound, taste, touch and smell, are subject to illusions and our language confirms this: "Your whistle *sounds* like that of a bird"; "This mock apple pie *tastes* like the real thing"; "I know it's not a silk scarf but it *feels* like silk"; "This new fragrance *smells* like roses."

TROMPE L'OEIL

Creating illusionistic images has a long recorded history that began in ancient Greece and extends to the sophisticated computer imaging we witness today. An incident is recorded by the Roman scholar Pliny regarding two Greek painters, Zeuxis and Parrhasius: "Writing about Zeuxis, who flourished about 400 BC, Pliny tells a story of his rivalry with a contemporary painter, Parrhasius. Challenged by the latter, Zeuxis drew aside the curtain covering his work to reveal a painting of grapes so realistic in effect that some birds attempted to peck them, but he had to admit defeat when, demanding that the drapery covering his rival's picture be drawn aside, he was chagrined to find the curtain itself was painted."[1]

What came to be known as *trompe l'oeil* (fooling the eye) has taken many forms over the years including some of the graffiti we see on walls and buildings. Trompe l'oeil dealt with a type of hyper-reality where two-dimensional (2-D) images took on a realistic three-dimensional (3-D) appearance that was so convincing that one had to reach out and touch the painting to confirm it was indeed a painting. (Some contemporary resin sculptures are so realistic that it is not unusual to see a person reach out and touch them to confirm they are not real.) "Trompe l'oeil painters… relied on the mutual reinforcement of illusion and expectation… the most successful trompe l'oeil I have ever seen was… a painting simulating a broken glass pane in front of a picture."[2]

A recent billboard in Times Square in New York City attests to the power artists and photographers have in fooling the eye (Figure 6.1). On a busy Broadway street corner atop a storefront is a huge photograph of a woman dressed in a fashion suit sitting on what appears to be a window ledge. Although this is a photograph, the illusion that the woman and window are three-dimensional is quite convincing and it is nearly impossible to see it otherwise. The illusion is enhanced by both the size of the picture and its high location.

What we know to be physical reality is not always in accord with what we see. Illusions, like puns, can be playful, interesting, and engaging.

Illusion—
contradiction between perceptual experience and its physical reality.

Allusion—
a reference to something else.

A picture is something which requires as much knavery, trickery, and deceit as the preparation of a crime.

Degas

Figure 6.1   Billboard in Times Square, New York City, 1995, Richard Zakia.

SPACE, TIME, AND COLOR ILLUSIONS

There are many different types of visual illusions, but most can be placed into three broad categories; *geometric, chronometric,* and *colorimetric.* The geometric illusions are a result of misperception of length, size, shape, and direction. The chronometric illusions involve time and movement, and colorimetric illusions testify to the fact that color is a chameleon whose perceived hue, saturation, and brightness can change with changes in the surround, color temperature of the light source, light level, and other factors (see Chapter 4).

GEOMETRIC ILLUSIONS

The whole is different from the sum of its parts.

An important aspect of human vision is that it does not see things in isolation but rather in relationships. As was noted in Chapter 2, "Gestalt Grouping," the whole is different from the sum of its parts. Instruments, like 1-degree light meters "see" in isolation; humans do not. Perceptually we cannot separate figure from ground. We see them in relation to each other and that relationship determines what we see. This is the key to understanding most illusions. By controlling the background, the *length, size, shape,* and *direction* of a line can be changed.

Figure 6.2A shows examples of illusions in which the *lengths* of lines appear to be different from their actual lengths. Perceptually they are different, physically they are not. If the surround were removed we would see them as having the same length. You may want to prove this by putting a piece of tracing paper over the illustrations and tracing the lines that appear to be different lengths.

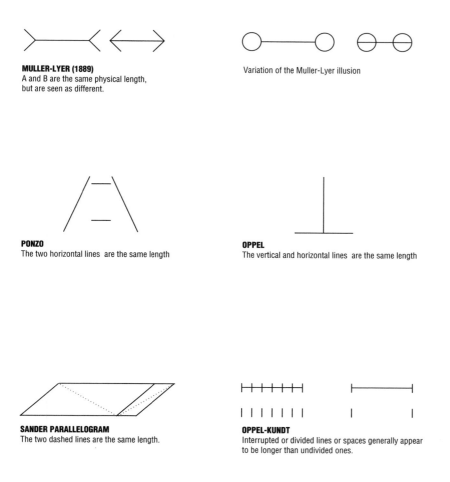

MULLER-LYER (1889)
A and B are the same physical length,
but are seen as different.

Variation of the Muller-Lyer illusion

PONZO
The two horizontal lines are the same length

OPPEL
The vertical and horizontal lines are the same length

SANDER PARALLELOGRAM
The two dashed lines are the same length.

OPPEL-KUNDT
Interrupted or divided lines or spaces generally appear
to be longer than undivided ones.

Figure 6.2A   Geometric illusion: Length.

The family of illustrations in Figure 6.2B shows how the surround can change the appearance of the *size* of a visual element. Notice that some illusions of size are just variations of others. Again, it is the relationship between figure and ground that creates the illusion.

Draw a straight line askew as long as it gives the impression of being straight.

Degas

Converging lines create an illusion of depth.
All three persons are the same height. The one
furthest, however, appears the tallest. Size is
traded for distance.

JASTROW
A and B are identical in size and shape.
A looks smaller because its' bottom
curvature is in close proximity to the
larger outer curvature B.

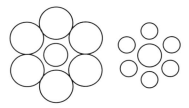

EBBINGHAUS
The two center circles are the same size, but one
appears smaller compared to the larger circles
that surround it; the other appears larger because
of the small circles that surround it. Size is relative
to the surround.

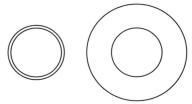

DELBOEUF
The two inner circles are the same size.
One looks larger than the other because
of the size of the surround circle.

Figure 6.2B   Geometric illusion: Size.

Figure 6.2C shows how angular and circular background lines
can change the perceived *shape* of a horizontal line, square, or
circle. In the Hering and Wundt illusions, horizontal lines bend
and become convex or concave depending upon how the background lines intersect the horizontal lines that are seen as figure.
The same is true for the Ehrenstein, Orbison, and Ponzo illusions.
They are all variations of the Hering-Wundt illusion.

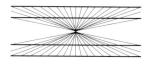

HERING
The horizontal lines bend away from
the vertex of the converging lines in
the background and appear somewhat
convex.

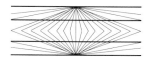

WUNDT
The horizontal lines bend away from the vertex
of the converging lines but now appear concave.
Both illusions have the same basis. The difference
is in the position of the verticies.

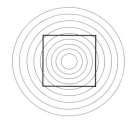

EHRENSTEIN
The angles at which the circular lines
intersect the square distort it.

ORBISON
The angles at which the spoked lines
intersect the circle distort it.

PONZO
The angles at which the converging
lines intersect the square distort it.

Figure 6.2C   Geometric illusion: Shape.

How the surround can change the *direction* of a line is seen in
Figure 6.2D. In the Zollner illusion the angle at which the short
lines intersect the longer lines causes the longer lines to be seen as
tilting in opposite directions. Figure cannot be separated from
ground.

*This is not an
optical illusion, it
just looks like one.*

Anonymous

ZOLLNER
The angles at which the small lines
intersect the longer parallel lines cause
them to appear non-parallel. *(To prove
this simply cover the even or odd lines
with a pencil)*

POGGENDORFF
Which line, A or B, connects with line C

Figure 6.2D   Geometric illusion: Direction.

A number of geometric illusions are related in that the lines
crossing or intersecting one another can appear to bend and change
shape. With the Zollner illusion the lines appear bent away from
one another rather than parallel. The Hering and Wundt illusions
exhibit similar characteristics. "Many other illusions are constructed on the basis... of an apparent tilting of certain lines away
from other lines that cross them. The distortion of the square
(Ehrenstein illusion) and the circle (Orbison illusion) are cases in
point."[3]

In looking at something we tend to see it in such a way that
it will cause the least amount of visual tension. Rudolf Arnheim
gives an explanation of the bending of lines in the Hering illusion
based on the principle of tension reduction (Figure 6.3). "An
objectively straight line crossing a sunburst of radii bends toward
the center. In this case the centric, expanding pattern creates an
inhomogeneous field, in which objective straightness is no longer
as devoid of tension as it would be in a homogeneous field (B). Its
equivalent in the centric field would be a circular line (C) because
all sections of such a line would be in the same relation to the field
and to its center. The straight line in A, on the other hand, changes
angle, size, and distance from the center in each of its sections. To
the extent that the line gives in to the tendency toward tension-
reduction we see it curving."[4]

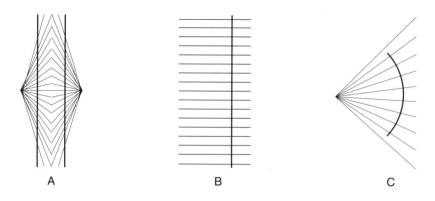

Figure 6.3   Hering illusion. Figure and ground are interdependent.

Reversibles

There is a class of illusions that could be called *reversible* images or "flip-flops." An article titled "Multistability in Perception" by Fred Attneave describes a number of these including the familiar Necker cube and works by artists Salvador Dali and Maurits Escher.[5] In Figure 6.4 all four reversible figures are related in that their geometry is similar and they are based on the initial configurations of Ernst Mach and Louis Necker.

Postage stamp, Sweden.

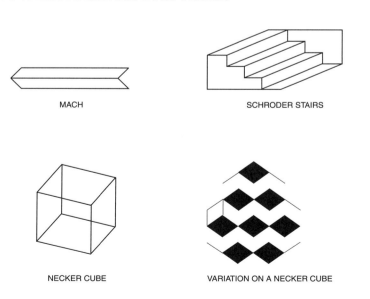

Figure 6.4   Reversibles. Variations on a theme; acute angles are critical to perception.

TIME (MOVEMENT) ILLUSIONS

Imagine two small lights a short distance apart in a darkened room. Number 1 light is flashed briefly, then goes off, and for a fraction of a second nothing is visible. Now number 2 light is flashed briefly, then goes off, and for a brief interval nothing is visible. The process continues with the lights going on and off.

Motion is the strongest visual appeal to attention.

Rudolf Arnheim

If the interval (dark time) between the light going on and off is right, the observer will see an apparent movement from 1 to 2. This illusion of movement by two stationary lights is so convincing that it cannot be distinguished from real movement. It has been referred to as the *phi phenomenon* or *stroboscopic* movement.

Without such a phenomenon, motion pictures, which are still pictures projected at a rate of 24 frames per second, would not be possible. A movie frame is projected at 1/48th of a second, followed by a dark period of 1/48th of a second (total time of 1/24th of a second per frame), and then the next frame is projected, and so on. The result is the perception of a moving image.

Movement on a video screen, which is made up of thousands of red, green, and blue phosphors (little colored lights) that go on and off, depends upon the same phenomenon. A series of alternating horizontal lines of phosphors is scanned and lit up every 1/60th of a second for a total time of 1/30th of a second per still image on the screen. (To capture a still image on a video screen the camera shutter must be set at 1/30th of a second or longer, otherwise the result will be only part of the image on the screen.)

Computer Graphics and Animation

Computer graphics, computer animations, and multimedia lend themselves nicely to creating an illusion of 3-D on a video screen. The illusion of depth on a two-dimensional surface is something artists and others have worked with since Renaissance times. The depth cues being used involve perspective, overlap, texture gradient, size differences, aerial haze, motion parallax, motion perspective, and color. What adds greatly to the illusion of depth with moving images is the visual experience of movement. As objects increase and decrease in size they appear to *move* forward and backward. They can move to the right and to the left, up and down, yaw, pitch, and roll—*movement* in every possible direction.

...The greatest grace and life that a picture can have is that it expresses motion, which the painters call the spirit of the picture.

Lomazzo

Colors add to the illusion—warm colors moving forward and cold colors receding. Movement is a powerful depth cue. Added to the other depth cues mentioned and to sound, the illusion becomes even more convincing. Sound can enhance the illusion of 3-D by increasing and decreasing in volume, in the type of sound, and also the direction it seems to come from relative to the moving image on the screen.

The Pulfrich Effect

If one were to look at a simple pendulum movement ("A" in the marginal figure) with a dark filter or sunglass covering one eye, what would be seen is an elliptical movement (B), rather than a linear movement (A). The filter causes a delay in the signals reaching the brain from the retina. "Since the target is moving, a temporal delay corresponds to a spatial displacement: the covered eye is seeing the target with a delay in time, and thus at a spatially lagging point in its trajectory. The lag produces a stereoscopic disparity, and therefore a shift in depth."[6] This is called the *Pulfrich effect*.

The Pulfrich illusion applies not only to a linear pendulum movement but to any object in a horizontal movement relative to the eyes. "In an ordinary television picture, for example, objects moving from left to right will appear displaced in front of the screen if the right eye is covered by a filter."[7] Some years back an experimental video advertisement, based on the Pulfrich effect, successfully presented a 3-D appearance on a video screen for those who watched the television commercial with filtered viewers that had been made available.

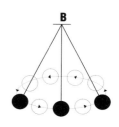

The Pulfrich effect.

The Waterfall Effect

If one were to stare at a waterfall for a period of a minute or so and then look away from it, the aftereffect would be a movement of the waterfall image in an opposite direction; up instead of down. A similar illusion occurs when looking at a rotating spiral; the aftereffect is an image of the spiral rotating in the opposite direction. It seems that our perceptual system, like our biological system, tries to restore a balance and maintain equilibrium by responding in an opposite way. This happens with color as well. For example, looking at a red circle for a period of time and then away from it results in a cyan afterimage.

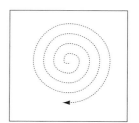

COLOR ILLUSIONS

The color of an object is highly dependent on its surround (see Chapter 4) and this can be used to advantage to overcome some of the physical limitation in color reproduction. Regardless of the medium used (photography, printing, xerography, video) none will faithfully reproduce all colors. For example, a video screen is not capable of reproducing an aquamarine color correctly. The problem is not in the recording of the color but rather in the display on a video screen.

To be able to reproduce the largest gamut of color, compromises had to be made in the choice of the red, green, and blue phosphors that make up the video screen. A better reproduction with projection video is possible, however, since such a system uses red, green, and blue *dichroic filters* instead of phosphors.

One way to overcome the problem of reproducing an aquamarine color on a video screen is to change the surround. A red surround can strengthen the hue, saturation, and brightness of the aquamarine color (simultaneous contrast), and make it appear more correctly. A similar problem exists with other precise colors to be faithfully reproduced on a video screen such as IBM blue, Coca Cola red and Kodak yellow. The choice of an appropriate surround color can improve the appearance of the color reproduction.

A color has many faces, and one color can be made to appear as two different colors.

Josef Albers

SIZE–DISTANCE TRADEOFFS

Size and distance are interrelated. You cannot judge one without the other. Perception is relative: We see relationships. The size or distance of something is dependent upon some familiar reference. Assumptions made about distance affect the perception of size and vice versa. This is the basis for a variety of interesting illusions, one of them being the *Ames Room* illusion seen in Figure 6.5.

We see what we expect to see.

Rudolf Arnheim

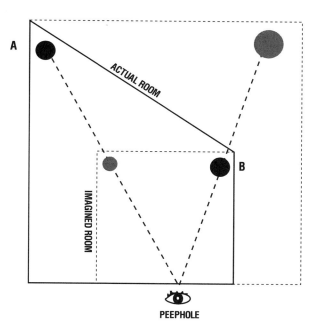

1. **Black circles A and B are the same size in a distorted room.**

2. **The room as seen with one eye through a peephole is assumed to be a normal room having square corners**

3. **The dotted circles show the perceived size; A is seen smaller and B larger.**

Figure 6.5   Ames Room, top view.

The room is located in an enclosure and can only be seen from a peephole (one-point perspective). The viewer assumes that the walls, ceiling, and floor meet at right angles, which is what one would expect and indeed they appear that way viewed from a fixed peephole position. The fact, however, is that the room is distorted; ceiling and floor are trapezoids that slope toward each other—the right wall being smaller than the left. The floorboards are not rectangular and the far left corner of the room is twice the distance from the peephole as the right. The result is that a person B standing on the right is assumed to be the same distance as the person A on the left; and in projecting person B to that distance would make the person appear much larger than he or she actually is.

The phenomenon is somewhat similar to the illusion that the moon or the sun at sunrise or sunset looks much larger at the horizon than in the sky above. Assumed distance determines size. Size-distance dependency provides opportunities for creative arrangements in imaging.

Dutch Cabinets

The Ames Room illusion is an interesting variation of the early rooms created by Dutch artists in the 1600s. They would construct a normal-size room with a peephole. Inside the room were chairs, tables, walls, hangings, and so on that looked normal from only the peephole position. The rooms were called *Dutch Cabinets*, and inside the room everything looked distorted when seen from another position. Samuel van Hoogstraten's "View Down a Corridor" and "Interior of a Peep Show" are wonderful examples.[8]

SIZE–SIZE DEPENDENCY

Since perception is relative, the size of an object is judged on the basis of context, its relationship to other objects, and to some extent familiarity. A classic example of this is the painting, "The Listening Room" by René Magritte. An apple squeezed into a room appears to be the size of an elephant (Figure 6.6).

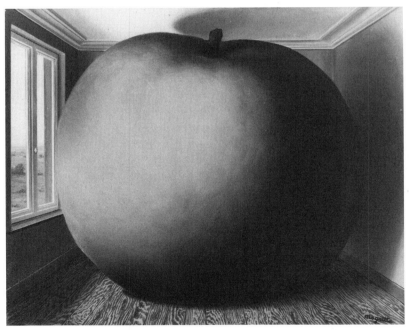

Figure 6.6   *"La chambre d'ecoute" ["The Listening Room"], René Magritte. © C. Herscovici, Brussels/Artists Rights Association (ARS), New York and the Menil Collections, Houston, Texas. The apple is seen as gigantic and filling the room. Why do we not see it the other way; the apple as normal size and the room being miniature?*

By assuming the room is normal size there is no alternative but to see the apple as huge, the "big apple." A question to be raised here, however, is why the room isn't seen as miniature and the apple as normal. Perception of size is, of course, relative, but why does it favor one perception and not the other? The same illusion occurs when normal-size people are photographed or filmed in miniature settings: We see the people as giants and not the furniture as miniature.

Sketch of an early photographic paste-up.

Magritte's "big apple" painting was done in 1952, but long before that photographers were creating paste-ups to create a similar size-size illusion. A number of them appeared on photographic postcards and can be seen in the book, *Larger Than Life*: a man standing next to a 6-foot ear of corn; men pitching horseshoes that are about 5 feet wide; a farmer harvesting sweet potatoes the size of hippopotami; a little girl dressed in white sitting atop three peaches the size of hot air balloons.[9]

Shrinking Size, Increasing Distance

A dramatic demonstration of the relationship between size and distance requires only a white balloon and a darkened vacant stage or area. With a spotlight on the inflated balloon, it is slowly deflated. As it becomes smaller and smaller it appears to be moving farther and farther away, distancing itself from the viewer. In fact the balloon has not moved at all, only gotten progressively smaller in size. Size determines distance and distance determines size. The two are inseparable. A video monitor and computer can be used to create the same illusion. As a white circular area with a dark surround on the screen is made to gradually become smaller, it will appear to be distancing itself.

Shrinking white balloon.

Emmert's Law

If a person sits next to a slide projector as a slide is first projected onto a screen at a distance of about 10 feet and then onto another screen at a further distance, the person will see the second image as being larger, even though the angles of the projected image (at the projector) and the received image (at the eye), and the size of the images formed on the retina are identical for the two images. One can experience the same effect when an afterimage is projected onto surfaces at different distances from the viewer: The apparent size of the afterimage increases with the distance of the surface. The relationship between the apparent size of a projected afterimage and the distance to the projection surface is known as *Emmert's Law*. The Ames Room illusion exhibits a similar phenomenon.

Emmert's Law

Size–Distance Reversal

The relationship between size and distance is reversed in this playful and surreal B.C. cartoon by Johnny Hart, Figure 6.7. A person sitting on a rock seems absorbed in a book titled, *The Law of Perspective.* A small figure in the distance approaches, but contrary to the laws of perspective and size-distance, he does not increase in size but challenges our perception by remaining the same size. In disbelief the person reading throws away the book on perspective and as he walks away into the distance increases in size instead of decreasing, as perspective and size-distance would dictate.

B.C.   By Johnny Hart

Figure 6.7   *B.C. cartoon. The world in which the Law of
               Perspective breaks down is depicted in this comic
               strip. (B.C. by permission of Johnny Hart and
               Field Enterprises, Inc.)*

AMBIGUITY

Words that can take on double meanings are said to be ambiguous. They are *double entendres*, plays on words, puns. Some words called *homonyms* sound alike: made/maid, rain/reign, board /bored, wood/would, and can be used as puns. The visual equivalent would be words that look alike: angle/angel, conservation/conversation, natural/neutral, public/pubic. During Edward Weston's career, a museum refused to display a couple of his photographs of nudes showing pubic hair. The letter from the museum stated that they would not display photographs showing *public* hair. From then on Weston referred to pubic hair as public hair.

Since words are context-dependent, they lend themselves nicely to ambiguity: "My professor's wife wakes up with a jerk"; "Our school cafeteria serves soup to nuts." Advertising thrives on such wordplay. A company wanting to increase their market share of product XXX in some of the larger cities ran a series of visually interesting ads showing the city in all its glory with headlines, *Boston Pops Over XXX, Chicago Goes For a Loop Over XXX, Don't Seattle for Less, Buy XXX.*

A wonderful cartoon that appeared some time ago in the *New Yorker* magazine shows a parking garage with a large opening for cars entering and exiting. A large sign above the garage opening reads, PARK. At the opening of the garage is a beautiful parklike setting of trees, shrubs, grass, and flowers.

Pictures, like words, can take on more than one meaning and this can add to their interest or to their confusion. A simple and striking example of ambiguity in depth perception is the *Necker cube*, described by the Swiss geologist Louis Albert Necker in 1832. The "Impossible Triangle" devised by Lionel S. Penrose provides another example of visual ambiguity and confusion (Figure 6.8). Seen as a 2-D representation, it is confusing and impossible. It just doesn't make sense. Isolating the three connecting angles from the triangular shape will reveal the source of the confusion (Figure 6.9).

The works of Maurits Escher rely on some of the same techniques to create ambiguity in depth and impossible construction as do the works of Salvador Dali, and others. They used their talent to exploit the dual interpretation that can be given an image. "The game had been played before in the 17th century by Archimboldo, who enjoyed creating two totally different interpretations of the same composition—a man's head could equally well be a pile of fruit."[10]

Picasso is noted for his visual double entendres. In one of them he used a bicycle seat and handle bars to create a sculpture of a bull's head, if you care to see it that way. The correspondence of what is and what appears to be can also be thought of as a structural equivalent or simply as a visual simile—it looks like a bull's head. In any case discovering such connections is a creative process independent of the medium used.

Photographers have used ambiguity to add interest and sometimes puzzlement in their photographs. Edward Weston's "Eroded Rock No. 51, 1930" (see Chapter 3, Figure 3.1) again comes to mind. It is a picture of a rock formation lying on a pebbled surface. The surface is a dark gray and the rock formation is just above a middle gray tone (a Zone VI flesh tone). Is the picture that of an

Some surrealist artists play hide-and-seek with the beholder, producing ambiguous pictures susceptible to different mutually exclusive views.

Rudolf Arnheim

Necker Cube

Sketch of "Bull's Head"
by Picasso.[11]

Figure 6.8   "Penrose Illusion" © Thomas J. Shillea. Photographing this model of the Penrose triangular form from a carefully selected position reduces the three-dimensional model to a two-dimensional illusion. From another perspective it would look quite different, not as a closed form but an open one.

Figure 6.9   The Penrose Illusion in 3-D. A three-dimensional model of the Penrose Illusion photographed from two different camera positions. (Three-dimensional model courtesy of Richard N. Norman.)

eroded rock as the caption states or of a reclining nude figure? In his diaries edited by Nancy Newhall, Weston has written, "Clouds, torsos, shells, peppers, trees, rocks, smokestacks are but interdependent, interrelated parts of a whole, which is life. Life rhythms felt in no matter what, become symbols of the whole."[12]

Objects having one form can be seen as taking on another form, a similar form. This similarity of form is called *isomorphism* and it creates interest and involves the viewer. It is an invitation to creatively participate in the viewing of the image. In Chapter 7, "The Morphics," this will be expanded further.

Recording unfelt facts by acquired rule results in a sterile inventory.

Edward Weston

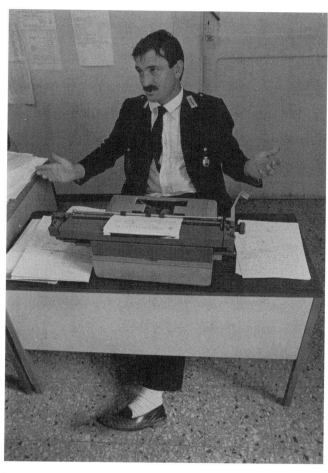

"Untitled," Barry Myers. Breaking up or interrupting space can make an object appear longer. Here, an Italian policeman sitting at his desk seems to have a rather long left leg. Not only does the leg look longer than it actually is, the man appears to be standing as well as sitting.

Visual illusions are visual realities. We see what we see.

KEY WORDS

Ames Room
chronometric illusions
colorimetric illusions
double entendre
Emmert's Law
geometric illusions
illusion
isomorphism
Necker cube
phi phenomenon
Pulfrich effect
stroboscopic movement
trompe l'oeil

Illusion and Ambiguity Exercises

1. Adjusting the Illusion

Refer to the Muller-Lyer illusion shown in the margin. Try extending the horizontal line in B so that it *appears* to be the same length as that in A. How much increase was required?

2. Visual Geometry

Play with some of the other illusions in Figures 6.2A–D to discover discrepancies between the physical geometry and the visual geometry.

3. Visual Puns

Think up some verbal puns and contradictions (oxymorons) and translate them into visual form. Examples: "The object fell to the ceiling"; "My friend is stone sober"; "The fleecy cloud in the sky weighs a ton"; "The 10-ton boulder floats like a feather in the sky."

4. Visual Double Entendrés

Photograph one thing so that it looks like something else as Weston did with his rock formation, peppers, and other vegetables.

5. The Big Apple

The Belgian artist René Magritte was a master of visual pun and paradox. Try creating a variation of his 1952 painting titled, "The Listening Room" (Figure 6.6) that had what appeared to be a gigantic apple in a normal-size room. Trade size for size as he did. Use a camera, a PC, or simply create it by hand as Magritte did.

(The Graphic Designer, Milton Glaser, did a Magritte-inspired variation in 1978 by putting what appears to be a huge tomato in a chair surrounded by a fancy, flowery carpet and wall.)

6. Emmert's Law

Stare steadily at a lighted opalized household light bulb from a distance of a few feet until the bulb appears to decrease noticeably in brightness, which usually occurs within 30 seconds. Then look at a sheet of white paper held at arm's length. You should see a dark afterimage that is the same shape as the light bulb. After a few seconds shift your gaze to a white or light-colored surface on the opposite side of the room and note any change in the apparent size of the afterimage. If the afterimage quickly disappears, it may be revived by blinking your eyes. (Never stare at the sun or a laser or arc light source, as such intense sources can damage your retina.)

7. One-Point Camera Perspective

Arrange some string or rope in such a way that from a camera position it takes on a shape that is of interest relative to its surround. The photographer John Pfahl in his early book, *Altered Landscapes*,[13] made a number of such photographs.

8. Found Illusions

An entire art form occurred some years ago based on "found objects." Marcel Duchamp, Dada artists, and others led the way. With your camera in hand, keep an eye out for potential photographic illusions. Here is one I found as I walked down a motel corridor to my room. At first I thought the framed window at the end of the corridor was a large mural of a palm tree.

9. Paste-up or Scan-in

Long before computers and scanners arrived on the imaging scene, photographers altered reality by doing "paste-ups." Photographic hair implants were put on the pictures of bald-headed men, students pasted portraits of themselves or girlfriends on covers of national magazines such as *Time* and *Vogue*, and then photographed the combination. It is much easier to create such combination pictures with electronic imaging, but it is still a lot of fun doing it by hand. In any case, regardless of how it is done, the most important thing is the idea. "Creativity drives the technology." Try your hand and use your imagination to create such images.

Creativity is a radical necessity, not a luxury.

Jean Houston

Notes

1. Martin Battersby, *Trompe l'Oeil*, New York: St Martin's Press, 1974, p. 9.

2. E.H. Gombrich, *Art and Illusion*, Princeton, NJ: Princeton University Press, 1969, p. 207.

3. Irving Rock, *An Introduction to Perception*, New York: Macmillan, 1975, p. 401.

4. Rudolf Arnheim, *Art and Visual Perception*, Berkeley, CA: University of California Press, 1974, p. 420.

5. Fred Attneave, "Multistability in Perception," *Scientific American*, December 1971.

6. Richard L. Gregory (ed.), *The Oxford Companion to the Mind*, New York: Oxford University Press, 1991, p. 663.

7. Ibid., p. 663.

8. M.L. d'Otrange Masti, *Illusions in Art*, New York: Abaris Books, 1975, p.191.

9. Cynthia Rubin and Morgan Williams, *Larger Than Life*, New York: Abbeville Press, 1990.

10. R.L. Gregory and E.H. Gombrich (eds.) *Illusions*, New York: Charles Scribner's Sons, 1973, p. 276.

11. Ibid, p. 244.

12. Nancy Newhall, *Edward Weston*, New York: Aperture, 1971, p. 41.

13. John Pfahl, *Altered Landscapes*, Carmel, CA: Friends of Photography, 1981.

7
The Morphics

Isomorphic, Anthropomorphic, Zoomorphic, Theriomorphic, Mechanomorphic, Anamorphic, Polymorphic, Amorphic.

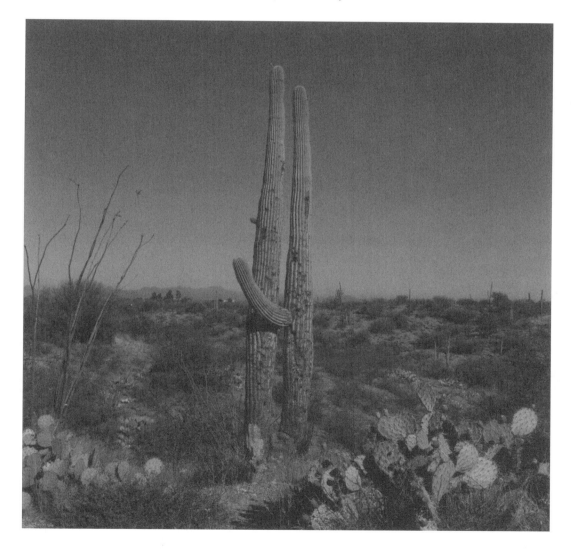

"Saguaro Cacti Couple, Arizona" © Jennifer Steensma

*Early primitive
anthropomorph*

1. Projection
2. Introjection
3. Confluence

The word *morphic* is from the Greek word *morphos,* which means form or shape. I recall giving a lecture on what I called "The Morphics" and having a Korean student inquire in private, "What's the word *morphic* mean?" I said that it simply meant *form.* She then politely advised, well why didn't I use that word instead of morph (morph was not in her Korean/English dictionary). I thanked her and used her suggestion in subsequent lectures.

This chapter on morphics is about form, and the different forms objects can take and be photographed as. Or put differently, we seek out and try to discover and then photograph the various forms that objects can express. A particular object such as a rock or cloud, for example, might be photographed so that it resembles something else such as a person, an animal, or a deity. Words that describe such resemblances are:

- *Isomorphic*—having similar form
- *Anthropomorphic*—having human form
- *Zoomorphic*—having animal form
- *Theriomorphic*—having beastly, scary form
- *Mechanomorphic*—having mechanical form
- *Anamorphic*—having a distorted form

A form that can take on and represent a number of other forms is called *polymorphic.* Something that has no form, such as the wind, is called *amorphic.*

Seeing and photographing objects as if they possessed human attributes is a form of *animism,* the belief that things animate and inanimate possess a soul. It is an old idea. Pythagoras and Plato hypothesized that there was an immaterial force present everywhere that animated the universe.

The *Oxford Companion to the Mind* defines animism in this way: "The belief, common among primitive peoples, that all things in the world (including stones, plants, the wind, etc.) are imbued with some kind of spiritual or psychological presence; this may imply that things are 'ensouled' or 'animated' by a universal 'world soul' or by individual spirits of various kinds."[1] How strongly one believes or disbelieves in animism is a personal matter.

What is important, I believe, is the relationship that photographers develop with whatever they are photographing, be it a person, a tree, a stone, a landscape, a flower, or whatever.

The relationship established between the photographer and what is being photographed is a critical one. At least three different approaches are possible. The first is called *projection;* the photographer projects onto the object what he or she feels at the time. If the object is a tree and the photographer sees the tree as standing tall and proud, then the photographer attempts to capture that feeling. The next level is one of *introjection.* Here the photographer spends time looking at the tree and studying it in a quiet way, attempting to "listen" to what the tree has to reveal. The photographer then tries to photograph that quality of the tree. The third approach, *confluence*, is a highly meditative one in which the tree and the photographer become as one and the photograph reveals that intimate relationship. (In Chapter 8, I explore these three approaches in terms of personality in photography.)

Native American Indians would put on the skins of animals such as deer or buffalo and become one with them, taking on their characteristics as they prepared for the hunt. The practice, in a way, exists today in sports with teams such as the Atlanta Falcons, Buffalo Bills, Chicago Bears, Cincinnati Bengals, Detroit Lions, Los Angeles Rams, Miami Dolphins, Philadelphia Eagles, and so on. The same can be said of the names given to perfumes that women *put on*: Tabu, Opium, Passion, Beautiful, Temptation. If a person becomes one with what they "put on," they can assume the characteristics of what is put on—glamour, sensuality, beauty, risk, danger, strength, power, or whatever. Music is also a "put on," and our body and mind respond to its tempo and rhythm. In some way, when we put something on, depending upon what our needs are, we can try to connect with someone or something else.

The photographer Aaron Siskind, when asked about the meaning of some of his photographs, pondered the question and after some thought responded, "Pressed for the meaning of these pictures, I should answer, obliquely, that they are informed with animism… Aesthetically, they pretend to the resolution of …sometimes fierce, sometimes gentle, but always conflicting forces…"[2] What we photograph becomes representative of our experiences at the time.

As a child, I noticed my mom and some of the women in the neighborhood talking to their flowers when they watered them. As a kid I thought it strange, but as I grew older I began to understand.

ISOMORPHIC

The word *isomorphism*, as used by the Gestalt psychologists in the early 1900s, suggested that there was a correspondence between what was looked at and how the brain functioned; between the stimulus pattern and the excitatory fields in the cerebral cortex. Used here, it refers to objects and things having the same or similar form or function. Turbulent water, for example, can be photographed in such a way that it looks like, takes on the appearance of, the turbulence of a flaming fire as seen in Figure 7.1.

When I looked at things for what they are I was fool enough to persist in my folly and found that each photograph was a mirror of my Self.

Minor White

Courtesy of Buffalo Bills

A man walks into an antique shop and asks "What's new?"

Marshall McLuhan

I attempt through much of my work to animate all things—even the so-called inanimate objects.

Clarence Laughlin

Figure 7.1   *"Maine" © Robert Walch. Isomorphism: Oncoming waves of water splashing against dark rocks take on the qualities of a flaming fire. Opposites can be seen as similar in shape and form.*

My God, Edward, your last photographs surely took my breath away, they contain both the innocence of natural things and the morbidity of a sophisticated distorted mind. They are mystical and erotic.

Tina Modotti[4] (in reference to Weston's Shell photographs).

Edward Weston's "Eroded Rock No. 51, 1930" (shown in Chapter 3, Figure 3.1), which resembles a reclining torso, is another example of isomorphism.[3] As photographed, it has a structure similar to that of a reclining nude. We relate and transfer meaning to those things that are similar; similar in form, shape, color, position, and so on. In short, we associate those things that have something in common. Other words that have been used to express similarity of form or function are:

- *Correspondence* by the Swedish scientist Swedenborg,
- *Predicate thinking* by the Austrian psychiatrist Sigmund Freud,
- *Structural equivalent* by the French poet Baudelaire,
- *Equivalent* by the American photographer Alfred Stieglitz.

The term *predicate thinking* was used by Freud to describe associations that are made at a subconscious or unconscious level. "The tendency of the id to treat objects as though they were the same in spite of differences between them, produces a distorted form of thinking which is called *predicate thinking*. When two objects, for instance a tree and a male sex organ, are equated in a person's mind because they both share the same physical characteristic of protruding, that person is doing predicate thinking."[5] Edward Weston's photograph, "Palma Cuernavaca II, 1925" is a possible example.[6]

Examples of objects and pictures suggesting a male sex organ have a long history, and how they are to be interpreted must be looked at in terms of both the culture and historical time. Barbara Walker writes that, "Phallic symbols are objects of either overt or covert worship in all patriarchal societies...."[7] As examples, she cites the *pillars* in India as representations of the lingam of Shiva, the Egyptian *obelisk* as representing the penis of Geb, and in Greece, the phallic pillar of the classic Herm.

Humans are very aware of and concerned about their own bodies. Advertising companies are well aware of, and attentive to this fact. Cosmetic products and jewelry capitalize on this concern. A careful look at the ads in any magazine, on billboards, or on television will readily confirm this. In looking at ads attend not to just what is being shown but more importantly, what is being suggested.

Shiva: the god of destruction and reproduction, a member of the Hindu triad along with Brahma and Vishnu.

Packaging design has not been blind to the power of the phallus to sell products. A number of packaged products in recent years resemble the *pillars* in India and Greece. These packaged pillars are contemporary, commercialized, sculptured equivalents. In his book *Visual Communications*, Paul Martin Lester writes, "Liquor, lipstick and cigarette advertisers also commonly use phallic imagery in the form of products' shape in the hope that potential customers will link the use of their products with possible sexual conquest."[8]

Herm: A statue of the head of the Greek god Hermes mounted on a stone post.

Graffiti can be looked upon as a form of advertising—of making a public statement. It has its own interesting history. It is an old art form that can be traced as far back as the scrawls on the walls of Neolithic caves. Some of the graffiti that litters the walls of buildings, bridges, and subways, particularly in large cities, mimic these scrawls. The intents of modern man and Neolithic man may differ, but the symbolism used is similar.

Predicate thinking, mentioned earlier, is not limited to the visual mode and can occur in any modality, including the verbal. Freudian slips are examples of predicate thinking. At a gala reception one evening an announcer introduced the *singer* for the evening (a prominent entertainer with quite a loose reputation) in this way, "Ladies and gentlemen let's all give a warm welcome to our wonderful *sinner* from California...." That was a *verbal* slip. Freudian slips can also be visual and many are, as some photographs and paintings will testify. Secondary images in paintings and photographs or other visual media can be considered visual

Freudian slips, unless, of course, they are intentional. (In Chapter 9 on subliminals, I will explore this idea further.)

ANTHROPOMORPHIC

The prefix *anthro*, from the Greek *anthropos*, means man. Anthropology is the study of man. Anthropomorphic refers to objects that can take on human form. The practice of attributing human characteristics to inanimate objects has a long history. Ancient drawings have been found in which facial features have been added to pictures of the sun, and no doubt early man as well as modern man was able to visualize a face on a full moon. Humans have a propensity to see faces in things. Facial patterns are one of the most distinguishing features among humans. "It can be argued and has been argued, that we respond with particular readiness to certain configurations of biological significance for our survival. The recognition of the human face, in this argument, is not wholly learned. It is based on some kind of inborn disposition. Whenever anything remotely face-like enters our field of vision, we are alerted and respond."[9]

Today, electronic photography provides all kinds of opportunities to anthropomorphize digitized images. Although this can provide challenges and be fun, there is still a wonderful sense of discovery in locating objects in the environment that exhibit human qualities. This not only provides the photographer with an exciting feeling of discovery, but when the photograph is executed with finesse, it provides the viewer with a similar feeling.

ZOOMORPHIC

It can be fun to discover inanimate objects in the environment that appear to take on animal forms. *Zoomorphic* (pronounced Zo-morphic) is the term used to describe such a characteristic.

Many of the early gods and goddesses were represented as animals. "There is abundant evidence throughout the world that primitive human beings regarded animals as highly spiritual creatures, even deities. The human-bodied, animal-headed gods and goddesses of Egypt were obviously priests and priestesses costumed as animal spirits, wearing elaborate headdresses and masks...."[10] (See Figure 7.2.)

*Figure 7.2   "Sphinx and Pyramid," 1944 Captain Les
Stroebel. The monumental Sphinx with the head
of a man and the body of a lion represents an
Egyptian deity.*

Zoomorphic expressions are often used in fashion design and
in advertising. One of the prime examples is that of jewelry and
leather products such as shoes and handbags taking on the qualities of a serpent. The snake/serpent was one of the oldest symbols
of female power. Together, snake and serpent were considered holy
in early civilization, since both seemed to possess the power of
life.[11] One reason some ads are so effective is that they are able to
continually transform myths and fairy tales into contemporary
images using both old and new iconography.

THERIOMORPHIC

Forms that take on the characteristics of an imaginary beast are
said to be *theriomorpic*. The term also pertains to a deity wor-
shipped in the form of a beast. Theriomorphic representations
have frightening appearances, such as the beastly gargoyles invented in the Middle Ages during the great age of cathedral
building. Gargoyles can be found on many Gothic cathedrals. They

*Whilst part of
what we perceive
comes to us
through our
senses from the
object before us,
another part (and
it may be the
larger part) al-
ways comes out
of our minds.*

William James

took on theriomorphic forms and were used to scare away evil spirits. Some were used as decorative water spouts.[12]

Creation of beastly, theriomorphic objects and images preceded the Middle Ages by many years and continues to this day in horror tales and horror movies, and will undoubtedly continue in the future. Early on, shamans and witch doctors made use of theriomorphic masks, many of which now adorn museums throughout the world. Halloween gives children an early encounter with theriomorphic masks. History has much to tell us about our culture and rituals; one has only to look at how some products are advertised (Figure 7.3) and at what passes as entertainment.

Figure 7.3   *Theriomorphic. Contemporary gargoyles in a surreal setting. "Pure Mischief," (Courtesy Smirnoff).*

Man can frame to himself ideas of things that are not actual as though they were actual.

Hegel

MECHANOMORPHIC

The converse of anthropomorphic is *mechanomorpic*, in which a human subject, or a picture of a person, is perceived as having mechanical characteristics (Figure 7.4).

Figure 7.4   "Consumer Service," Vincent Comparetto. A mechanomorphic image using mixed media.

Thus, an elbow can be seen as a hinge, and as many young children have observed, when the hands are clasped together, "Here's a church, here's the steeple, open the doors and see all the people."

Photomontage provided early photographers a means of manipulating photographs to make social and political statements visually. A German artist, Helmut Herzfelde, who assumed the English name John Heartfield in protest to Adolf Hitler's Nazi regime, was prominent in using photomontage to show the mechanical nature of the regime. The Dada artist, Picabia, created many mechanomorphic pictures, most with strong sexual statements. He was fascinated by machines and the use of machine parts to represent human features and human functions. On a visit to New York City in 1915, he declared, "...upon coming to America it flashed to me the genius of the modern world is in machinery and that through machinery art ought to find a most vivid expression...I mean to work on and on until I attain the pinnacle of mechanical symbolism."[13] (One could substitute computers for machines in this quote to reflect some of today's images.)

I want to reveal in my work the idea that hides itself behind the so-called reality.

Max Beckman

ANAMORPHIC

The word *anamorphic* refers to a distorted image that can be re-formed visually, optically, or electronically using computers. It is forming anew, transforming, from the Greek *ana* (again) and *morphos* (form).

Anyone who has looked at their reflection in a non-flat mirror, such as one found in an amusement park, has seen a distorted image that is very difficult to reform into a normal image. Reflections from any non-flat reflecting surface will distort an image. The mirror-like surface of Mylar, a thin and flexible sheeting, can be twisted into a variety of curved surfaces and has been widely used to create anamorphic images.

Perhaps the most famous anamorphic image in art, "The Ambassadors," was painted in 1533 by Hans Holbein. Two gentlemen are standing side by side alongside expensive nautical instruments. In the bottom middle of the painting is a large, skewed, distorted image. When squinted at from the right-hand side of the frame, the distorted image is transformed into a skull—a reminder of the vanity of earthly possessions and power, and life's end.

One of the interesting aspects of Hans Holbein's painting is that only part of the image is distorted; the larger part is seen in normal perspective. When a camera or enlarger is used to create an anamorphic image the entire image is distorted. This is unavoidable since conventional photography is an *analog* system of image creation. With electronic photography, however, photographs can be scanned and digitized, lending themselves to partial or complete distortion as well as to every conceivable form of image manipulation.

Albrecht Dürer in 1506 had made reference to anamorphic images as having a "secret perspective"—a point of view that allows the distorted image to be reformed and seen in its proper perspective. Anamorphic images can be found in early Chinese art where the technique was used to hide erotic images—images that could only be seen from a "secret perspective."

One of the earliest anamorphic photographic images was a self-portrait made in 1888 by a French photographer and experimenter, Ducos du Hauron (Figure 7.5).

He distorted the camera image by using crossed slits instead of a lens. "... his technique was published in amateur magazines as 'trick photography'—along with anamorphic images, exaggerated perspective, 'worms-eye' and 'bird's-eye' views, double exposures, composite prints, photomontages. A whole book of them [these special effects] was published in 1896 under the title, *Photographic Amusements.*"[14] The creative and effective use of anamorphic technique in an advertisement is shown in Figure 7.6.

*Figure 7.5   Anamorphic. An early photographic anamorphic
image; a self-portrait created by Ducos du Hauron
in 1888. (George Eastman House.)*

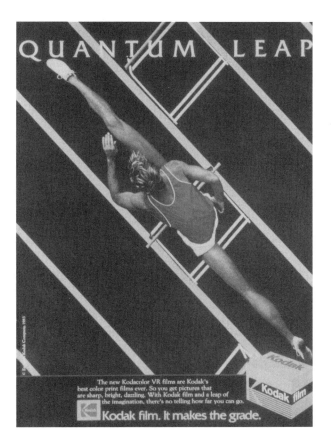

This overhead pho-
tograph of a run-
ner, legs extended
and exaggerated,
and the dynamic
composition, gives
a feeling of the
enormous strides
runners must take
to win an event—
to be a winner.
And by analogy,
this winning spirit
reflects the prod-
uct advertised.

(Courtesy
Eastman Kodak.)

Figure 7.6   Anamorphic ad.

A few years ago while at a conference in Stockholm, Sweden, I came upon a metal gate made up of anamorphic letters. After taking a photograph of the gate, I tried to make out what the letters spelled. Later I made a line drawing from the photograph to make the letters stand out more clearly (Figure 7.7).

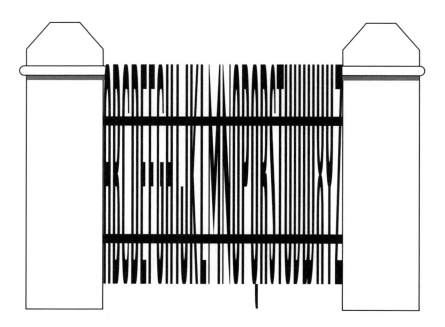

Figure 7.7   *Anamorphic Gate, Stockholm, Sweden. Re-form the anamorphic letters on the gate and discover what is being stated. (See Appendix B, "Answers to Selected Exercises," if necessary.)*

I began looking at the letters from different perspectives hoping to re-form them. I was successful in re-forming many of the letters but could not make out any words. Not knowing whether the words were in English or Swedish added to the problem. After some time, however, I did succeed.

"Reclining Figure" © Deborah Ditchoff

KEY WORDS

amorphic
anamorphic
animism
anthropomorphic
confluence
correspondence
equivalent
introjection
isomorphic
mechanomorphic
morphos
numen
polymorphic
predicate thinking
projection
structural equivalent
theriomorphic
zoomorphic

The mysterious way in which shapes and marks can be made to signify and suggest other things beyond themselves had intrigued me since my student days.

E. H. Gombrich

Morphics Exercises

*Biomorphic—
any object that
appears to take
on living form.*

1. Morphics

Look at some of the photographs of earlier photographers such as Wynn Bullock, Clarence Laughlin, Minor White, Frederick Sommer, André Kertész, and Bill Brandt to discover examples of the various morphics.

2. More Morphics

Create a series of photographs that suggest:

*The mind knows
more than the eye
and the camera
see.*

Isomorphics (similar forms),
Anthropomorphics (human forms),
Zoomorphics (animal forms),
Mechanomorphics (machine forms),
Theriomorphics (beastly forms).

Jerry Uelsmann

3. Predicate Thinking

Search out photographs, paintings, advertisements that may suggest predicate thinking. Review some of the photographs of Guy Bourdin, Helmut Newton, Paul Outerbridge, and paintings by Georgia O'Keeffe.

4. Anamorphics

*Subjects may be
reformed or de-
formed to express
the most telling
qualities.*

Pierre Bonnard

Make several photographs having distorted images that can be visually re-formed. There are a number of ways this can be done: by the use of a special anamorphic lens on a camera or enlarger, by tilting the film plane in a view camera or the easel on an enlarger, by bending or buckling the printing paper, by photographing images reflected from non-flat surfaces, shadows that fall on curved surfaces, and shadows that are compressed or stretched due to the angle of the sun or other light source.

5. More Anna Morphics

*Let ancient times
delight other folk.
I rejoice that I
was not born till
now.*

Ovid

If you have access to a computer imaging system, scan in some of your photographs and try distorting them in interesting ways. Distort part of the image or the entire image. You might even try scanning in photographs that are distorted and using the computer to try to correct the distortion.

(In wide-screen cinematography, anamorphic lenses are used on the camera and projector to "squeeze" a wide-angle scene onto standard-width film and then "unsqueeze" the anamorphic film image when it is projected onto a wide screen.)

6. Animistic Photographs

Think about this statement by the anthropologist Ladislas Segy, and try to create photographs that support his statement:

> *The unrecognized part of man's psyche below the threshold of consciousness, defies understanding in terms of causality... this is the domain of Being, the transrational, transpersonal, nondimensional region of the mind in which man's intuitive faculties are rooted. By reanimating his Being, man is able to sense and experience that essential part of reality which is numinous, which being beyond phenomenon gives a sacred dimension to his existence. All men have the potential to "take Being out of concealment" as Heidegger put it.*[15]

numinous: *spiritually elevated;* numen: *the spirit believed by animists to inhabit certain natural objects.*

"Domain of Being," George DeWolfe. "With my camera, I bring my hands together in prayer as I patiently wait for the all-consuming mystery of nature to reveal itself—a mystery of oneness—of primordial energy—one in which I and nature share a unique private moment."

7. Photography as Prayer

When asked why he photographed, a Jesuit priest, noted photographer, and friend, remarked, "For me photography is a form of prayer." Minor White, on a similar note while at MIT in the 1960s, put together a photographic exhibition called "Octave of Prayer."

Prayer takes on many forms. Think of this as you photograph and try to capture the spirit in nature, in people, in animals, and in all forms of the animate and inanimate.

My photography is the best way I know of bringing me closer to some of the mysteries of existence.

Wynn Bullock

Notes

1.   Richard L. Gregory (ed.), *The Oxford Companion to the Mind*, New York: Oxford University Press, 1991, p. 27.

2.   Carl Chiarenza, *Aaron Siskind and His Critics, 1946–1966*, Tucson, AZ: Center for Creative Photography, University of Arizona, 1978, p. 7.

3.   Nancy Newhall (ed.), *Edward Weston*, New York: Aperture, 1971, p. 40.

4.   Ibid., p. 23.

5.   Calvin S. Hall, *A Primer of Freudian Psychology*, New York: New American Library, 1954, p. 40.

6.   Beaumont Newhall, *The History of Photography*, New York: Museum of Modern Art, 1964, p. 124.

7.   Barbara Walker, *The Woman's Dictionary of Symbols and Sacred Objects*, San Francisco, CA: Harper and Row, 1988, p. 321.

8.   Paul Martin Lester, *Visual Communication*, Belmont, CA: Wadsworth Publishing, 1995, p. 66.

9.   E.H. Gombrich, *Art and Illusion*, Princeton, NJ: Princeton University Press, 1969, p. 103.

10.   Walker, op cit., p. 360.

11.   James Hall, *Dictionary of Subject and Symbols in Art*, New York: Harper and Row, 1979, p. 20.

12.   Harold Osborn (ed.), *The Oxford Companion to Art*, London: Oxford University Press, 1975.

13.   Robert Hughes, *The Shock of the New*, New York: Alfred Knopf, 1981, p. 51.

14.   Beaumont Newhall, *The History of Photography*, New York: The Museum of Modern Art, 1964, p. 162.

15.   Ladislas Segy, *Masks of Black Africa*, New York: Dover, 1976, p. 18.

8
Personality

I photograph to heighten and strengthen my awareness of the sublime beauty and grandeur of nature—to become one with nature.

Thomas L. McCartney

"Mount McKinley, Alaska" ©Thomas L. McCartney

*Tain't what you
do, it's the way
you do it.*

Fats Waller

Personalities are unique and so are photographs. Photographs can and do exhibit personalities, the personality of the photographer. Some understanding of personality differences can be helpful in relating to different kinds of photographs and to other people. It requires us to see things from different points of view, even though we may not relate or agree with them.

PROJECTION, INTROJECTION, AND CONFLUENCE

In Chapter 7, "The Morphics," it was stated that photographers can relate to the things they photograph in three different ways: projection, introjection, and confluence. In projection, the photographer projects onto the object what he or she feels. With introjection, the photographer tries to understand the essential quality or essence of whatever he or she is photographing and then to capture it on film, tape, or disc. In confluence, the photographer and the subject become one.

Projection

*Sometimes trees
strike me as laugh-
ing or crying and
occasionally as
nurturing or even
threatening.*

John Sexton

As originally defined by Freud, projection is one of several defense mechanisms used for protection against certain anxieties. Thus, if people feel anxious because they dislike someone without cause, projection enables them to convert "I hate him" into "He hates me" and allows them to express their impulses under the guise of defending themselves against an enemy.

A broad view of projection suggests that people can find expression for many of their feelings and thoughts by projection onto the environment, including people, animals, pictures, motion pictures, television, music and a variety of objects.

One of the oldest projective techniques is the word-association or free-association test. A word is presented and the subject responds quickly with the first word that comes to mind. The type of word used and the length of time required for a response are clues for identifying certain personality characteristics. The more ambiguous a projective test, the more the subjects depend upon their own memories, feelings, and thoughts to make the word stimulus meaningful.

The *Rorschach test* consists of a series of ambiguous ink blots that were designed to arouse emotional responses. The test was devised by the Swiss psychiatrist Hermann Rorschach after discovering, during some experimental studies in form perception, that certain forms produced quite different responses among his patients. Rorschach's diagnostic method was reported in 1921.

The *Thematic Apperception Test* (TAT), worked out by Henry Murray and his colleagues in 1938, requires the subject to interpret a somewhat ambiguous picture by telling a story. The person attempts to reconstruct the events that led up to the situation presented in the pictures, and to predict the outcome. The responses can reveal significant information about the subject's experiences, memories, anxieties, feelings, needs, and aspirations. Essentially, subjects project themselves into the picture and identify with one of the characters represented.

Projective techniques can be useful in triggering ideas for creating photographs. During the Renaissance period Botticelli remarked to Leonardo da Vinci that "...by merely throwing a sponge full of paint at the wall it leaves a blot where one sees a fine landscape."[1] Leonardo agreed and added that in such a blot of paint you may see whatever you wish to see in it.

In his *Treatise on Painting*, Leonardo speaks of this method of "quickening the spirit of invention": "You should look at certain walls stained with damp, or at stones of uneven colour. If you have to invent some backgrounds you will be able to see in these the likeness of divine landscapes, adorned with mountains, ruins, rocks, woods, great plains, hills and valleys in great variety; and then again you will see there battles and strange figures in violent action, expressions of faces and clothes and an infinity of things which you will be able to reduce to their complete and proper forms. In such walls the same thing happens as in the sound of bells, in whose stroke you may find every named word which you can imagine."[2]

Chinese artists used projective techniques to "quicken the spirit" long before the Renaissance painters did. An 11th-century artist Sung Ti, is reported to have criticized the landscape paintings of a fellow artist in this way, "The technique in this is very good but there is a want of natural effect. You should choose an old tumbledown wall and throw over it a piece of white silk. Then, morning and evening you should gaze at it until, at length, you can see the ruins through the silk, its prominences, its levels, its zig-zags, and its cleavages, storing them up in your mind and fixing them in your eyes. Make the prominences your mountains, the lower part your water, the hollows your ravines, the cracks your streams, the lighter parts your nearest points, the darker parts your more distant points. Get all these thoroughly into you, and soon you will see men, birds, plants, and trees, flying and moving among them. You may then apply your brush according to your fancy, and the result will be of heaven, not men."[3]

Projective techniques used in a superficial way will lead to superficial images. Used with great concentration and imagination, in which the heart, mind, and memory unite, it can quicken

I am unable to make any distinction between the feeling I get from life and the way I translate that feeling into painting.

Henri Matisse

The mind of the painter must resemble a mirror which permanently transforms itself into the color of its objects and fills itself with as many images as there are things placed in front of it.

Leonardo da Vinci

For me form is never abstract. It is always a sign for something. It is always a man, a bird, or something else.

Joan Miro

the spirit and serve as a launching pad to creativity. Projection can be used as a mirror reflecting only the personal concerns of the photographer or as a window to the mystery of the world and universe. Minor White in *Mirrors, Messages and Manifestations*,[4] was perhaps alluding, in some way, to this.

The photographer and art historian, Dr. Carl Chiarenza, a student of Minor White when White taught at the Rochester Institute of Technology, uses projection in a very unique and creative way to arrive at his *Landscapes of the Mind*.[5] In his home studio, Carl arranges still-life landscapes using torn and crumpled pieces of various kinds of paper, cellophane, aluminum foil, and other material. He then spends hours arranging the crumpled material and the lighting, studying it quietly and reverently, rearranging it as the spirit moves him and then photographing it with Polaroid negative/print film. The print is studied and the negative is then projected with an enlarger. The image on the easel is again studied in the quiet darkness where it is further played with and manipulated using burning and dodging techniques. The result is a never-seen-before imaginative landscape that is somewhat understated, allowing the viewer, in the words of the anthropologist Ladislas Segy, "…to place himself in the action and complete it in his own imagination—and thereby enable him to share the creative process with the artist."[6]

The New Orleans photographer, Clarence John Laughlin (1905–1985), used projection to give life to what he photographed. "I attempt, through much of my work, to animate all things—even so-called 'inanimate objects'—with the spirit of man. I have come, by degrees, to realize that this extremely animistic projection rises, ultimately, from my profound fear and disquiet over the accelerating mechanization of man's life; and all the resultant attempts to stamp out individuality in all spheres of man's activities.…"[7]

The art critic Michael Brenson calls attention to the primal energy he finds in Van Gogh's paintings: "The foliage in Van Gogh's paintings is so alive, so much a cauldron of primal energy, darkness and light, that it shoots us back to the ages of animism and tree worship…It is in the trees that we see most clearly the degree to which Van Gogh personified and projected himself into the natural world."[8]

Introjection

The title that John Sexton used for one of his books, *Listen to the Trees*, can be thought of as a way for the photographer to approach any subject he or she may wish to photograph—introjection, not

Follow your vision, do not adhere to any theory, school, or preconceived notion.

Hans Richter

With my inward eye tis an old man grey. With my outward a thistle across the way.

William Blake

projection. Look and listen, let the object look at and speak to you to reveal its presence and essence.

In the introduction to Sexton's book, Steward L. Udall wrote, "The truth is, trees are shy; they reveal their essence rarely. To capture these moments on film takes endless perseverance and prodigious labor."[9] One might add: to capture similar moments when looking at John Sexton's photographs or any artist's images requires quiet, patience, and perseverance. Listen, be quiet and let the photographs of the trees speak to you. Henry Thoreau would say, "Go not to the object; let the object come to you."

In his unpublished manuscript ("Visualization Manual," 1975), Minor White had a number of exercises to assist the photographer in capturing the essence of what is to be photographed. One exercise directed the photographer to sit quietly in front of the object, close his eyes, listen, and let the object speak. When you heard what the object is allowed to reveal, then, and only then, were you to open your eyes and create the photograph.

A man has not seen a thing who has not felt it.

Henry Thoreau

Confluence

Confluence suggests a deep commitment to what is being photographed. The photographer, for a fleeting moment or two, actually feels a kinship with the object being photographed—object and photographer become one and the photograph mirrors that union. Some statements made by persons in various disciplines attest to this precious moment in which union is experienced. The painter Paul Klee has written, "Color possesses me. I don't have to pursue it. It will possess me always, I know it. That is the meaning of this happy hour; color and I are one."[10]

Minor White used a circle as a metaphor for confluence, "Close the circle from the features of my inner landscape, I relate, take part, participate when I close the circle of joy. Image and I united, *joyous.*"[11]

Fritjof Capra, author of *The Tao of Physics*, says it this way: "The experience of oneness with the surrounding environment is the main characteristic of the meditative state. It is a state of consciousness where every form of fragmentation has ceased, fading away into undifferentiated unity."[12] D.H. Lawrence writes, "If we think about it, we find that our life consists in...achieving of a pure relationship between ourselves and the living universe about us. This is how I 'save my soul' by accomplishing a pure relationship between me and another person, me and other people, me and a nation, me and a race of men, me and the animals, me and the trees or flowers, me and the earth, me and the skies and sun and stars, me and the moon: an infinity of pure relations, big

Too often we attempt to force a photograph out of a situation rather than allow the situation to speak to us.

John Sexton

and little..."[13] One of the short prayers of Pope John XXII was, "Oh Truth! My God, make me one with thee in eternal love."[14]

I believe that confluence elevates a photograph beyond its content so that it expresses a dimension deep within the human psyche—a universal dimension inherent in all of us. I believe this is what constitutes art, regardless of the medium, for essential to any medium are the individuals' personalities and their ability to commune with their surroundings.

PERSONALITY TYPES

Carl Gustav Jung (1875–1961) was a Swiss psychiatrist and contemporary of Sigmund Freud (1856–1939). Some of the highlights of Jung's brilliant career were his elaboration of the theories of the *collective unconscious* and *archetypes* (which will be discussed in Chapter 9, "Subliminals"), and *personality types*, to be discussed in this chapter.

Jung believed that every judgment an individual makes is related to his personality type. Based on a large number of therapy sessions with a variety of patients and on observations of how people in general relate to one another, Jung published *Psychological Types* in 1921, in which he proposed a topology for classifying different types of personalities. The four types of personality can be thought of as points on a compass (Figure 8.1). Each point represents an opposite personality type. Thinking and feeling are considered rational functions while sensing and intuiting are considered nonrational. A personality can locate anywhere within the circle. A personality could, for example, locate somewhere within the upper left, sensing-thinking quadrant. A personality located near the center would be one that has integrated all four functions—a "self-actualized" personality.

As a generalization, Edward Weston could have been considered a sensing type; Minor White, intuiting; Harold Edgerton, thinking; and Ansel Adams, feeling. In addition, each personality can be extroverted or introverted, making a total of eight personality types. Again, as a generalization, Ansel Adams and Harold Edgerton tended to be extroverts; Edward Weston and Minor White, introverts.

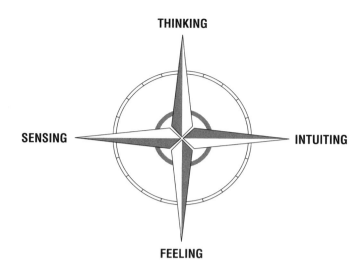

Figure 8.1   Jung's personality types.

Jung's topology, then, consisted of two general attitudes people have, *introversion* and *extroversion* and four functions, *thinking, feeling, sensing* and *intuiting*. Attitudes and functions in combination make up eight basic personality types. Surprisingly enough, most people, despite their differences, fall into one of the eight types of personalities. Such classification is of importance to a photographer because personality strongly influences how and what we see, how we relate to others, and how they relate to us.

Thinking and feeling are called rational functions. Thinking is logical and is concerned with ideas. It tells us what it is that we are experiencing at any one time. People use thought in attempting to understand the world and themselves. Feeling is a value function. It tells us whether something is desirable or not, and is responsible for such experiences as pleasure, pain, fear, and love.

Sensing and intuiting are nonrational functions. Sensing is part of the perceptual process that tells one that something exists. It provides concrete information about the world through the senses of seeing, hearing, smelling, tasting, and touching. Intuiting is an unconscious function; it is a way of attempting to gain knowledge through such means as hunches, guesses, and mystical experiences.

In establishing these functions, Jung cautioned that there is nothing dogmatic about them and that they should be considered as just four useful viewpoints or classifications. Further, they are not necessarily mutually exclusive. Some persons tend to be more feeling and less thinking, some more intuitive and less sensing. One can think of the illustration in Figure 8.1 as a personality "compass" that points in the direction of one's most prominent personality characteristic. Another way to look at it is as a personality

The mark of a first-rate intelligence is the capacity to entertain two contradictory propositions in one's mind simultaneously without going crazy.

F. Scott Fitzgerald

The meeting of two personalities is like the contact between two chemical substances, if there is any reaction both are transformed.

Carl Jung

Movie stars project a variety of personality types with which we can identify.

I am the first to recognize that daring is the motive force of the finest and greatest artists.

Igor Stravinsky

map in which one's personality locates somewhere within the mapped area.

Personality also affects the way one perceives time. In a study of time perception, Mann, Siegler, and Osmond found that people experience time differently.[15] Generally, thinking types experience events in terms of a linear time dimension, continually relating past to present to future. The other types seem to concentrate on one dimension of time: feeling types on the past, sensory types on the present, and intuitive types on the future. Different perspectives on time result in different experiences of reality. One only has to travel from one culture to another to discover this firsthand.

Jung's eight personality types can be helpful in relationships with others on both a professional and personal level. First, one must decide on his or her own personality type. Is your tendency to be more thinking, feeling, sensing, or intuiting? Most people have personalities and ways of perceiving that favor one of the functions. Thinking photographers are highly analytical and logical (left-brained) in their approach, sensing photographers see things as they are without much thought, feeling photographers are concerned about the potential values of a photograph, while intuitive photographers are concerned primarily with trying to capture something that transcends what is being photographed.

Included within each personality type are the two attitudes; introvert and extrovert. Photographers who tend to be introverted probably take pleasure in being by themselves when they are photographing and probably avoid photographing strangers. Photographers who are extroverted would probably prefer to photograph strangers and to attend all kinds of events that provide such opportunities.

These eight different personality types that Jung has formulated are not intended to be rigid, as Jung has suggested. Rather they are tendencies people have in the way they perceive things and react to things. Personal experience reminds us that it is possible to be a thinking type and introverted in one situation, such as a work situation, and to assume another personality type in a different situation such as a sporting event.

RIGHT BRAIN AND LEFT BRAIN

The idea of a right and left hemisphere in the brain relates to Jung's personality types. Thinking-feeling types are rational and tend to be left-brain oriented, while sensing-intuiting types are nonrational and tend to be right-brain oriented.

The two hemispheres of the brain are of special interest since each seems to serve a quite different function in our everyday activities. Although both work together, the left hemisphere tends to be highly analytical, logical, sequential, verbal, and mathematical, while the right hemisphere tends toward the opposite, being qualitative and intuitive (Figure 8.2).

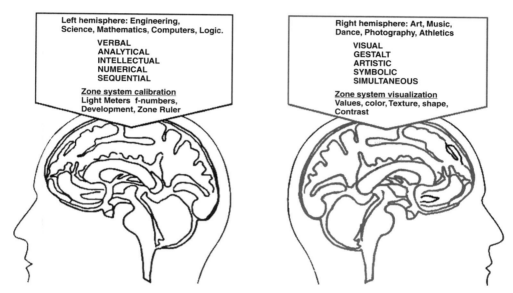

Figure 8.2 *Right and left brain. As a generalization, one can think of the left brain as serving a thinking-feeling personality type and the right brain as a sensing-intuiting type.*

The artist tends to be a right-hemisphere person, the engineer a left-hemisphere person. A visual artist depends heavily on pictorial language, the engineer on verbal and mathematical language. One tends to operate more on sensing-intuiting and the other on thinking-feeling. There is no value judgment attached to this. These are just different ways of responding to our world.

A photographer who has an underdeveloped right hemisphere may be unsuccessful in making highly aesthetic photographs, but may excel instead in the technical aspects of photography. Some photographers have been able to combine both, such as Edward Weston, who wrote, "There seemed to be two forces warring for supremacy, for even as I made the soft, artistic, work with poetic titles, I would secretly admire sharp, clean technically perfect photographs..."[16] Highly creative effort requires the use of both hemispheres of the brain. If the interest and desire are present, a left-brain-dominant person can strengthen the less dominant artistic side of the brain and vice versa.

For me, the intellect is always the guide but not the goal of performance. Three things have to be coordinated and not one must stick out. Not too much intellect because it can become too scholastic. Not too much heart because it can become schmaltz. Not too much technique because you become a mechanic.

Vladimir
Horowitz

Our right and left hands connect to the two hemispheres of the brain in reverse order; that is, the right hand to the left brain and the left hand to the right brain. The word *left* in Latin is *sinister*, implying evil, and in French it is *gauche*, anyone who is awkward. On the other hand *right* in Latin is *dexter* (dexterous), and in French it is *adroit,* meaning nimble or quick-witted. The literature is full of examples on how the right and left hand have been used as a metaphor for good and evil, and the metaphor is found in many cultures. An early Iroquois Native American myth reads, "Twin brothers grew up representing two ways of the world which are in all people. The twins were identified as right-handed and left-handed, straight mind and crooked mind, upright and devious."[17] Fritjof Capra writes that in China, "The contrast of yin and yang is not only the basic ordering principle throughout Chinese culture, but is also reflected in the two dominant trends of Chinese thought. Confucianism was rational, masculine, active and dominating. Taoism, on the other hand, emphasized all that was intuitive, feminine, mystical, and yielding."[18]

Right-handedness, left-handedness, left-brain, or right-brain should not be looked upon or judged as foolish or wise, trusting or not trusting, good or evil, but simply as preferences people have, both of which are valid and essential to a healthy society.

PERSONAL SPACE

Space, the distance between the photographer and what is being photographed, is especially important when photographing people, with or without consent.

How we experience and react to space is a personal matter. In a conversation or photographic situation one person may feel uncomfortable if the distance is only two feet while another may feel quite comfortable. What is perceived as "appropriate" personal space is an elastic balloon that changes depending upon such factors as the person, the culture, and the senses involved. For example, two people in love feel comfortable at very close range, Mediterranean people accept closer personal space than the English, and some people may require a greater visual than acoustical space.

A person who is a criminal or suspected by the police would not want his or her picture taken at any distance. An example of such a situation is a photograph taken by Lisette Model titled, "Gambler Type, French Riviera, 1938." The photograph shows a man in a dark suit sitting in a cane chair with his legs crossed. His elbows rest on the arms of the chair, his head is tilted back slightly and he projects a piercing, threatening stare at the photographer. John Szarkowski wrote of it, "Model has made her photograph from very close, and from a low vantage point, which foreshortens the gambler's figure. It is an unfamiliar and menacing perspective. If she moves one step closer, he may kick the camera neatly from her hands."[19]

The photograph is worth studying as an example of the importance of personal space. "Some photographers, particularly press photographers, have taken that extra step closer and have indeed had their cameras kicked and have been roughed up in the process...Model, I believe, reached the brink of disaster just before she clicked the shutter and, if she had not, the photograph would have lost its intensity and terror."[20]

Edward T. Hall, an anthropologist, has studied the reaction of people to the space around them and how they relate to it. In an attempt to structure some of the observations, he suggested four distinct zones in which most people function (Figure 8.3). These should be attended to by photographers to avoid unintentional intrusion into the personal space of their subjects.

Between photographer and subject there has to be distance. The camera may intrude, trespass, distort, exploit.

Susan Sontag

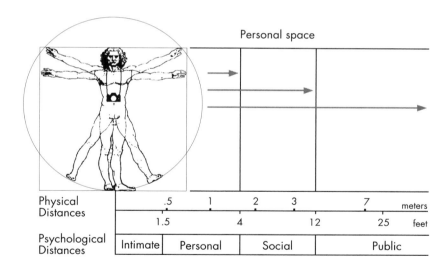

Figure 8.3   Personal space. Humans and animals require a certain distance between themselves and others in which to feel comfortable and not threatened. Photographers must keep this in mind when photographing people, particularly at close range (intimate and personal space).

As between the soul and the body there is a bond so are the body and its environment linked together.

Kahlil Gibran

My joy as an actor is to live different lives without risking the real-life consequences.

Robert DeNiro

The artist is a man himself, nature and a part of nature within a natural space.

Paul Klee

Photographers can get around some of these intrusions by using long focal length lenses, which allow them to keep a reasonable distance from their subjects and still produce images of satisfactory size. Photographers should be alert and sensitive to nonverbal clues when they are posing persons for group shots and when they are trying to take intimate pictures. If the subject signals nervousness, it is best to back off. The cliché "never touch the model" is a statement about personal space. It is, however, too general a statement. Whether or not you touch the model is an understanding to be reached by you and the model. Some areas of the body are less personal than others. The important thing to remember is that in order to touch the model you must come close—you must enter the model's intimate space. This includes not only tactile space but also visual space, auditory space, and olfactory space. "Do not touch the model" really means "Do not violate the model's intimate space."

In motion pictures and television, actors and camera people are well aware of the need to use exaggerated gestures for long shots, whereas in closeups emotion is conveyed by small changes in facial expression, such as a raised eyebrow or a quiver of the lips. The extent of gesture used is dictated by viewers' perception of the distance or the personal space between them and the person on the screen.

Similar consideration should be given to making still photographs. For example, with pictures of people the viewer may have vicarious feelings of personal space that vary with image size and cropping, eyes directed at or away from the lens, and so on. A picture to be used in a magazine might require a different treatment from one to be shown in a gallery. A person looking at a photograph in a magazine, newspaper, or book looks at it from a fixed distance of about 8 inches.

In a gallery the photograph is viewed at a larger and variable distance, as it is on a video screen, where the viewing distance depends upon the size of the screen. The anticipated viewing distance and what the photographer intends to express in the photograph dictates the size of the print. If the intent is to create an intimate space, and the viewing distance is fixed as in a magazine, then the print size should be as large as possible. Take note of the size of the face of models on fashion magazine covers (or *in* magazines). The ultimate intimate space of a photograph in a magazine is one that is based on a "scratch and sniff" invitation. Here the viewer actually makes nose-to-page contact with the picture or ad.

Photographers sometimes exhibit small prints in galleries to invite the viewer to move closer to the print, from a distance of personal space to intimate space. A small print, like a whisper, becomes intimate as one comes closer to it.

CHILDREN

When photographing children, photographers should be particularly sensitive to personal space. Children have their own personal space and at times parents and others are not sensitive to this when photographing them. I was not when taking a photograph of Reneé, my daughter, then 5 years old. She was sitting on her tricycle, having fun and not wanting to be bothered posing for a photograph. My insensitivity to her wishes and my determination on getting the photograph violated her privacy. To protect herself against my intrusion, she partially covered her face and spoke to me in the visual language of gesture and eye, telling me she did not want her picture taken (Figure 8.4).

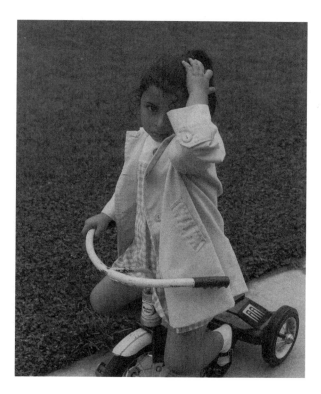

Figure 8.4   "Reneé," Richard Zakia. Her mournful expression
and hand-on-head gesture is a strong body
language response to the photographer (her dad)
who inadvertently violated her personal space.

So intent was I on taking the picture that I failed to see her plea. Every time I look at this photograph of Reneé on her little bicycle, I am reminded of the incident and feel a bit of pain for having violated her personal space, and having been visually deaf to her plea for privacy. It taught me firsthand the meaning of personal space and the protective bubble we all occupy to shield ourselves, whether we are adults or children.

FIELD DEPENDENCY

Tilted objects can cause visual tension.

For a few minutes, pay careful attention to your visual field and notice that much of it is either vertical or horizontal—tables, chairs, desks, windows, walls, pictures, tree trunks, the horizon, and so on. The orientation of your visual environment tends to relate your body positions to the vertical and horizontal lines. Without hesitation you know whether your body is upright or tilted.

Such an ability to relate the position of your body to the vertical/horizontal axes of space has two bases. The first has to do with the gravitational field and the second with the visual field. The force of gravity acts on the kinesthetic sense in the muscles, tendons, and joints and the static sense in the inner ear so that you experience yourself as being upright or not. This is independent of the visual field and is easily experienced by tilting your body with the eyes closed. Immediately you know you are not upright and can usually sense the direction and degree of tilt. Spatial orientation is also influenced by tilting the visual field with the body in an upright position.

Everyday experiences are such that you find yourself upright relative to both the gravitational field and the visual field much of the time. It is difficult, therefore, to determine whether people perceive their body position on the basis of gravitational forces, visual forces, or both. One of the first perceptual researchers to investigate the extent to which the gravitational field and the visual field influence perception of the upright was Herman Witkin.[21] To separate and control both fields he built a "tilting-room/tilting-chair" apparatus (Figure 8.5).

(A)

(B)

Figure 8.5   *Field dependency room. In an experimental room the chair in the room or the room itself can be independently rotated (tilted) without the subject's awareness. How the subject reacts to the tilted situation determines whether he or she is responding to the visual field or to the gravitational field for balance. (A) The room and the chair are shown in normal upright position. (B) The room (the visual field) has been tilted.*

If the subject in Figure 8.5 tilts the chair to coincide with the tilted room or the room to coincide with the position of the chair, the subject is considered field-dependent: dependent upon the visual field for the sensation of balance. If, on the other hand, the subject does not tilt the room or chair, he or she is considered field-independent: not dependent upon the orientation of his visual field for balance but rather on the gravitational field.

Both chair and room can be rotated independently and the extent of rotation or tilt is measurable in terms of angle. A person sitting in the chair is tested under various tilted-room/tilted-chair combinations. For each situation the person is put into a nonupright position and is instructed to tell the experimenter to adjust either the room or the chair, and by how much, until an upright position is perceived. The results of Witkin's experiments, and others that followed, showed that people differed consider-

What lies behind us and what lies before us are tiny matters compared with what lies within us.

Ralph Waldo Emerson

ably in how they attempted to adjust to an upright position—some changed the visual field (tilted the room) and others the gravitational field (tilted the chair). The terms *field-dependent* was coined to describe those who adjusted the tilted room (the visual field) and *field-independent* for those who adjusted the tilted chair in which they were seated. Similar results were found with embedded-figure tests in which a geometric shape is hidden in a larger geometric pattern.

People who can easily separate the hidden geometric shape from the larger pattern and see it as figure tend to be visually field-independent. Field-dependent persons will feel uncomfortable when something within their visual field is tilted. The tilt creates a visual tension, a feeling of imbalance. I am such a person. If I am sitting in a room with a tilted picture on a wall, I either get up and straighten it or look away to avoid my feeling of imbalance. Aboard ship in the Navy, the ship for me was like Witkin's tilted room experiment. Every time the ship tilted it would cause me to feel an imbalance, which would at times, depending upon the degree of tilt and how long it lasted, result in sea sickness, a common problem for field-dependent sailors. I have similar problems with tilted images on a movie screen or video screen, and severe problems with nausea during high-tech movies that have 180-degree screens or seating that moves in rhythm with the movement on the screen, such as those in Epcot Center.

Field dependency is a factor when taking pictures. Often photographers find themselves in situations in which their body posture is not upright relative to the gravitational field or visual field, and must somehow make adjustments. Examples include photographing while leaning out a car window, airplane, or other vehicle; intentionally tilting the visual field in a motion picture camera for effect, operating swings and tilts on a view camera to adjust the vertical and horizontal perspective, and mounting prints in which the subject matter is not vertical relative to the mount board. In these situations, field-dependent photographers will experience a certain level of disequilibrium and visual tension that could affect their work.

How a picture is composed and printed will affect the viewer. If the intent is to create a bit of disequilibrium and visual tension, tilt the horizon line when photographing a landscape or seascape, or tilt objects within a vertical horizontal frame (Figure 8.6).

Does this picture make you feel a bit uncomfortable?

FOLIO

A tilted letter attracts attention and can be unsettling.

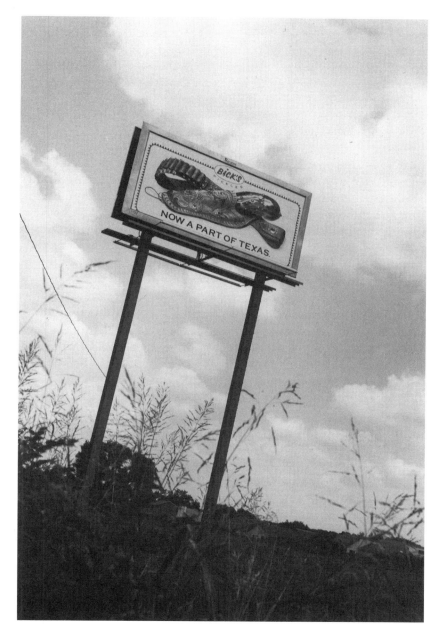

Figure 8.6   *"Texas Pickle, San Antonio, 1995," Richard D.*
Zakia. A field-dependent person, compared to one
who is field-independent, will experience more
imbalance and visual tension when a photograph is
tilted within a vertical and horizontal frame.

LEVELING AND SHARPENING

The aspects of things that are most important for us are hidden because of their simplicity and familiarity.

Ludwig Wittgenstein

The concepts of leveling and sharpening were put forth by the early Gestalt psychologists. People who *sharpen* tend to remember the detail and sequence of things they see and hear, whereas those who *level* tend to simplify their experience. Sharpeners attend more to detail and differences than do levelers.

I recall a situation in which a young couple were describing how they first met. The gentleman, a thinking type, recalled the sequence of events in minute detail (a sharpener). His girlfriend, however, a sensing type, related not the details of their first meeting but rather how she experienced the entire event (a leveler). Her description of their first meeting was somewhat poetic and romantic while his was analytical and detailed.

Rudolf Arnheim describes the difference between leveling and sharpening: "Leveling is characterized by such devices as unification, enhancement of symmetry, reduction of structural features, repetition, dropping of nonfitting detail, elimination of obliqueness. Sharpening enhances differences, stresses obliqueness. Leveling and sharpening frequently occur in the same drawing, just as in a person's memory large things may be recalled as being larger and small ones as being smaller, than they actually were, but at the same time the total situation may survive in a simpler, more orderly form."[22]

Nobody really sees a flower—it is so small it takes time—we haven't time—and to see takes time like to have a friend takes time.

Georgia O'Keeffe

In Figure 8.7, Arnheim gives an example of early Gestalt research regarding leveling and sharpening. Illustrations A and B are not quite symmetrical. The two wings in A are a bit off-center as is the small rectangle in B. In making drawings of A and B, some subjects created symmetry to increase the simplicity (leveling), while others exaggerated the asymmetry (sharpening). The different shapes that result affect the dynamics. Leveling reduces the tension inherent in a visual pattern while sharpening increases it. Photographers who are sharpeners are the ones who often create the more interesting photographs (Figure 8.8). They take their time and study the subject in great detail; the geometry, the color, texture, lighting, relationships, and so on.

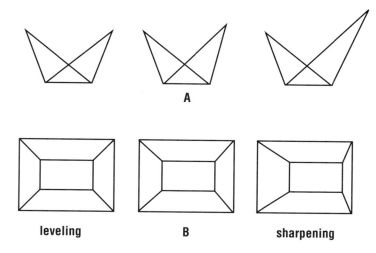

A

leveling   **B**   **sharpening**

Figure 8.7   *Leveling and sharpening. If illustrations A and B are adjusted to look more symmetrical, the person is leveling. If they are adjusted to exaggerate the asymmetry, the person is sharpening.*

Figure 8.8   *"East Hill Farm," Steve Kurtz. In this dramatic photograph of a worker in a dark hole, is the hole seen as a diamond shape, square, or somewhere in between? What shape is the brilliant white reflection in the upper center? Would the photograph have been as dramatic if the camera were positioned to record a perfect square or rectangular reflection?*

*More visual infor-
mation on the ret-
ina is filtered out
than filtered in.*

Richard Norman

*Little of what we
look at do we see.*

Richard Fahey

The unconscious act of leveling or sharpening a picture invites participation. In Figure 8.8, note the metaphorical play of the man submerged in the dark hole and the brilliant patch of white light directly above him.

Some of the most difficult things to photograph are those that are familiar and have been given a name or label. We continually search for new things to photograph, things we haven't seen before. It is difficult to get inspired when photographing in an environment that is familiar. Perhaps this is the reason photographers do most of their work away from their daily surroundings. Photographing close to home is a real challenge. I recall some years ago when a colleague, Bea Nettles, had a sabbatical leave but could not travel because she had two young children she had to care for. To solve the problem she decided to do her photography "close to home." It forced her to see the familiar in an unfamiliar way and provided a number of interesting photographs and an exhibit called "Close to Home." Familiar things do not have to be photographed in a familiar way. Take time to "sharpen" what is familiar and see it in a new way.

In looking at photographs and pictures in general, a lot is missed because insufficient time is spent in studying the images. When looking at an image, look at what stands out as figure in the picture; look at the ground surrounding the figures; look at the tonalities, the colors; keep looking, look for relationships. Let your mind wander. Think of associations, metaphors. Take time and study the pictures. Look for the unexpected, study the unfamiliar.

I recall a cartoon some years ago in which a group of bird watchers are standing on a ledge, binoculars over their eyes and their heads tilted upward as they look up to study the birds across the way. I kept looking at the cartoon hoping to see something humorous. All I could see were the bird watchers with their binoculars and that was not funny. Suddenly, as I was studying each individual birdwatcher, I noticed that one had his binoculars in the "wrong" place, covering his mouth instead of his eyes. Aha!! One of the birdwatchers, head tilted like all the rest of the watchers, was having a little nip. The binoculars looked like all the rest but served a different function; the form was the same but the function wasn't. Had I leveled the cartoon, as I almost did, rather than sharpened it, I would have missed the subtle humor it contained and not seen the one pair of unique binoculars as a flask.

"Beaumont, Ansel and Willard," Barbara Morgan, 1942. Left to right: Beaumont Newhall, Ansel Adams, and Willard Morgan frolicking in front of the camera as Barbara Morgan tests a 1942 Harold Edgerton strobe unit attached to her 4×5 Graflex camera. (Courtesy Willard and Barbara Morgan Archives.)

KEY WORDS

confluence
extrovert
field-dependent
field-independent
intimate space
introjection
introvert
Jung's personality types
leveling
personal space
personality types
projection
right and left brain
Rorschach test
sharpening
Thematic Apperception Test (TAT)

The flow and shift of distance between people as they interact with each other is part and parcel of the communication process.

Edward Hall

Personality Exercises

1. Your Personality Type

There are a number of personality tests available at counseling centers that can be taken to suggest your personality characteristics. The Meyers-Briggs test is a popular one and is available in hard copy as well as on a floppy disc. With the disc the results are immediate. Knowing your personality type will help you in understanding yourself and those you work for and with.

On the Myers-Briggs test I found that I am more intuitive than sensing, more feeling than thinking, more perceptive than judging, and midway between being an introvert and an extrovert.

2. Projection

Find a subject to photograph that interests you. Study it for awhile and see it as being beautiful. Photograph it. Now see the same subject as ugly and photograph it. You may make whatever changes you feel necessary: lighting, focus, exposure, position, printing, and so on. You may want to take several photographs for each situation and choose the best. Compare the two photographs. Ask others to compare them and to describe any differences they see regarding the portrayed mood.

3. Chinese Photography

Carry out the advice that the 11th-century Chinese artist, Sung Ti, gave his artist friend. Find an old wall that is visually interesting, cover it with a piece of gauze or equivalent to diffuse the surface of the wall. Study the covered area and make some closeup photographs of areas that might suggest something else, such as surreal landscapes, patterns, abstractions, etc.

4. Contemporary Animism

Look over some of Van Gogh's paintings of trees to discover the "primal energy" art historian Michael Brenson mentions. Study the trees John Sexton has photographed and writes about in his book, *Listen to the Trees*.[24]

Journey into a wooded area, "listen to the trees," and try to capture their primal energy as Sexton has. Ponder some of these statements by the naturalist, Henry Thoreau:

> "A man has not seen a thing who has not felt it."
> "The question is not what you look at but what you see."
> "Go not to the object; let it come to you."

No one can make you feel inferior without your consent.

Eleanor Roosevelt

Meaningful images...should in some way be a photographer's self portrait.

John Sexton

5. Thinking/Sensing

Take a series of photographs that are very carefully and thoughtfully composed. Take another series in which they are not—without looking through the viewfinder, aim your camera at what looks interesting and take a picture. Compare the two series of photographs.

6. Right and Left Brain

In her book, *Drawing on the Right Side of the Brain*,[25] Betty Edwards has a number of exercises that can be helpful to a photographer. Locate the book in a local or school library and look it over. Try some of the exercises. They will sharpen your visual awareness. Here is one to try:

Find a picture you like, turn it upside down, and draw it. Put what you have drawn to one side and draw the picture again, but this time right-side up. Compare the two copies. Looking at things upside-down has a tendency to engage the right side of the brain. Some photographers believe that looking at an upside-down image on the ground glass of a view camera has this desired effect.

7. Personal Space

(a) In a conversation with someone, see how close you can get to that person, face to face, before one of you begins to feel uncomfortable. Try it with friends and acquaintances, male and female. Now try the same procedure with your eyes closed. Is there a difference?

(b) Take a portrait of a friend as you normally would and then make a series of prints of various sizes; from 4×5 to 16×20 or larger. Place them all on a wall and ask friends to look at them and to tell you which one they like or feel a closeness to and which they feel distant from. While they are studying the prints make a note of their distance from the print, whether they moved closer or further away.

8. Field Dependency

(a) Make a series of photographs in which everything in the scene is vertical or horizontal. Now photograph the same situation with something tilted in the scene. Make prints and have friends look at the prints in pairs and comment as to which print they felt more comfortable with.

(b) Look through magazines and collect pictures that exhibit tilted objects within the picture and see with which ones you feel the most visual tension, if any.

Creativity with portrait involves the invocation of a state of rapport when only a camera stands between two people, mutual vulnerability and mutual trust.

Minor White

You may want to try the same by taping some of the events on television and studying them.

Notes

1. E.H. Gombrich, *Art and Illusion*, Princeton, NJ: Princeton University Press, 1969, p. 189.

2. Ibid., p. 188.

3. Ibid., p. 188.

4. Minor White, *Mirrors, Messages and Manifestation*, New York: Aperture, 1969.

5. Carl Chiarenza, *Landscapes of the Mind*, Boston: David R. Godine, 1988.

6. Ladislas Segy, *African Sculpture*, New York: Dover, 1958, p. 17.

7. Charles Laughlin "Beyond Documentation and Purism," New Orleans, LA: 1977, (unpublished manuscript).

8. Michael Benson, "The Faces that Haunt Van Gogh's Landscapes," *New York Times*, January 4, 1987.

9. John Sexton, *Listen to the Trees*, Boston: Little Brown, 1994, p. 11.

10. Richard D. Zakia, *Perceptual Quotes for Photographers*, Rochester, NY: Light Impressions, 1980, p. 74.

11. Ibid., p 93.

12. Ibid., p 94.

13. Ibid., p 93.

14. Ibid., p 93.

15. Harriet Mann, Miriam Siegler, and Humphry Osmond, "Four Types of Personalities and Time," *Psychology Today*, December 1972, pp. 76–84.

16. Nancy Newhall (ed.), *The Daybooks of Edward Weston*, Millerton, NY: Aperture, 1973, p. 57.

17. Richard D. Zakia, *Perceptual Quotes for Photographers*, Rochester, NY: Light Impressions, 1980, p. 112.

18. Fritjof Capra, *The Tao of Physics*, New York: Bantam Books, 1977, p. 111.

19. John Szarkowski, *Looking at Photographs*, New York: Museum of Modern Art, 1973, p. 128.

20. Richard D. Zakia, "Spaced-Out," *Exposure*, Journal of the Society for Photographic Education, 15:1, February 1977, p. 318.

21. Herman Witkin, "The Perception of the Upright," *Scientific American*, February 1959, pp. 50–56.

22. Rudolf Arnheim, *Art and Visual Perception*, Berkeley, CA: University of California Press, 1974, p. 67.

23. Ibid., p. 66.

24. John Sexton, *Listen to the Trees*, Boston: Little, Brown, 1994.

25. Betty Edwards, *Drawing on the Right Side of the Brain*, Los Angeles, CA: J.P. Tarcher (New York: St. Martin's Press, distributor), 1979.

9

Subliminals

The most important feature of subliminal perception is not that people can respond to stimulation below the awareness threshold, but that they can respond to stimuli of which, for one reason or another, they are unaware.

N. F. Nixon

"Stonehenge, Summer Solstice," ©1987, Wes Kemp

199

The word limen *(Latin) means threshold;* subliminal *means below threshold.*

Complex arrays of visual information can be read into the nervous system and produce subsequent effects without ever achieving phenomenal representation.

N.F. Nixon

Much is perceptible which is not perceived by us.

Democritus

The word *subliminal* refers to something that is below conscious perception—stimuli received by the eye, ear, nose, tongue, or skin that is not strong enough to be consciously seen, heard, smelled, tasted, or felt.

Subliminal perception suggests that there is unconscious awareness, that we can be affected by stimuli that we do not consciously experience. This notion may be a bit unsettling, knowing that we may not have complete conscious control of our experiences and behavior. The fact of the matter is that we do not, anymore than we have control of our dreams or with whom we fall in love. Our experiences are a result of both our conscious and unconscious perceptions. "Few hypotheses in the behavioral sciences have occasioned so much controversy as the suggestion that people may be affected by external stimuli of which they remain wholly unaware."[1]

A number of research studies support the phenomenon of subliminal perception and the fact that much of the information on the retina is not attended to at a conscious level. If it were, we would be overwhelmed; there is simply too much information. "Since the span of consciousness is severely restricted, selective processes evolved whereby only a limited proportion of available sensory information could be admitted to consciousness. Subliminal stimuli constitute some part of the remainder—stimuli which, though insufficiently strong or important to warrant entry into consciousness, may nevertheless be received, monitored, and reacted to."[2]

The idea of subliminal perception is not new and has a rather long history. Perception without awareness was taken for granted by such philosophers as Democritus, Socrates, Aristotle, and Leibniz. Despite this historical acceptance and research supporting it, subliminal perception remains somewhat controversial.

I would like to suggest a second meaning to the term subliminal perception that can be more relevant to photographers and other image makers, and perhaps less controversial. Subliminal perception need not be restricted to physical stimuli below the perceptual threshold. It could well include physical stimuli above the threshold of perception—stimuli that are visible or audible but not seen or heard—not attended to—unseen and unheard stimuli. We only see a small fraction of what we look at, and more often than not we "level" what we look at rather than "sharpen" it. (Leveling and sharpening were discussed in Chapter 8.)

A painting of the human eye by René Magritte called "The False Mirror" is a reminder that the eye mirrors all that is in front of it on the light-sensitive retina. The optical system of the eye forms inverted images on the retina in much the same way a camera lens forms inverted images on film. What we see, however, is what we choose to see, and it is only a fraction of what is optically imaged on the retina.

THE RETINA

The retina is not flat, like film, but roughly spherical like the inside of a ping-pong ball and slightly smaller. This provides a visual field of a little over 180 degrees. (To experience a 180-degree field, look straight ahead and with your arms extended sideways, draw an imaginary arc. This represents a 180-degree field.)

Figure 9.1A shows a cross section of the human eye and the location of the curved retina. The retina contains millions of tightly packed light-sensitive *rods* and *cones* (Figure 9.1B). About 5 million cones are located in a small central area of the retina called the *fovea*. This assembly of cones is responsible for perception of the colors (hue, saturation, and brightness) we see and for visual acuity—the ability to see fine detail. The fovea occupies a very small area of the retina, and the millions of closely packed cones are about 3 microns wide—about the size of the point of a pin. The remaining area, which surrounds the fovea and makes up most of the retina, consists mostly of larger rod receptors. The rods are responsible primarily for movement and sensitivity to low light levels.

An average digital camera had 300,000 sensors, the best has about 6 million. Our retina, consisting of rods and cones, has over 100 million sensors.

The eye jumps around in what are called *saccadic* movements to fixate on areas of interest so that it can use foveal vision to pick up color and detail. Surrounding the small foveal area is a much larger area that makes up about 95 percent of the retinal surface and it consists mostly of rods.

The rods are much more sensitive to light than are the cones, but they do not respond to the hue content of color, only to brightness or lightness. Although rod vision is very sensitive to movement within the visual field, it has low acuity. Since the rods are located around the fovea and extend to the periphery of the retina, rod vision is referred to as peripheral vision.

Some writers have described peripheral vision as a scout that is continually searching and telling the eye where next to focus and pick up information. An important aspect of peripheral vision regarding subliminal perception is that we may not be aware of the image information there even though we are affected by it in some way.

Although identification requires foveal vision, more information reaches us at an unconscious level than at a conscious, foveal level.

Mihai Nadin

We would be overwhelmed if we were consciously tuned in to all the information on the retina. In other words, peripheral vision is attended to at a subconscious level. Everyday experiences in driving a car, and many other visual activities, will confirm this.

(A)

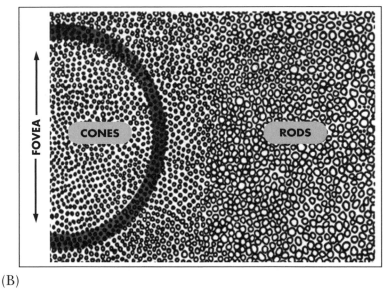

(B)

Figure 9.1   *The human eye and retina. Studies have shown*
             that portions of an image that fall in the peripheral
             area of the retina (rod receptors) can
             subconsciously influence perception. The retina is
             made up of two kinds of photoreceptors called
             rods and cones. Within the fovea area (described
             here by a partial circle) are most of the millions of
             small cones responsible for color vision, resolution,
             and sharpness.

What we see and how we see is a very complex process involving billions of nerve cells and memory, as well as expectations.

EMBEDS

A critical look at some photographs, paintings, and advertisements reveals embedded information that viewers are often not aware of until it is pointed out to them (Figure 9.2).

*Figure 9.2   Embeds. An advertisement with a playful embed—
            a secondary image. In this Guerlain fairytale, a
            handsome young man gazes into the billowing
            clouds just to the left of the castle, and bears
            witness to the magic and charm the product
            promises. (Courtesy of Guerlain.)*

Whether the embedded information is intentional or not (a possible *visual* Freudian slip) is not important; what is important is whether such unnoticed stimuli—part of our peripheral vision—affect our foveal vision, that is, what we consciously attend to. Peripheral vision is, to a large extent, unconscious vision.

In her book on the Mexican artist Remidios Varo, Janet Kaplan writes of how, as a young girl growing up in Spain, Remidios found herself in a strict convent school sitting with a group of other young girls embroidering images into a continuous fabric. Kaplan quotes Varo telling how she embedded a picture of herself and her lover in an embroidery and much later in a painting, "Embroidering Earth's Mantle." Varo referred to her embed as a "trick."[3]

The writer D.H. Lawrence used embedding to express a concern of his. "In his paintings, as in his writings, he tried to break the Victorian moralistic traditions which bound his generation. He would embed phalluses in his paintings, as a letter to a Buddhist friend reveals, 'I try to put a phallus, a lingam you call it, in each of my paintings somewhere.'"[4]

In the summer of 1977, a disgruntled employee embedded a phallus in an ad for Caterpillar tractors. The ad appeared in the *Wall Street Journal*, to their embarrassment. The embed evidently had not been noticed during the preparation and production stage but it did get noticed shortly after it appeared on the newsstands. One does not expect to see such an obvious phallus in an advertisement. Embeds are usually more subtle such as the possible one "Camel Joe" sports for Camel cigarettes.

Secondary Images

Art historians have referred to embedded images as *secondary images* and as *physiognomic intimations*. As photographers we might think of them as "latent" images—images not seen that are developed by the chemistry of our unconscious.

Michael Brenson, art critic for the *New York Times*, in his column, "Art View" calls attention to secondary images in some of the paintings by Van Gogh and Cézanne. In a 1987 review of an exhibition of paintings by Vincent Van Gogh at the Metropolitan Museum of Art he wrote, "Of the issues that suggest the problem in distinguishing between the rational and irrational in Van Gogh's work, none has more urgency than the one of 'secondary imagery.' The phrase refers to images that are rarely noticed at first glance, that refuse to get lost once they are found, and whose meaning, importance, or role is hard to define. Van Gogh's landscapes are inhabited. What faces and heads are doing in his trees and clouds, whether they are intended—and indeed *whether*

It is a mistake to enclose the subconscious in an outline and to situate it at the border of rationality.

Georges Braque

Superficially insignificant or accidental looking detail may well carry the most unconscious symbolism.

Anton Ehrenzweig

they are even there—are questions that can mobilize impressive rational and irrational resources. What cannot be denied after this show is that these faces and heads exist."[5]

In an earlier article on an exhibition of some of the paintings by Paul Cézanne he wrote, "There seem to be expressive heads in Cézanne's work... some of them almost visionary in their force. The problem is that they are not part of the primary imagery but rather of what has been called his 'secondary imagery.' These heads do not seem to have composed themselves; it is as if they had used whatever imagery was available to will themselves into being. The heads are never obvious and sometimes they remain inaccessible even after the person who notices them points them out. What gives the issue a scope that goes well behind Cézanne is that the history of art is filled with these kind of subliminal images."[6]

Statements by Anton Ehrenzweig and by Arthur Koestler are relevant in this context. Ehrenzweig writes, "While the artist's conscious attention may be occupied with shaping the large-scale composition, his (unconscious) spontaneity will add the countless hardly articulate inflections that make up his personal handwriting...We cannot define their hidden organization and order any more than we can decipher their unconscious symbolism."[7] Arthur Koestler writes, "Perception is loaded with unconscious inferences, from visual constancies, through spatial projections, empathy, and synesthesia, to projection of meaning into Rorschach blot, and the assigning of purpose and function to the human shape. The artist exploits these unconscious processes by the added twist of perspective, rhythm, and balance, contrast, 'tactile value', etc."[8]

An interesting story about faces in photographs is told by Joan Murray in an article that appeared in *Popular Photography.* Edward Weston was showing Moholy Nage some of his photographs while Beaumont Newhall looked on. Beaumont tells how Moholy upset Weston by calling attention to what he saw as secondary images in the photographs. "Moholy kept finding in the photographs hidden and fantastic forms, which were often revealed when—to Weston's obvious but politely hidden annoyance—he would turn the prints upside down. These after-products of Weston's vision fascinated Moholy; he considered photographs not interpretations of nature, but objects in themselves fascinating."[9] (If one assumes that Weston was using a view camera, then the images composed on the ground glass would have been upside down, as Moholy Nage viewed them.)

Arnold Newman tells about what he called a "happy accident" while photographing the surrealist artist Max Ernst. As Ernst was sitting for his portrait and smoking, Newman asked him to let the smoke out slowly. As he did, Newman took the photograph. Upon viewing the print, Max Ernst noticed, in the cloud of smoke, at

Perceive those things which cannot be seen.

Miyamoto Musashi, Samurai, 16th C.

If supraliminal stimuli are not attended to, they become like subliminal stimuli...

N.F. Dixon

A work of art must narrate something that does not appear within its outline.

Giorgio DeChirico

the left of the photograph, an image of a bird. This fascinated Ernst since he was drawing birds during that period of time.

Of significance to the photographer is the fact that the elements of a photograph not consciously perceived may have a profound influence on the viewer. Nondistinct imagery and peripheral placement of information can be perceived subliminally. What is consciously seen as figure is influenced by the subliminally perceived ground.

Faces

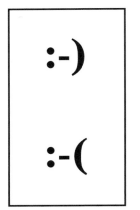

Just why the face should constitute such a powerful basic schema for our experiences is an unsolved mystery.

John Liggett

We know that just by being born human the infant fresh from the mother's womb is especially attracted to the features of the human face.

Adrian McFarlane

The art historian, E.H. Gombrich, calls attention to the importance of faces, sometimes hidden, to human vision, reminding us of its importance to our survival and that it is inborn and not learned.[10] Faces fascinate us from birth with a "language" that is simple and direct. The face is made up of many muscles, and is capable of hundreds of different expressions.

The research pediatrician René Spitz has written extensively on the importance of the face, particularly the mother's face, to an infant. "In the course of the first six weeks of life a mnemonic trace of the human face is laid down in the infantile memory as the first signal of the presence of need gratifier; the infant will follow all the movements of this signal with his eyes."[11]

We learn to read the information expressed in a human face long before we learn verbal language. The language of the face is a visual language that we learn in infancy. In psychoanalysis few patients can verbally remember much prior to about age two. Between infancy and two years a large, latent reservoir of visual experience and visual information is stored.

"The image of the face seems to take precedence over all others when the visual scene is at all unclear. The face seems to be, for all of us, a preferred shape. We can see faces in fire, faces in rocks, faces in clouds... It is strange to discover, too, how artists...seem to be impelled, in their creative work by the same hidden image of the face."[12]

It is as if we are "imprinted" at birth to respond to a human face as a way of survival. When a mother walks away from her infant and she is no longer in sight, the child experiences the mother as having disappeared. This is perhaps why the game "peek-a-boo" is so fascinating to an infant. A mother covers her face with her hands and, to the infant she actually disappears; she removes her hands from her face and suddenly she reappears. In the infant's world it is magic: She actually disappears and reappears. I remember a student telling me that as a child she did not want to have her mother watch her when she went "potty." Her mother, being cautious and perhaps recalling earlier experiences, told her to cover her eyes and she would disappear, which the child did.

Embedded figures can be playful and one cannot help but remember the fun, as children, of discovering hidden animals, faces, and such in pictures (Figure 9.3). Today's children experience the same. Hidden figures provide a sense of discovery that begins early in the infant stage with "peek-a-boo," and progresses to that of the child playing the game "hide-and-seek" and finding things hidden in "hidden pictures."

Figure 9.3   *"Johnny, 1944." Edward Weston. © Center for Creative Photography, Arizona Board of Regents. Edward Weston was a great lover of cats, many of which roamed the hills surrounding his modest home in Carmel, California. In this wonderful and compelling photograph, his cat, Johnny, drapes himself comfortably over a piece of bulbous driftwood with focused attention. He proudly sports long white whiskers as he peers directly and perhaps quizzically, at the photographer and his camera. The patterned plywood board that completely fills the background is also of interest. Not only are the patterns similar to the markings of Johnny's fur, but they also present the potential for secondary images.*

Perhaps photography is a variation of this need to discover things, searching for something to photograph that is hidden in the sense we have yet to discover it and reveal it in a photograph. Other activities could also be "hide-and-seek" discovery variations; visits to a flea market, searching for knowledge in books and libraries, all forms of research, and so on. Searching for something "hidden" is a lifelong pursuit that can be thought of as archetypal.

PUPILLOMETRICS

The study of how the size of the pupil changes when a person becomes emotional is called pupillometrics. It was mentioned earlier that considerable research confirms subliminal experiences. Research on the effect of pupil size on perception of images is of particular interest. It demonstrates how important unseen stimuli are to perception, and such research does not need any sophisticated lab equipment.

*Pupil size auto-
matically changes
with strong emo-
tional responses.*

It is common knowledge that the size of the pupil in the eye increases (dilates) as the light level decreases and decreases (constricts) when the light level increases. By analogy, the same thing happens to the automatic diaphragm control in a camera. In a dim room it increases (f/5.6), and in sunlight is decreases (f/16).

An interesting aspect of the eye is the automatic change in pupil size that can result from changes other than in light intensity. There is a high correlation between a person's pupil size and his emotional response. When something is seen that excites a person, pupil size tends to increase. It decreases when something unpleasant or scary is shown, such as bloodied bodies, and menacing sharks or snakes.

Automatic changes in pupil size are not limited to the visual sense. Changes can also be observed when a person is smelling, tasting, touching, or hearing something pleasant or unpleasant. Mental activities such as intense concentration can also cause changes in the pupil size. The eye is an extension of the brain.

This pupil size phenomenon has been known for a long time and has, for example, been effectively used by magicians, card sharks, and early Chinese jade merchants. Dilation and constriction of pupils are a direct and reliable means of nonverbal communication. They tell your friend or adversary that something has triggered you and changed your mental or emotional state.

The uniqueness of the early photographs by Barbara Morgan that captured the essence of dance was due in part to her ability to read the dancer's eyes, to "dance" with the dancer. Her son

Lloyd remembers watching his mother photograph dancers in her New York studio. "From a low position on the floor, her favorite position, and with a 4×5 Speed Graphic in hand, she would fixate on the eyes of the dancer and the dancer's movements. Her vision, concentration, and incredible reflexes were as sharp as a hawk's. Patiently she would study and track the dancers' movements and concentrate on the pupils of their eyes. Dancer and photographer would actually carry on a dialogue. They developed a rhythm with each other and would resonate together. At times it almost seemed as if Mom helped choreograph the dance. Mom would say 'ready-go.' Dancer and the photographer's eye, hand and shutter were in sync for the planned gesture. At the very instant the pupils of the dancer's eyes dilated—CLICK—'the decisive moment,' the unique moment."[13]

With portrait photography in a studio, the use of electronic flash with low wattage modeling lights has an advantage over the bright tungsten lights that cause pupils to constrict. The dim modeling lights allow the pupils to enlarge and remain enlarged while the lighting is being adjusted. The bright electronic flash exposure captures the image before the pupils can constrict. Most portrait photographers are aware that large pupils in portraits are more interesting than small pupils and that they tend to provide a more romantic appearance. Women as far back as the Middle Ages knew of this and some used the drug belladonna ("beautiful woman") as a cosmetic to dilate their pupils. Perhaps one of the reasons dinner by candlelight is considered romantic is that the low light level induces larger pupils.

In a 1965 research study by Dr. E. Hess of the University of Chicago, a large number of students were asked to look at two photographs that appeared to be identical and to choose one of them.[14] The task was difficult and students would often remark that they were both the same. When forced to make a choice most picked the photograph having the larger pupils. Asked later whether they were aware of the difference in pupil size nearly everyone said no.

I conducted a similar study in 1988 using a total of 80 male and female college students. Shown the "identical" portraits in Figure 9.4 and forced to make a choice, 87 percent of them preferred the portrait with the larger pupil size. There was no difference between male and female preferences. Only two of the subjects were aware of the difference in pupil size when they made their choice.

I feel myself one vibrating center in a galaxy of vibrations.

Barbara Morgan

The pupil can expand as much as 45 percent when looking at something exciting and pleasant.

Figure 9.4   *Pupillometrics. Both of the original photographs were identical except for the size of the pupils. Most subjects preferred the photograph to the left without being aware of the larger pupil size.*

© Richard Gicewicz

The myths of ancient peoples are still meaning- ful to us because they express pre- occupations and moods which are universal and eternal.

René Dubos

One might conclude from such studies that we can be influenced by things of which we are not consciously aware, things that are subliminal, in the sense that the difference in pupil size did not register as such but somehow affected choice.

ARCHETYPES

Pictures with embedded images such as latent faces, skulls, sexual parts, and the like are universal and may be more effective unseen in an image than seen—subconscious rather than conscious.

One of the early theories of Carl Gustav Jung was that of the *archetype*. The word archetype means an original model after which other things that have a similar quality are patterned. Jung distinguished between our unique *personal unconscious* and our *collective unconscious*, which all humans, past and present possess. The collective unconscious is a universal memory that contains the archetypes, variations on the original models. Some of the more important models that all humans possess in memory are the hero, mother, trickster, wise old man and woman, God, giant, demon, birth, death, rebirth, and many natural objects such as trees, sun, moon, river, and fire. "Endless repetition has engraved these experiences into our psychic constitution, not in the form of images filled with content, but at first only as *forms without content*, representing merely the possibility of a certain type of perception and action."[15]

Consider any one of the many archetypes and the number of different ways that the original model, the prototype, can be represented. The mother archetype takes many forms: mother, grandmother, mother of God, mother earth, nurse, church, synagogue, mosque, university, in music Ave Maria, Mother McCree. Photographs of modern-day madonnas, plowed fertile fields, gardens, and landscapes are archetypal.

"The primordial image or archetype, is a figure...be it a demon, a human being, or a process...that constantly recurs in the course of history and appears wherever creative phantasy is freely experienced."[16]

The hero archetype remains with us throughout our lifetime but takes on different forms. As children our heroes might have been our parents or playmates, certainly Superman, Batman, The Lone Ranger, GI Joe, Wonder Woman, Cat Woman, Barbie, Ninja Turtles, Power Rangers. All of the over 20,000 Westerns produced by Hollywood had a cowboy hero and of course a villain (another archetype). As we matured we got interested in other heroes, heroes in sports, music, literature, history, politics, religion, science, military, space exploration, space odysseys (Star Trek), and so on. The success of the movie *Star Wars*, according to its creator George Lucas, was the inspiration he derived from reading Joseph Campbell's book, *The Hero with a Thousand Faces*.

The scenes of a chase we often see in movies are archetypes in which someone is being pursued and is having difficulty in getting away. The chase is seen in many different ways and places: on land or water, in the air, in space, underwater, across rooftops, in the streets, deserts, or woods. The chase can occur on horseback over rugged terrain, in cars racing through busy streets and intersections, in airplanes in a dogfight, on boats, underwater in scuba gear, on trains as in some old movies, or simply on foot, running as the pursuer closes in with each step. The chase also occurs in our dreams where someone or something pursues us and we feel completely helpless—the dream becomes a nightmare.

Adolf Bastian (1826–1905), who preceded Sigmund Freud (1856–1939) and Carl Jung (1875–1961), termed recurring themes and features such as hero, mother, birth, and so on *elementargedanken* (elementary ideas), and the various ways they represent themselves in the arts, *volkergedaken* (folk ideas). The motifs that Bastian listed as "elementary ideas," Jung called archetypes of the collective unconscious.

The mother archetype is associated with things and places standing for fertility and fruitfulness: the cornucopia, a plowed field, a garden.

Carl Gustav Jung

As we become familiar with more objects of art, we discover certain similarities between images which are thousands of years and miles apart.

Graham Collier

Freud used the term "archaic remnants" to refer to archetypes.

KILROY

MR. CHAD

ORIGINAL?

Two cognitive scientists in a 1992 article, "The Problem of Consciousness" wrote, "...the information available to our eyes is not sufficient to provide the brain with its unique interpretation of the visual world. The brain must use past experiences (either its own or that of our distant ancestors, which is embedded in our genes) to help interpret the information coming into our eyes."[17]

KILROY

During and shortly after World War II, Kilroy graffiti began appearing everywhere, a childlike caricature of a face with a long phallic nose and the words "Kilroy was here." Similar features persist in comic strips, cartoons, drawings, illustrations, advertisements, paintings, and photographs. The salient features are two eyes and an elongated nose. (As a secondary image in detailed pictures, the eyes are usually two dark shadows.) The Kilroy figure contained a horizontal line representing the edge of a wall, an extended nose hanging over it and hands holding on to the edge of the wall. The English had their own Kilroy, a chap they named Chad. In Australia Kilroy took on the same features using the symbols of positive (+) and negative (−) for the eyes, and a distorted sine wave for the eyes and nose; which was probably the first way Kilroy was portrayed.

The pervasiveness of this Kilroy symbol suggests a subtext, a hidden meaning. As it is displayed, it is direct, confrontational, and a bit humorous. It is not a secondary image, although in some pictures it appears as such (Figure 9.5).

One British author writing on "Depth Psychology of Thing Perception" explains Chad in this way, "May I suggest that its [Chad] astounding expressiveness is due to the thinly veiled phallic exhibitionism expressed by the nose... In primitive dancing or infantile play the heroic display of the phallus represents provocation; little wonder, therefore, that the strongly symbolic 'Mr. Chad' should have appeal to the military (heroic) sense of humour."[18]

In this context one cannot help but recall the advertisement featuring Joe Camel, that pervasive anthropomorphized camel (really a dromedary) that has become an icon for Camel cigarettes. Joe has features equivalent to Kilroy and Chad, but perhaps a bit more subtle. Not everyone would agree with this. In an article in *Artforum*, Stuart Ewen refers to Joe Camel as an example of "desublimated advertising." Ewen writes, "The 'smooth character' is truly the Henry Ford of phallus worship... this desublimated ad is seen as relatively benign, an amusing form of blue entertainment...."[19] Regardless of how adults read Joe Camel's features,

Deep rooted symbols are used subliminally and cynically in advertisements, and even in the images and rhetoric of political campaigns.[20]

David Fontana

Figure 9.5   "Kilroy and the Rhinemaidens." (Courtesy Dover Publications.) An illustration by Arthur Rackham from the book, Arthur Rackham's Color Illustrations for Wagner's Ring, New York: Dover, 1979. Notice the Kilroy equivalent in the form of a tree root just to the left of the Rhinemaiden hand.

"Alice" (Reprinted with special permission of King Features Syndicate.)

he has been an attraction to children. He is the second most recognizable character for children, Mickey Mouse being first.

Some other Kilroy equivalents that have appeared over time are worth noting since the Kilroy image is a variation of a prototype that can be found worldwide—that is, the phallus. Some time back a Popeye comic strip series featured a character called "Alice the Goon" whose features were very similar to Kilroy's. On March 10, 1978 the comic strip, "Dr. Smock" featured Kilroy grafittied on a hospital wall as "Dr. Kildare." A December 1990 ad for Jim Beam Kentucky whisky, with the headline, "You always come back to basics," had a vintage Kilroy illustration representing the war year 1944.

Kilroy and Chad continue to be with us for they serve to represent an archetype. Their image appears in many places, at different times, in different ways, with an inexplicable similarity of meaning. The Kilroy archetype is not only seen on walls but can be found in early sculpture, rituals, folklore, fairy tales (Figure 9.6), mythologies, dreams, and perhaps even on the Internet.

Xerox presents 90 minutes with one of literature's most celebrated heroes.

Bilbo Baggins, the reluctant adventurer created by J.R.R. Tolkien and idolized by millions of readers of all ages, comes to tele-vision in a spectacular animated special from Rankin/Bass Productions.
    Everyone will want to see how the timid Bilbo finds the courage to confront the fearsome Gollum, the mighty Great Goblin and, finally, the awful Smaug.
    Once you've seen this Xerox presenta-tion, you'll never again believe animated specials are only for children.

"The Hobbit."
Sunday, November 27, NBC-TV Network.

Figure 9.6   Kilroy lives on. Kilroy appears again as a tree root with dark eyes peering at the Hobbit just to his right. Compare this Kilroy structural equivalent (likeness) to the Pinch bottle with the two dark eyes and phallic nose on the Key Words page of this chapter. (Courtesy Xerox Corporation.)

The very edge of the human retina…gives primitive uncon-scious vision.

Richard Gregory

Archetypes are important to the photographer and other image makers because they feed the collective unconscious, our universal memory that transcends time and culture. A powerful image, regardless of the medium, is one that can trigger an archetype. Memorable images do this and some are called works of art.

Kilroy in a bottle? From how many different perspectives can a bottle be photographed? What makes this representation of a bottle of Pinch Scotch so interesting and engaging? (Courtesy Pinch Scotch)

KEY WORDS

archetype
Chad
collective unconscious
cones
foveal vision
Kilroy
lingam
peripheral vision
personal unconscious
phallus
pupillometrics
rods
saccadic
secondary images
subliminal
unseen stimuli

The unconscious depth-messages of ads are never attacked by the literate, because of their incapacity to notice or discuss nonverbal forms of arrangement and meaning. They have not the art to argue with pictures.[21]

Marshall
McLuhan

Subliminals Exercises

1. Secondary Images

In the two articles by Michael Brenson in the *New York Times*, he cites paintings by Van Gogh and Cézanne that have, in his opinion, secondary images. Look up some of these in art books and form your own opinion. Remember that what you will be looking at are reproductions. There is no substitute for actually viewing the original whenever you can. Here are some of the paintings Brenson mentions:

Ninety-nine percent of what our brain does is not available to us in terms of consciousness.

Michael
Gazzaniga

- *By Cézanne*: "The Large Bathers," "Montagne Saint-Victoire," "Rocks at Fountainbleau," "Trees Near a Road," "Great Pine."
- *By Van Gogh*: "Pine Trees with Setting Sun," "Olive trees with the Alpilles in the Background," "Cypresses," "Olive Orchard," "Road with Cypress and Star.'

The work of other painters mentioned in Brenson's articles are Gauguin (to whom he refers as the third member of the Post-Impressionist triumvirate), Odilin Redon, and Jackson Pollock. Works by Surrealist artists such as Salvador Dali and Max Ernst are also a potential source of secondary images as are the works of Paul Klee and illustrations by Arthur Rackham in early children's books. It is also enlightening to look for examples in non-Western art.

... advertising is a subliminal pill designed to massage the unconscious.

Marshall
McLuhan

2. Photographs

Look for secondary images in some of the photographs in photographic books, or when possible on exhibit, by photographers such as Edward Weston, Brett Weston, Ann Brigman, Ruth Bernhard, Minor White, Charles Laughlin, David Hamilton, Wynn Bullock, Lucien Clergue, Jerry Uelsmann, Judy Dater, and others. If you are holding the photograph in your hand, look at it in different orientations, as Moholy Nage did when he turned Edward Weston's photographs upside down. Attend to the background in the photographs, and in particular to fuzzy backgrounds.

The very edge of the human retina... gives primitive unconcious vision.

Richard Gregory

3. Advertisements

Advertisements are a rich source of secondary images, particularly those for non-essential items such as cosmetics, jewelry, alcohol, and cigarettes, as seen in the following figure. When you find ads with such images, show them to friends, and without revealing your discovery, see if their vision is the same as yours.

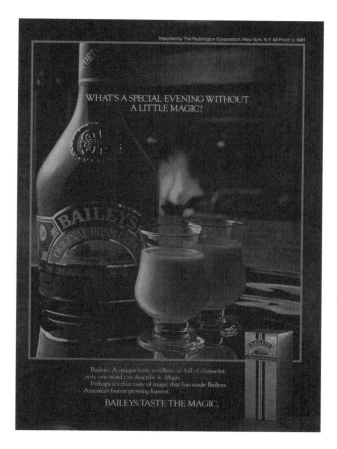

Take another look at the Pinch scotch bottle and notice the two dark, peering eyes.

A little magic. In this cleverly designed ad, notice the two small white circles to the right of the Baileys bottle. According to Picasso, Two holes—that's the symbol for a face, enough to evoke it without representing it. A number of research studies with infants over the years support this. (Courtesy Baileys.)

4. Subliminal Time?

Look for advertisements for watches and clocks and notice the time. More often than not the hands on the face are arranged so that the time is ten minutes to two or ten minutes after ten. Had you noticed this before? What do the hands in an upward position signify or suggest? How would you experience the same watch if the hands read twenty minutes after eight or a quarter past nine?

5. Photographing

Create some photographs that have potential secondary images. Attending to things in the background and at the periphery of the camera frame is important. Look through the viewfinder in a single-lens-reflex or view camera and study what happens to the background when you move it progressively out of focus. Try large diaphragm openings such as f/5.6 and 3.5 to decrease depth of field and cause fuzzy backgrounds.

6. Photo Rorschach

Sharpen your vision by searching out interesting facial patterns in natural things such as cut wood, old tree bark and roots, and flowers. (Edward Steichen saw hundreds of faces in a large cluster of pansies and photographed them.) Look for potential images in the variety of patterns in marble and graffiti.

You may want to create your own chance images by splattering ink or paint on a paper surface. Try the Jackson Pollock technique of "drip-painting," only use "drip-developer" on photographic paper and then develop it.

7. Pupillometrics

Carry out the pupillometric experiment cited in the text by photographing a friend, making matched prints, and then increasing the pupil size of one of the prints. This is easily done on a computer with software such as Photoshop. You may want to make three or four matched prints with increasing pupil size. Ask a number of men and women, boys and girls their print preference. Shift the prints' position each time, for position can be a factor; some people will prefer the print on the right and some on the left.

8. More Pupillometrics

Study the eyes in some of the close-up photographs of models in magazines. Look for pupil size and position of the iris of the eye relative to the white area that surrounds it. Also look to see where the catch light falls and the shape of it as it reflects off the eyeball.

9. Archetypes

Look at paintings, photographs, sculptures, advertisements, and movies to discover the importance of archetypes and the different forms they take now and have taken in earlier days. Some good references to look at are:

Joseph Campbell, *Hero with a Thousand Faces*, Princeton, NJ: Princeton University Press, 1968.

Carl Gustav Jung (ed.), *Man and His Symbols*, New York: Doubleday, 1964.

Jolande Jacobi, *Complex Archetype Symbol*, New York: Princeton University Press, 1959.

Carol S. Pearson, *Awakening the Heros Within*, New York: HarperCollins, 1991.

Environments by reason of their total character are mostly subliminal to ordinary experience.

Marshall McLuhan

The primordial image or archetype is a figure, be it a daemon, a human being, or a process, that constantly recurs in the course of history and appears wherever creative phantasy is expressed.

Patricia L. Musick

10. Kilroy Lives

Keep an eye open for Kilroy-type graffiti and pictures. You will be amazed to discover the proliferation of such archetypal imagery. Search though some books on mythology such as *Myths* by Alexander Eliot (New York: McGraw-Hill, 1976), with contributions by Joseph Campbell and Mircea Eliade. Books on symbols such as Barbara Walker's book, *The Woman's Dictionary of Symbols and Sacred Objects* (San Francisco, CA: Harper and Row, 1988) are good sources.

11. The Human Eye

(A) The Dominant Eye

The dominant eye is the one that tends to determine perception when images formed by both eyes fail to fuse. It is the eye we tend to use when looking through a camera viewfinder or gun. To determine which eye is dominant, look at an object at a distance of about 10 feet with both eyes open. Now with your arm extended and both eyes open, align your upright thumb (as an artist does when studying perspective), with the object. Close one eye and then the other as you continue looking at the object. The eye that causes the most displacement when you close it is your dominant eye.

(B) Blind Spot

Holding this book at a comfortable reading distance, close your left eye and fixate on the X with your right eye. Slowly move the book back and forth between about 4 to 12 inches (about 10 to 30 cm) until a position is reached where the black dot disappears. When this happens, the image of the black spot has fallen on the region of the retina where there are no photoreceptors, just nerve fibers that group together and leave the eye. This area is called the blind spot or optic disk.

I claim not how man thinks in myth but how myth operated without his being aware of the fact.

Lévi-Strauss

What you have to do, you do with play.

Joseph Campbell

X   ●

(C) Astigmatism

Look at the center of the following radial pattern without glasses or contact lenses. If some of the spokes look less sharp than others it is an indication of astigmatism. Try the same thing with corrective lenses if you wear them.

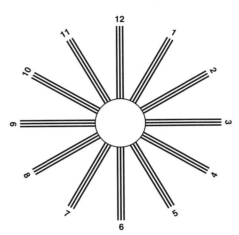

Work begins when you don't like what you are doing.

Joseph Campbell

(D) Foveal and Peripheral Vision

While looking straight ahead and not moving your eyes to the right or left, have a friend hold a colored object a foot or so behind your head and then *slowly* move it in a circular arc past your ear toward a position directly in front of your eyes. Notice when you can first (1) detect movement of the object, (2) identify the approximate shape of the object, and (3) identify the color of the object.

(E) Convergence: Boy meets Girl

Introduce this couple to each other and have them hold hands by slowly moving this page toward your nose.

Notes

1. Richard L. Gregory (ed.), *Oxford Companion to the Mind*, New York: Oxford University Press, 1991, p. 752.

2. Ibid., p. 754.

3. Janet A. Kaplan, *Unexpected Journeys*, New York: Abbeville Press, 1988, p. 21.

4. Stephen Foehr, "D.H. Lawrence, the Forbidden Paintings," *Horizon*, July 1980, p. 66.

5. Michael Brenson, "The Faces that Haunt Van Gogh's Landscapes," *New York Times*, January 4, 1987.

6. Michael Brenson, "Head-Hunting in the Landscapes of Cézanne," *New York Times*, October 14, 1984.

7. Anton Ehrenzweig, *The Hidden Order of Art*, Berkeley CA: University of California Press, 1971, p. 29.

8. Arthur Koestler, *The Act of Creation*, New York: Dell, 1975, p. 392.

9. Joan Murray, *Popular Photography*, December 1975.

10. E.H. Gombrich, *Art and Illusion*, Princeton, NJ: Princeton University Press, 1969, p. 103.

11. René Spitz, *The First Year of Life*, New York: International University Press, 1965, p. 52.

12. John Liggett, *The Human Face*, New York: Stein and Day, 1974, p. 174.

13. Lloyd Morgan (Private conversation, November 12, 1994).

14. E. Hess, "Attitude and Pupil Size," *Scientific American*, April 1965, p. 212.

15. Calvin S. Hall and Vernon J. Nordby, *A Primer of Jungian Psychology*, New York: New American Library, 1973, p. 42.

16. Hull, R. (ed.), *The Portable Jung*, New York: The Viking Press, 1971, p. 72.

17. Francis Crick and Christof Koch, "The Problem of Consciousness," *Scientific American*, September 1992, p. 153.

18. Anton Ehrenzweig, *The Psycho-Analysis of Artistic Vision and Hearing*, New York: George Braziller, 1965, p. 214.

19. Stuart Ewen, "The Public Eye," *Art Forum*, January 1991, p. 28.

20. David Fontana, *The Secret Language of Symbols*, San Francisco, CA: Chronicle Books, 1994, p. 8

21. Marshall McLuhan, *Understanding Media,* New York: Signet, 1964, p. 205.

10
Critiquing Photographs

Criticism of my work ... now means something to me, whereas previously my self-deception admitted nothing.

Paul Klee

"Katharine, Upper Taughannock Falls, NY, 1992" © John D. Carroll

Pictures are made to be looked at as original images or as reproductions in printed media such as magazines, newspapers, books, brochures, catalogs, billboards, and electronic media such as video, computer monitors, Photo CD and CD-ROM. The medium used to display the image and its context will have an effect on how the picture is experienced. A matted and framed photograph displayed in a well-lit gallery will be seen differently than an unmounted photograph pinned to a wall. A photograph reproduced in a quality magazine will look much better than one in a newspaper. A color print viewed as an original (object color) and viewed on a video screen (illuminant color) represent different color modalities and will be seen differently.

The total context in which a photograph appears will influence how it is perceived. Placement of a photograph in a magazine with text, with other photographs, or with advertisements surrounding it, can have different meanings. Any title or caption given the photograph can affect the meaning as well. Some photographers have titled their photographs "Untitled" to allow the image to speak for itself. Jerry Uelsmann's surreal images are an example. Others have used a title to identify a location, as did Dr. Thomas McCartney in his mountain landscape titled "Mount McKinley, Alaska" (the opening photograph in Chapter 8). Mary Ellen Mark identified person and place in her photograph "Tiny, in Seattle." Sheila Metzner uses a title to echo the sensuality of one of her photographs, "Jako Passion." Duane Michals not only provides philosophical titles for his photographs such as "All Things Mellow in the Mind," but also adds handwritten narrative; a contemporary Illuminated Manuscript.

In addition, time is part of the context—our perceptions can change throughout the day and evening. Historical time is also a factor. Photographs that were considered unworthy of museum exhibits when they were made are now admired and collected, such as Weegee's photographs of accidents taken in New York City in the early 1900s. The high-speed stroboscopic photographs pioneered by Dr. Harold Edgerton while at MIT are another example. Edgerton's work can be seen as a continuation of the earlier motion studies of animals and humans by Muybridge and Marey.

CRITIQUE AS EVALUATION

The word *critique* refers to a critical review or commentary, written or spoken, regarding someone's work, usually artistic work but certainly not limited to that. For anyone to critique or

The photographs are not illustrative. They and the text are coequal, mutually independent, and fully collaborative.

James Agee,
Walker Evans

I'm willing to be judged by posterity, it's not important what people think now.

Frederick Remington

If I could tell the story in words, I wouldn't need to lug around a camera.

Lewis Hines

pass judgment on a photograph involves evaluation, and for the evaluation to be fair and reasonable there must be some type of criteria or purpose. Photographs take on many different expressions, from, for example, the artistic (fine art) to the informative (photojournalism), to the highly technical (high-speed photography). One cannot critique a photograph without some overt or covert criteria, either one's own or those of the photographer. (There are exceptions, as will be noted later.) Remarks such as "I like it" or "It's not interesting" may be based on the critic's unspoken criteria but are of little help to the photographer. I am reminded of the remark the writer James Thurber made when someone asked him, "How's your wife?" His sharp reply was, "With respect to what?"

VALIDITY

Evaluation of any kind, artistic or otherwise must assume some kind of a purpose to be valid. The criteria can be based on the intention of the photographer or on the stated purpose of the client or instructor. An assignment to go out and photograph a tree is quite loose and would be difficult to judge with any validity unless the photographer is asked what his or her intentions were and then judged on that basis. Students sometimes complain about a test question not being fair and their complaint is often justified. It is not valid to teach one thing (for example, how to use a 35-mm camera), and then test for something else (how to use a view camera).

Valid:
Well grounded, sound, supportable, convincing.

VARIABILITY

Critiquing a photograph is a subjective task and more often than not there will be differences of opinion among different critics. This is easily demonstrated by showing the same photograph to several critics, independently telling each of them what the criteria are, then having them rate the photograph on a scale from 1 to 10 and write a short statement supporting their rating. Regardless of how expert the critics are, they will rarely be in agreement in their evaluations. Photographers must accept this variability of response to their pictures, listen to what others have to say, but also believe in themselves and their work.

The Impressionist painters believed strongly in their style of painting regardless of the criticism they received from the classical

No individual symbolic image can be said to have a dogmatically fixed generalized meaning.

Carl Jung

Beauty, like truth, is relative to the time when one lives and to the individual who can grasp it.

Gustave Courbet

Be what you is, 'cuz if you be what you ain't, then you ain't what you is.

Boot Hill Cemetery, Arizona

painters and the French Academy at that time and their inability to initially find one gallery or museum willing to display their work.

"The first Impressionist exhibition was held in 1874, and for much of the ensuing century Impressionism—at first so disconcerting that cartoonists predicted it would cause pregnant women to miscarry—has been the most popular of all art movements."[1] The importance of their work took time to be realized as did the importance of the modern art paintings that Dr. Albert C. Barnes was collecting in the early 1900s. He was severely criticized by the art establishment of Philadelphia for wasting money collecting questionable work by painters such as Cézanne, Matisse, Picasso, Degas, and Renoir. The photographer/painter Barbara Morgan, as a young art teacher at the University of California, realized the importance of his modern art collecting and studied with him.

She and her husband Willard were the first photographers to photograph Barnes's entire collection. It was put on lantern slides and made available to schools. His collection now is recognized as one of the largest and most important private collections of modern art and is on display at his home in Marion, Pennsylvania.

PHOTOGRAPHERS' COMMENTS

A thought may be an expression of the person's feelings and convictions. It is rooted in his total personality and has an emotional matrix.

Erich Fromm

Listen to what some photographers have to say about their most popular photographs. About his photograph, "Rock Wall," Paul Caponigro writes, "In an unexpected moment the print spoke to me as if with a voice. The words were registered in my head or my heart, of course, but I was aware that my rational mind had not shaped that sequence of words which I now heard."[2]

Sally Mann writes, "My work appears to have turned irrevocably from the decorative to a commitment best described as humanistic. 'Jessie at 6,' however, is evidence that the documentary impulse I am yielding to need not be without occasional lyricism and grace."[3] Duane Michals' photograph, "All Things Mellow in the Mind," is in his words, "... a traditional momento mori, which illustrated my awareness of being and not being. It is about youth, our illusion of permanence, and our unawareness of the moment of now, which is all there is or ever will be."[4] Tom McCartney recalls his experience when photographing Mount McKinley in 1982: "The Indians of Alaska gave the name *Denali* ('The High One') to the mountain...I decided to try to show this mountain in all its majesty. Darkening the shadowed glacier bed and contrasting it with numerous glacier rivers and streams would produce the richness and luster the print deserved. Brilliance would be supplied by maintaining the values of the sunlit snows while increasing the separation of the mountain peaks from the sky."[5]

Regarding her most popular photograph, "In the Box," Ruth Bernhard, who studied with Edward Weston, writes, "I was photographing a friend and, briefly glancing out the window, saw a United Postal Service driver carrying a very large box over his shoulder. I immediately envisioned her in it...I obediently followed my intuition and posed the model in the box, precisely as I imagined. It was not until ten years later that it suddenly occurred to me that this image might have come to me from reading D.H. Lawrence's book, *The Man Who Died*."[6] Bernhard's photograph reminds me of a section of a painting by René Magritte titled, "Le Dormeur téméraire" (The Daring Sleeper). One writer describes it thus: "...suspended in the night, lies the sleeper in an upturned wooden box—a coffin."[7] There are probably other references to this painting and to Bernhard's photograph suggesting that they might be archetypal images, prototypes taking on different literary and visual forms.

The production of artists and writers represents rich, unmined beds of hard data on how man perceives.

Edward Hall

Birth, death, and rebirth are archetypes.

CRITIQUING

Different styles of critiquing are used by different critics and by a given critic in different situations. A critique can be one-on-one or can be done with a group, somewhat like a counseling session. Either way, it should be fair and constructive, not confrontational, although some critics are able to use confrontation in a positive way. The critic should serve as a counselor helping photographers gain insight into their work, which in some ways is an extension of the photographers, a *projection* of feelings on the object photographed.

One of the most difficult tasks in critiquing is having to use words to discuss the content of the photograph, which itself is wordless. The same problem exists in critiquing music and other forms of nonverbal expression. Words are inadequate but they are the basis for our spoken and written language, and we are limited by them. Some photographers are uncomfortable with words and are "at a loss for words" to express themselves when talking about a photograph.

Group critiques in which photographs are arranged on a wall and the group is asked to start talking about them usually begin with an extended dead silence. Everyone is a bit guarded and waiting for someone else to begin. The first person to speak can set the direction for the entire group. The direction can be useful or detrimental. Many research studies in the social sciences have

One repents having written succinct and lapidary phrases upon art.

Pierre Bonnard

shown how easy it is for the first speaker in a group to influence the response of the others. What might be called "open-ended" critiques, which are unstructured, have their place, but they also present problems in that the most talkative members control the direction of the critique.

When judging a photograph or a series of photographs:

- Try to maintain a neutral position and not be influenced by the remarks of others.
- Take sufficient time to seriously study the photographs before making any remarks.
- Consider not just the content of the photograph but also the photographer's viewpoint in making the photograph.
- Identify issues that are being expressed and determine whether the issues deal with specifics or universals.
- Consider whether the approach is historical, political, sociological, psychological, and so on, and whether it is unique or represents a cliché.

It is not just what you photograph but how you photograph. How are you seeing what you are seeing?

Nathan Lyons

CLUSTERING

Free-association: A spontaneous unconstrained association of feelings and ideas.

The idea of clustering is based on the open-ended use of words as pioneered by the free-association techniques of Freud and Jung. To bypass a conscious response, clients were asked to respond quickly to each word in a list of words spoken. Their responses and quickness of response gave insight into the person's feelings and problems.

With Freud and Jung, a spoken word was used to respond to a spoken word (word-word association). With clustering, words are used to first respond to a picture and then words are used to respond to those words (photo-word-word association). When a large enough cluster of words are gathered, they are studied, edited, and grouped in an attempt to find relationships that will provide insight into the photograph. One advantage of such a technique is that it allows spontaneity, and the words spoken are associated less with thinking and more with sensing and intuiting. In a way, clustering is similar to brain-storming techniques.

How clustering can be used to unveil the layered and latent meanings in the photograph of boats shown in Figure 10.1 will serve as an example.

The procedure took place in a classroom setting. We began by using a word to literally identify the photograph. In this case the word "Boats" was used. The word was written on the chalkboard and a circle drawn around it. "Boats" now served as a centering word upon which other word associations could be made. Students were then invited to look at the photograph in Figure 10.1 and quickly say or write whatever words came to mind. In this way the right brain is engaged and words that describe how one feels about the photograph are given without much thought. The words most frequently given were "serenity," "tranquility," "quietness," "peacefulness," "idyllic."

And what is word knowledge but a shadow of word-less knowledge?

Kahil Gibran

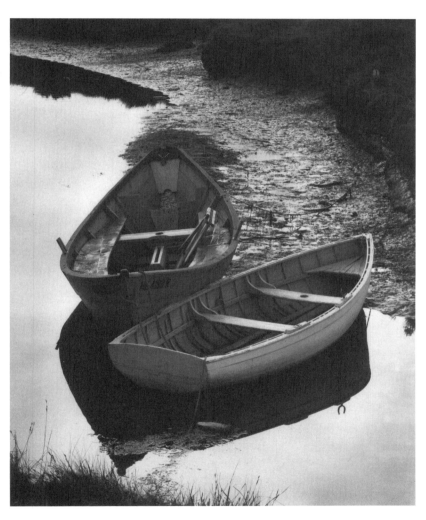

Figure 10.1   "Eventide," © Tom McCartney. At a literal level this is a photograph of two boats tied to the shore by a rope, but at a connotative, poetic level it is much more. (As Minor White would remind his students. "Yes, it is a photograph of two boats but what else is it?).

The title of the photograph, "Eventide," conveys the same feeling. A number of other words were given, the most significant being *relationships, direction, serenity,* and *nostalgia*. As shown in Figure 10.2, these became key words that set off other word associations.

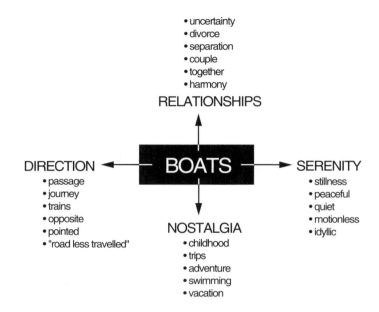

Figure 10.2 *Word clustering. Word associations around a centering word (Boats) serve to trigger a number of word relationships that provide insight into the meaning of a photograph.*

Relationships

The words associated with relationships suggested two opposing interpretations. One, that the two boats serve as a metaphor for an older couple who have journeyed through life in a loving relationship and have now reached shore and departed gracefully. The title of the photograph supports this idea of the later years in life. (It is important to note here that a title given to a photograph becomes part of the photograph, and directly influences how it is experienced.)

An opposite interpretation, one of separation and divorce, was suggested by another student who probably had experienced such an event as a child of separated or divorced parents. The shape of the boat on the left suggested the woman and the boat on the right, the man. (When I later asked the basis for this interpretation, the response was that the boat on the left was more almond shape.)

Trope:
A figure of speech; a word or picture used in a nonliteral way. A metaphor or simile is an example.

Notice also that the dark shadows of the two boats could suggest a feeling of sadness, remorse, and the uncertainty of what the future holds.

Direction

The two boats that are moored point in different directions. This reminded one student of a poem by Robert Frost, "The Road Not Taken." Recall the line,

> "Two roads diverged in a wood, and I —
> I took the one less traveled by,
> And that made all the difference..."[8]

Boats suggest a journey and they have been used in various art forms as metaphors for our journey through life, and in some cases the journey into the afterlife.

Nostalgia

For other students the photograph was reminiscent of earlier days—of childhood. They recalled summer days rowing with friends and docking along the shore, taking their oars with them for security, and then walking into the darkness in search for new adventures. One student, in recalling his childhood, revealed a rather sad experience. His single mother would put him on a train each summer to go to camp so she could be free to work. He did not want to leave his mother and felt isolated and afraid, and was never sure where the train was to take him. He also mentioned that whenever he hears a train whistle he has the same experience.

"Eventide" is rich with meaning, and other interpretations are certainly possible depending upon the personal experiences and memory of the reader/viewer. The associations made are all valid since they are based on personal experiences. We all see things a bit differently and should not deny this to please someone else's vision.

Paramount to the photograph "Eventide," of course, is the feeling of serenity and tranquillity—peacefulness, which is probably archetypal, a collective experience based on a universal memory we all harbor.

Composition

Some students who were deeply into design were attracted to the compositional features of the photograph and free-associated with

Education is man's going forward from cocksure ignorance to thoughtful uncertainty.

Kenneth G. Johnson

Everything I see and experience in Kentucky is to some extent colored and shaped by the thoughts and emotions I had when I first came to the monastery. It cannot be otherwise.

Thomas Merton

such words as, "nice lines," "symmetrical," "hour-glass look," "almond shapes," "curvatures," "tonalities," and the like.

As a side note, the photographer, who was in the class when our clustering critique was going on, was asked what *he* saw in his photograph. He remarked that he certainly was not aware of all of these associations and that something had drawn him to the boats and compelled him to make the photograph. When he first looked at the print he made he remarked, "WOW!!" The photograph, for him, represented what he had experienced in taking it and it is one of his favorite photographs.

On Location

This technique of clustering to derive meaning from photographs can be used in reverse. It can be used in planning where to take photographs and what kind of photographs to take. For example, in arranging for a photographic trip to Florida, personal or on assignment, a clustering procedure can provide a useful start. Beginning with the nucleus or centering word "Florida," free-associate the first words that come to mind as shown in Figure 10.3.

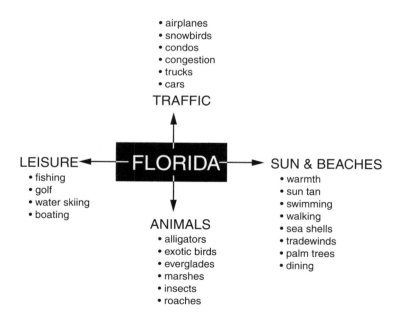

Figure 10.3   Location planning. Word clustering can be used to develop a theme for things to photograph when preparing to photograph in a particular location.

Some of the key words to build upon to portray a favorable side would be "sun," "seashore," "sports," and "Everglades." If a negative image is to be portrayed, then perhaps words such as "heat," "humidity," "crime," "poverty," "traffic," or "insects" are recalled. Once this is done, and depending upon how you want to portray Florida, pick out one or two of the key words and expand on them in some detail. On the positive side, sunshine and seashore might be considered; on the negative side, perhaps heat and crime. Once this is done, a focus is provided for the photographic journey. The result would be a series of photographs having a common theme and such a series could serve as a portfolio of work.

More information on clustering technique can be found in a book by Gabriele Lusser Rico called *Writing the Natural Way*.[9] The author has found the technique very successful in helping college students write papers for class assignments and even to compose poetry.

SEMANTIC DIFFERENTIAL

Another method for trying to gain insight into the meaning of a photograph is by using a *semantic differential* scale, which consists of a series of bipolar adjectives.[10] The scale was developed to investigate the meaning a person gives to a word as compared to the dictionary definition of the word.

Given a phrase such as "Photo CD," for example, a person is asked to rate the phrase on a seven-point scale between each pair of oppositional (bipolar) adjectives. The instructions specify that the closeness of the mark to each of two adjectives indicates the closeness of the relationship, with the middle position being neutral. In the example given below, the rater felt neutral about whether the phrase Photo CD was bad or good, but felt that it was slightly complex, moderately pleasant and intimate, strongly active, and very useful.

Each word means something slightly different to each person, even among those who share the same culture.

Henry James

Photo CD

Bad	__ __ __ X __ __ __	Good
Simple	__ __ __ __ X __ __	Complex
Pleasant	__ __ X __ __ __ __	Unpleasant
Intimate	__ __ X __ __ __ __	Remote
Active	__ X __ __ __ __ __	Passive
Useful	X __ __ __ __ __ __	Useless

It is not often that we use language correctly; usually we use it incorrectly, though we understand each other's meaning.

St. Augustine

The limits of your language are the limits of your world.

Ludwig Wittgenstein

When words become unclear, I shall focus on photographs. When images become inadequate, I shall be content with silence.

Ansel Adams

There are a number of different ways of interpreting the responses. One is to look for relationships. A thinking person might rate a Photo CD as complex and very good while a sensing person might rate it complex and remote.

In a group session it would be of interest to summarize the data and determine what the average response of the group is and how consistent or inconsistent (variable) the responses are for each bipolar adjective. Group responses that are quite inconsistent should be studied to determine the reason.

Connecting the Xs with a line for each bipolar adjective will show a pattern of responses—a graph—that can be compared with other individual responses for agreement and disagreement.

Bipolar adjectives can be classified according to three major dimensions for additional study:

- Evaluation (good or bad)
- Potency (strong or weak)
- Activity (active or passive)

These three dimensions, Evaluation, Potency, and Activity, represent important aspects of connotation in a wide variety of languages. By studying the responses to the different bipolar adjectives, one can separate the three related qualities of responses.

Although the semantic differential has been used mostly to determine connotative meanings of words, it has also been used to determine the meanings associated with paintings and photographs. In a study to find out if there was a difference between the meanings that a group of artists and a group of nonartists gave paintings, it was found that meanings for representational paintings were similar for both groups but quite dissimilar for abstract paintings. This suggests that artists have worked out and agreed upon a system of evaluation of abstract paintings.

A study of the effect of captions on photographs revealed that the captions could shift the meaning associated with a picture. For example, on a scale of happy to sad, a scene of a couple at an airline terminal captioned "Reunion" would be marked happy while the one captioned "Parting" would be marked sad. Captions that were quite the opposite of the pictorial content, however, did not alter the judgment of the photograph.

Figure 10.4 is a semantic differential scale with a number of bipolar adjectives. The scale can be added to or edited to suit a particular photograph (portrait, landscape, scientific, architectural, fashion, nude, medical, forensic, and so on).

SEMANTIC DIFFERENTIAL

pleasant								unpleasant
vibrant								still
repetitive								varied
happy								sad
chaotic								ordered
smooth								rough
superficial								profound
passive								active
simple								complex
relaxed								tense
obvious								subtle
serious								humorous
violent								gentle
static								dynamic
emotional								rational
bad								good

*Figure 10.4   Semantic differential scale. This rating scale of
bipolar adjectives can be used to measure the
word meanings a person associates with a
photograph or other type of image. An X in the
middle of the scale designates a neutral position.
This scale was originally constructed to derive the
meaning people gave to different words as
compared to a dictionary definition.*

CRITIQUING WITHOUT WORDS

Photographs that are not being made for some kind of an assignment such as a classroom assignment or a commercial assignment are often not specified in terms of intent or criteria. These are personal photographs that are created out of some need for individuals to express themselves. Photography, like other arts, including performing arts, is a wonderful means for personal expression. Personal photography involves approaching a subject from a *sensing* or *intuiting* position, in Jung's terms, from a nonrational position. Here we look for clues in the photograph

*I have nothing to
say, and I have
said it.*

John Cage

Work with the images, don't talk about them. Let the photographs speak for themselves.

Nathan Lyons

A photograph is always seen in some context; physical, remembered, imagined.

Rashid Elisha

A sequence of photographs is like a cinema of stills. The time and space between the photographs is filled by the beholder.

Minor White

that will reveal what is being expressed at a level below consciousness. This will require more than a single photograph—a series of about thirty or more photographs would be required.

Once the series is completed, the prints are viewed and studied by both the photographer and the critic. Considerable time is spent in studying each photograph individually and in relationship to the other photographs in the series. As insight into the series is gained, the critic may edit out some of the photographs that do not seem to be relevant and reposition others. In effect what the critic is attempting to do, without using words, is to have the photographs speak for themselves—to reveal the latent information in the pictures that is waiting to be discovered. Words are not necessary, but attention to the photographs and what they are saying is. It is as if one were given a scrambled text and had to edit out some words and rearrange others in order to find the statement being made.

Similar procedures have been used in a movement called *Photo Therapy*, the use of photographs in a counseling situation. A client may be having difficulty resolving some nagging problem, and sessions with a counselor, based on words, may not provide an avenue for insights into the problem. The counselor may then ask the client to bring in a family album of photographs or a series of photographs that the client has taken recently or over the years. The counselor then goes through the same procedure a critic does, carefully studying the photographs, editing out some and sequencing the remainder.

I recall a situation told to me by a psychiatrist friend from Toronto. One of his clients had a severe problem that seemed to revolve around her childhood relationship with her father. Each time the psychiatrist would inquire about her childhood she would become defensive and tell about their closely knit family and her closeness to her father. After weeks of no progress, she was asked to bring in a family album, which she did. She and the psychiatrist then went through the album looking at the series of photographs taken over time. As the psychiatrist was looking over the photographs he was also editing out some and rearranging others. He noticed that in most of the group photographs, his client was at one end of the photograph near her mother and her sister was at the other end close to her father. Her sister was often smiling and very often the father had his arm around her. When the psychiatrist pointed this visual evidence to her, she broke down in tears and was then able to admit to herself and to her psychiatrist the roots of her problem. This led to more productive therapy sessions and a resolution of her problem.

Photographs are statements that can be read and that provide useful information, but like all statements they must be read in context—in context with other photographs or verbal information, and in historical context, for all photographs to some extent are historical. Traditional disciplines such as sociology and anthropology, realizing the importance of photographs as a source of information, now have offshoot groups specializing in visual sociology and visual anthropology. Their research involves not only utilizing photographs others have taken but also photographs they have taken to document events.

SEMIOTICS

Yet another way to find meaning(s) in photographs is through the use of *semiotics*. Semiotics can be described as the study and application of *signs*, signs being anything and everything that conveys meaning. Think for a moment of the number of ways that meaning is conveyed: through words, numbers, symbols, color, music, dance, body language, aroma, texture, movement, movies, and on and on. Photographs are signs, signs that can convey both information and emotion.

Semiotic is the Greek word for sign.

Saussure and Peirce

Two of the early pioneers in the field of semiotics were Ferdinand de Saussure, a Swiss linguist, and Charles Peirce, an American philosopher. Saussure referred to signs as *signifiers* and the information or emotion conveyed as that which is *signified*. The flag of the United Nations, for example, is a signifier. What is signified is a gathering of nations in search of peaceful ways to solve conflicts. The familiar and famous photograph of the first man setting foot on the moon is a signifier, and one of the things it signifies is adventure, the spirit of man to conquer the unknown. The flight of the first man in space, a Russian, is another example of man's spirit. The clustering technique, used earlier with the photograph "Eventide," can also be used to arrive at the various significations or meanings of an image.

In Europe semiotics is called semiology. Their meaning is the same.

Charles Peirce described a *sign* as a relationship between an object or idea, how it is *represented*, and how the object or idea is communicated. This relationship can be visualized as a triad shown in Figure 10.5.

Sporting events display a variety of signals and signs (codes), many of which are not understood by the opposing team or the spectators.

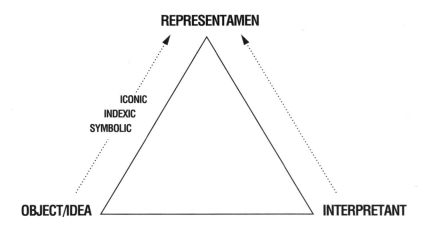

Figure 10.5   Charles Peirce's triad. There are three ways to represent something: iconically, indexically, and symbolically.

Semiotics is an old concept that can be traced back to the writings of St. Augustine in about the year 397.

In Peirce's triad, the object or idea is what is signified and the signifier is the *representamen* (represent + amen), a word Peirce coined. A photograph is a representamen or sign. The *interpretant* (interpret + ant), another word he coined, is the process of interpreting the representamen—that which represents or signifies the object or idea. In concrete terms, the object might be a product such as an automobile, the idea being to represent it as something luxurious. The representamen would be a photograph taken in such a way as to suggest luxury. The process of interpretation includes the person looking at the photo/ad along with how and where the photo/ad was exhibited—in an expensive magazine, in *USA Today*, *The New York Times*, in a slick brochure, on television, on a billboard, or whatever.

Representation

Representation is the process of having one thing stand for another.

According to Charles Peirce, there are three ways to represent something: *iconically*, *indexically*, and *symbolically*. In an iconic representation the representation looks like the object. A photograph of a car looks like a car. An indexical representation is an indirect reference, such as the shadow of a car or the wet tread marks of the tires left on a dry road. A symbolic representation would include the car's logo.

Fossil remains are indexical, as are train whistles, police sirens, and the like.

Other examples of indexical representations are a person's fingerprints, the smell of smoke, a fragrance in an empty room, an empty chair on the porch of an old home, footprints on a sandy beach, an arrow or finger pointing to something. In short, an indexical representation is an index to something else. Indexical representations are often more interesting than iconic ones, for they are more involving.

Symbolic representations are culturally agreed upon things, our language being a prime example. Words are symbolic, as are flags of different countries, crests, logos, religious symbols, trees, animals, and colors, among other things.

The three methods of representation are not mutually exclusive. For example, a picture of a serpent or snake is iconic but it can also, depending on context, be symbolic of sin or temptation. A tree is a tree but it can also symbolically represent life (as in the tree of life), or strength (an oak tree); the rock of Gibraltar is a rock but it's also a symbol for security and safe haven. The color red of a traffic light means one thing but the color red on a flag or in a photograph of a sunset means something else.

Another point to be made is that an iconic representation can have various levels of iconicity. On a scale of 1 to 10, a color photograph would be a 10, a black-and-white photograph about a 5 and a line drawing about a 1 or 2. As a general statement, the more you show the less interesting it becomes. Always try to leave something for the imagination.

Indexic

Symbolic

Analyzing an Ad

A semiotic triad can be used to interpret the photograph of the model in the Fidji perfume ad shown in Figure 10.6.

Looking at the photograph (the original is in color) and free-associating as in the clustering technique, a number of descriptive words are found.[11] By editing them down to about four they suggest that the ad is *sensual*, *sophisticated*, *exotic*, and *androgynous*. How is this so? What is it about the photo/ad (a representamen) that conveys this? We can find an answer to this by identifying the iconic, indexic, and symbolic elements in the photo/ad that suggest sensual, sophisticated, exotic, and androgynous.

Sensual

Iconic: Partially opened lips, long flowing neckline, long loose hair
Indexic: Feminine finger pointing to the product
Symbolic: Interlocking fingers, warm red, amber, yellow colors

Sophisticated

Iconic: Elevated face, fancy bottle laced and sealed
Indexic: Paris address, placement of the ad in *Vogue* magazine
Symbolic: Serpent as danger and risk (take a chance)

People's behavior makes sense if you think about it in terms of their goals, needs, and motives.

Thomas Mann

Figure 10.6   *Fidji advertisement. A semiotic analysis of this photo/ad reveals the way in which the various elements convey its exotic, sensual, sophisticated, and androgynous qualities. The original ad was in an array of rich warm colors. (Courtesy Guy Laroche, Paris.)*

Exotic

Iconic:	Foreign-looking flower in upper left
Indexic:	Paris, France, Fidji (Fiji) islands
Symbolic:	Native woman, serpent (Garden of Eden), text is in French—"Fidji: le parfum des paradis retrouves"—(paradise regained with Fidji perfume)

Androgynous

Iconic:	Female: face, neck, fingers, fingernails; Male: flat chest, broad shoulders
Indexic:	Ad is half light (female) and half dark (male)
Symbolic:	Yellow flowers and finger interlocking; male and female forms, long phallic neck

Not everyone will agree with this interpretation and that is to be understood, for perception is a personal matter. A good photograph or advertisement is one that is layered, one that lends itself to several meanings. Semiotics provides yet another way to get a handle on what photographs and advertisements convey.

Designing a Photograph for an Ad

This semiotic procedure of interpreting a photo/ad can be used in reverse as was done with the clustering technique earlier. It can be used to plan a photograph for an advertisement. Given information on what is to be signified to sell a product (romance, nostalgia, power, guilt, sexiness, Americana, and so on), give some thought to the kind of iconic, indexic, and symbolic elements (props, signifiers) that would work well together, including the model or models (casting), the lighting, styling, and so on.

Perception is personal. We see what we see.

Richard Fahey

The use of semiotics, as well as clustering and free-association, is not limited to photographs and advertisements but can be applied to any medium being used to convey meaning.

Semiotic Operations

The terms *syntax*, *semantics*, and *pragmatics*, borrowed from linguistics, can be used in a visual mode. Syntax refers to the visual grammar, the design or composition of a photograph—how the various elements are arranged to convey a particular message. Semantics refers to the meaning that the reader/viewer gives the photograph—what is signified. Pragmatics refers to the context in which the photograph is viewed, which includes not only the space or environment in which it is displayed but also the time in history. Some photographs that were not considered of importance years ago are now valued as art.

The empires of the future are the empires of the mind.

Winston Churchill

If one changes the syntax of a photograph or the pragmatics, the meaning (semantics) will change. In this way photographs can be altered or displayed differently to clarify, amplify, or alter their statement. There are four distinct and practical ways to change the syntax of a photograph or other form of communication and expression:

1. Add something to the message.
2. Subtract or remove something.
3. Substitute one thing for another.
4. Exchange one element for another.

As an example, consider the Fidji ad in Figure 10.6, and how the meaning of the advertisement can be altered by using any of these four operations or combination thereof. Here are some possibilities:

1. Add a bust line to emphasize the sensuality of the model and therefore the product.
2. Remove the serpent or the flower, two important signifiers that suggest temptation and the sexual act.

Flower as
metaphor

3. Substitute a red, yellow, or white rose for the exotic flower shown. Flowers and colors are signifiers that can alter what is signified. (Barbara G. Walker writes, "There is an old maxim: the language of flowers is the language of love. It is true not only in a metaphorical sense, but also in the sense of botanical biology, since flowers are the genitalia of plants. Perhaps the beauty of flowers is not the only reason, then, that they so often symbolize human sexual relationships. The arum plant called a Jack-in-the-Pulpit in the United States had many European names that identify it as a *lingam yoni* symbol more than anything else."[12])

4. Exchange the position of the flower and the serpent. Now the serpent crawls out of the forest of the model's hair.

BC (Before Computers), changing the syntax of a photograph required great manual skill on the part of a retoucher. Now, with the aid of computers and appropriate software, photographs can be scanned and digitized, lending themselves to all kinds of manipulation. Capturing a photographic image is only the beginning of the creation of an image. Using semiotic operations of addition, subtraction, substitution, and exchange allows the photographer to "postvisualize" the image, change its syntax and therefore its meaning.

Other Applications

A lecturer and consultant to businesses on how to think creatively bases his technique on the notion that every new idea is simply a variation of something that already exists. His advice for creating new ideas is the same as that for semiotic operations: Combine something with something else, eliminate something, substitute one thing for another, rearrange something.

Some examples of how these techniques can be used on word statements will reveal their usefulness:

DOG
DODGE
DO
LOG
GOD

- The Sesame Street program "Monsterpiece Theater with Alistair Cookie" is a playful example of substitution and addition, a play on the early successful TV program, *Masterpiece Theater* with Alistair Cook.
- New book titles are sometimes a play on familiar clichés. With a simple substitution, *Fountain of Youth* becomes the title for an optimistic book on aging titled, *Fountain of Age*.

- A decorative and humorous book on women's bras uses addition to connect it to the familiar German design school, The Bauhaus. The title of the book is *Brahaus*.
- A book called *A World Without Women* features a back cover with the familiar 1504 painting of "Adam and Eve" by Albrecht Dürer. The front cover has the same painting, except that the picture of Eve has been air-brushed out.
- Clichés can be put to good use in coming up with new ideas. "Pay now or pay later" can be given a religious tone using addition of one letter, "Pray now or pay later."
- "One if by land, two if by sea, three if by World Wide Web (WWW)" gives a well-remembered historic and patriotic call a contemporary twist.
- The first day of an international golf game held in Rochester, New York, in 1995 began on a rainy day. On the sport page a photograph of a golfer swinging his club in a drizzling rain was cleverly captioned, "Swinging in the Rain."

Add

Subtract

Substitute

Exchange

What is also significant in all of these manipulations is the use of the semiotic code of recognition. In creating any new message there must be some level of recognition—something that will connect with information and emotions held in memory. Perception is a process that is memory-dependent. The new message should pull something out of memory and add something new and novel.

For example, I recall a political cartoon depicting the growing influence of the religious right that shows a representative pushing and turning the letter "p" upside down, in the letters, *gop*. As the "p" is inverted, it is exchanged for the letter "d" and the billboard now reads, *god*.

Many cartoons, political and humorous, use these simple semiotic operations.

The power of these operations comes from their universal application to all forms of message creation and communications. One can even make a game out of these operations that can be a fun way to spend an evening with a friend or friends. For example, football is a game that attracts quite a following. The culmination of the football season is the Super Bowl. If you're sitting down for dinner during the game it becomes the Supper Bowl. If you're cheering a team that has just made a touchdown, it becomes the Super Howl, and so on.

In 1919, Duchamp, in a satire on art, added a mustache to the Mona Lisa and titled it L.H.O.O.Q., which, reads "look" in English, and something else in French.[13]

For the November 1967 cover of Esquire *magazine, George Lois used a portrait of Svetlana Stalin, who had defected to the United States, and added her father's mustache.*

There is an art of reading, as well as an art of thinking, and an art of writing.

Isaac D'Israeli

Right makes might.

Abraham Lincoln

Might makes right.

Anonymous

RHETORIC

Rhetoric has been defined as the art and study of using language in an effective and persuasive manner to influence the thoughts and actions of listeners. It relies heavily on rhetorical devices such as metaphor, simile, and illusion.

This traditional definition seems to restrict oratory to the written and spoken word. In a larger sense, rhetoric deals with any and all means of communication—persuasive communication. In this day and age persuasive communication is highly visual—pictures, pictures combined with musical background, and depending upon the message, voice-overs. Films, animations, multimedia, and advertisements in particular, all use rhetoric. If we extend the concept of rhetoric to visual imaging, it can be, and has been, most useful.

In 1970, a French researcher, Jacques Durand, reported on an extensive and systematic study on the use of visual rhetoric in advertising, which is applicable to any visual message. His analysis of thousands of ads provides a very useful rhetorical matrix for analyzing the syntax of an ad, photograph, or any visual statement, and also for showing how easily one can alter pictures and words to modify or change meaning.

For each semiotic operation of addition, subtraction, substitution, and exchange there are five things that one can do to alter the message in a particular direction. For example, in the case of addition, one can add:

- Identical elements   (A A)
- Similar elements   (A a)
- Different elements   (A Z)
- Opposing elements   (R Я)
- Ambiguous elements   (B)

Which one of the five elements is added will determine how the meaning of the message is altered. Durand developed a Rhetorical Matrix (Figure 10.7A) to show these relationships. You will note that he uses the word "suppression" rather than "subtraction." Suppression can be partial or complete, which would be total subtraction. Also note that Similarity and Opposition have two subcategories; form and content.

Figure 10.7B looks a bit more complex, as it adds the various rhetorical terms used to identify each rhetorical operation. These operations can be applied to any form or combination of forms of communication. Some of the terms, such as *hyperbole* and *metaphor*, are familiar, while many others are not, and some are tongue twisters.

What is important here is not the peculiar terms used to describe each operation, but the operation itself. One will recognize that these operations are used routinely in computer manipulations of images. Durand's rhetorical matrix provides a map that can be helpful in deciding which operation to use to emphasize or alter the meaning of a visual message.

Palindrome:
A word (or sentence) that is spelled the same backward and forward, such as radar, level, civic, noon, tenet, eye.

Relation between elements	Rhetorical operation			
	Addition	Suppression	Substitution	Exchange
1.Identity				
2.Similarity				
Form				
Content				
3.Difference				
4.Opposition				
Form				
Content				
5.False homologies				
Ambiguity				
Paradox				

Figure 10.7A   Jacques Durand's rhetorical matrix (1970).

Metonymy:
A figure of speech in which the name of one thing is substituted for the name of something that can be associated with it. Example: The "mustache" looks suspicious (in a detective movie, the villain often has a mustache).

Relation between elements	Rhetorical operation			
	Addition	Suppression	Substitution	Exchange
1.Identity	Repetition	Ellipsis	Hyperbole	Inversion
2.Similarity				
Form	Rhyme		Allusion	Hendiadys
Content	Simile	Circumlocution	Metaphor	Homology
3.Difference	Accumulation	Suspension	Metonymy	Asyndeton
4.Opposition				
Form	Zeugma	Dubitation	Periphrasis	Anacoluthon
Content	Antithesis	Reticence	Euphemism	Chiasmus
5.False homologies				
Ambiguity	Antanaclasis	Tautology	Pun	Antimetabole
Paradox	Paradox	Preterition	Antiphrasis	Antilogy

Figure 10.7B   Rhetorical matrix with identifiers

Ernst Haas (right) with professor John Head and students at a 1985 exhibit of his work in the RIT Photo Gallery. One of the freshman students, puzzled as to why his recent work was exclusively of flowers, asked, "Mr. Haas, why are you photographing flowers?" After a quiet moment of reflection, silence, and student anticipation, he replied quite honestly and simply, "I like flowers." "Ernst Haas." Photo by Richard D. Zakia

KEY WORDS

bipolar adjectives
clustering
critiquing
evaluation
free-association
iconic
indexic
interpretant
open-ended critique
personal photography
Photo Therapy
picture-word-word association
potency
pragmatics
projection
representamen
semantic differential

Language can become a screen which stands between the thinker and reality. This is the reason why true creativity often starts where language ends.

Arthur Koestler

semiotics
signified
signifier
signs
symbolic
syntax
validity
variability
word-word association

Critiquing Photographs Exercises

1. Word Critique

Every discipline has its own specialized vocabulary for describing things and it is no different with critiquing. Compile a list of the words and phrases most frequently used to critique artistic work in the fields of photography, painting, sculpture, music, film, video, dance, theater.

A good place to start is by looking through the Sunday Art and Leisure section of a major newspaper such as *The New York Times, Washington Post, Philadelphia Inquirer, Los Angeles Times*, or in magazines such as *Time* or *Newsweek*.

Try relating the words and phrases in writing a critique about your own photographs or those of others. Being able to verbally articulate your photographs can be helpful in promoting your work, but never let the words interfere or take precedence over the photographic statement.

2. Clustering

Use the clustering technique on one of your photographs or on someone else's that interests you. Begin by using a centering word to literally identify the photo and then, looking at the photograph, do a word association. Now edit the words to about four descriptors and use these descriptors to talk or write about the photograph. You may want to do the same exercise in a group setting to take advantage of the group dynamics and the rich exchange of ideas.

All the arts appertaining to man have a common bond.

Cicero

3. Location Preparation

Use clustering to prepare for a location shoot. Decide on the location, have it become your centering word, and then free-associate around it. Collapse the words to about four word descriptors, and then photograph on select locations based on those words.

After the work is printed and edited, compare the photographs with the themes you intended to record.

4. Semantic Differential

Put together your own semantic differential scale or use the one in this book to have friends rate one or two of your photographs. Before you do, however, rate the photograph yourself. Compare your assessment with those of your friends. Where you agree will be of interest but of greater interest will be where there is disagreement. Search out the reason for the disagreement. Sometimes the problem is simply a different interpretation of the bipolar adjectives. Other times it is the fact that we see the photograph differently, we see it from our own personal point of view. Once the photograph is exhibited or published, the photographer has no control over how his photograph will be interpreted by others.

5. Famous Photographs

Use the semantic differential with friends to rate some famous photographs that are of interest, depending upon the type of photography you practice: fine art, documentary, photojournalism, landscape, nude, advertising, technical, scientific, biomedical, architectural, forensic, and so on.

6. Applied Semiotics

Find an ad that has a strong photographic presence. Using free-association, list several words that you feel signify the intent of the ad, and then identify the relevant iconic, indexic, and symbolic elements to support the words you have chosen.

7. Props As Signifiers

Look over photographs and advertisements that interest you. Study them and make a list of the iconic, indexic, and symbolic signifiers that you think can be useful to you in your future work. Then record what each signifier signifies. You may want to organize your list under different categories such as trees, animals, flowers, birds, fruit, body language, and the like.

8. Individual Critique

Seek out an instructor or knowledgeable friend with whom you find it easy to relate and are comfortable with, and ask him or her to look over your work. A one-on-one critique and dialogue can be a very rewarding experience (Figure 10.10).

*Be ever so soft
and pliable like a
reed, not hard
and unbending
like a cedar.*

The Talmud

*Figure 10.10   An individual critique can provide a more
intimate understanding of your work than a
group critique.*

Notes

1. Robert Hughes, *The Shock of the New*, New York: Alfred Knopf,
    1981, p. 113.

2. Stephen Carothers and Gail Roberts, *Photographer's Dialogue*, Boca
    Raton, FL: Boca Raton Museum of Art, 1989, p. 106.

3. Ibid., p. 114.

4. Ibid., p. 119.

5. Ibid., p. 116.

6. Ibid., p. 105.

7. Sarah Whitefield, *Magritte*, London: The South Bank Centre, 1992,
    p. 35.

8. Robert Frost, *The Complete Poems of Robert Frost*, New York:
    Holt, Rinehart and Winston, 1968, p. 131.

9. Gabriele Lusser Rico, *Writing the Natural Way*, Los Angeles, Jeremy
    P. Tarcher, 1983.

10. C. Osgood, G. Suci, and P. Tannenbaum, *The Measurement of
    Meaning*, Urbana, IL: University of Illinois Press, 1971.

11. Mihai Nadin and Richard Zakia, *Creating Effective Advertising Using Semiotics*, New York: The Consultant Press, 1994, p. 101.

12. Barbara Walker, *The Woman's Dictionary of Symbols and Sacred Objects*, San Francisco: Harper and Row, 1988, p. 422.

13. Robert Hughes, op. cit., p. 66.

Appendix A
Additional Concepts

If metaphor is a verbal strategy to evoke images, then as a photographer I'm interested in combining images to alter associations by extending the image itself...It is this act of transformation, interactivity between images, that I find the most challenging.

Nathan Lyons

"Tina Tan" Photo by Cheng-Sung Chan

Aftereffect   The change in perception that occurs after looking at a bright and contrasty image, such as a line graphic on a video screen, and then looking away from it. For example, looking at a curved line for some time and then looking at a straight line can make that line appear curved and bending in the opposite direction. (See also Waterfall Effect.)

Afterimage   The visual image that is experienced after looking at a bright and contrasty image for some time, and then looking away from it. The image is seen as similar in shape but complementary in color, or in the case of black-and-white images, reversed in tonalities. The more intense the light source used for looking at the picture, the longer the duration of the afterimage.

Agnosia   Introduced by Freud in his writings, the word means the absence of recognition. A person afflicted with agnosia can identify the characteristics of an object, but fails to recognize what the object is. In visual agnosia, for example, a person looking at a face can identify all the facial features but cannot recognize the face. In auditory agnosia, a person can hear but is not able to interpret sounds, including speech.

Allusion   A pointed reference to something or someone, either directly or implied—an indexical sign. (Refer also to Indexical.)

Many people are strong in anima— full of imagination, close to life, empathetic and connected to people around them.

Thomas Moore

Anima and Animus   "Jung called the persona the 'outward face' of the psyche because it is that face which the world sees. The 'inward' face he called the *anima* in males and the *animus* in females. The anima archetype is the feminine side of the male psyche; the animus archetype is the masculine side of the female psyche... Every person has qualities of the opposite sex... in a psychological sense of attitudes and feelings."[1]

Androgynous   The combination of both male and female characteristics in one person. In mythology the Asian Androgyne, Hermes and Aphrodite were a united deity and called Hermaphroditus.

Aspect Ratio   The format proportions for motion pictures and television are normally expressed as *aspect ratios*, obtained by dividing the width by the height. (See also Golden Section.)

The numbers below represent the shorter dimension divided by the longer for comparison with the golden section. The aspect ratio for television and conventional motion pictures is 1.33 (0.75). Wide-screen motion picture aspect ratios range from 1.8 (0.56) to 3.0 (0.33).

Film Formats Arranged in Increasing Aspect Ratios

Format	Ratio
6 × 12 cm.	0.50
24 × 36 mm., (6 × 9 cm.)	0.67 (Golden Section)
2 1/4 × 3 1/4 in.	0.69
3 1/2 × 5 in.	0.70
5 × 7 in.	0.71
6 × 4.5 cm.	0.75 (film, video)
11 × 14 in.	0.79
4 × 5, 8 × 10, 16 × 20 in.	0.80
2 1/4 × 2 3/4 in.	0.82
6 × 7 cm.	0.86
6 × 6 cm.	1.00

Bit   A contraction for binary digit. It is the primary unit for measuring information. The bit is an on-off, 1-0, yes-no decision. In imaging, it is the number of tones that can be displayed in a digitized image. A 7-bit image can display 128 tones including black-and-white ($2^7 = 128$).

Byte   One byte contains a group of 8 bits.

Caduceus   A universal emblem of the medical profession having its origin in Mesopotamia. Intertwined snakes represent a healing god.

Chiaroscuro   The arrangement of dark and light, shadows and highlights, in a picture. (From two Italian words meaning light and dark.)

Chimaera (chimera)   A demonized monster from classical mythology.

Cognitive Dissonance   Inconsistent thoughts that can cause a person, in an effort to favorably resolve differences, to distort or otherwise alter the facts. For example, a person buys a photograph as an investment for a large sum of money only to find out later that it is ordinary and not worth much. Embarrassed, the person then tries to justify the expenditure in terms other than money.

Color Preference   Although color preference is a personal matter and somewhat culture-dependent, in general, studies find this order of preference: BLUE, RED, GREEN, VIOLET, ORANGE, YELLOW.

Color in its tremendous variety of hues and shades organizes our feelings according to precise connotations related to whatever society generated them and reads them in a codified manner.

Massimo Vignelli

Common Fate   The Gestalt principle in which visual elements that function, move, or change in unison will tend to be grouped and seen as a pattern or movement (similarity of movement).

Constancy   The perception of the attributes of an object, such as color, shape, size, and lightness do not change much, even though the viewing conditions may change. For example, with color and lightness constancy, objects look the same indoors as they do outdoors, even though the lighting is quite different in color balance and intensity. This of course is not true for films, and it is the reason for having outdoor and indoor film types.

Direct Perception   Perception requiring little cognitive processing. For example, the letters AA are identified as being the same faster than are the letters Aa.

Doppelganger   "A visual hallucination in which the 'other person' is recognized as being oneself. The concept of the phantom 'double' seems to have perturbed mankind since ancient times. It figures in folklore and fairy tales throughout the world, and is still prevalent in the religious beliefs of many primitive societies."[2]

Eidetic Imagery   A somewhat rare visual effect in which a vivid and accurate memory image that is capable of being scanned persists after looking away from what is being looked at.

Eye of Horus   This symbol appears on the back of every United States one-dollar bill and represents an Egyptian solar deity —an all-seeing deity.

Expectancy   A condition in which a person is more receptive to seeing what he anticipates or wants to see rather than what is.

Feature Detectors   A specific cluster of receptor cells in the retina that are excited by stimulus configurations such as lines, angles, curves, color, and movement.

Fibonacci Numbers   A series of numbers created by adding the number that follows to the number that precedes it: 1, 2, 3, 5, 8, 13, 21, 34, 55, and so on. The series represents a mathematical equivalent of many of the spiral shapes in nature such as seashells, sunflowers, and galaxies.

Golden Section and expanding logarithmic spiral

Gestalt Therapy   A holistic problem-centered approach to psychotherapy giving equal emphasis to mind and body and taking into consideration environmental factors. It is noninterpretative and nonjudgmental. It is sometimes referred to as family therapy.

Golden Section   A ratio of proportions between two dimensions of a plane that is approximately 3 to 5, an aspect ratio of 0.60. Similar proportions are evident in photography, film, and video. (See also Aspect Ratio.)

Hallucination   A false perception in which one experiences something that is not there—perception without the presence of an object. These false perceptions can occur in any sense modality: seeing, hearing, tasting, smelling, touching. (See also Negative Hallucination.)

Hallucination: From the Latin hallucinan, *meaning to dream, to wander in mind.*

Hybridization   A term used by René Magritte to describe two familiar objects combined to produce a third interesting, engaging, and bewildering one.

Hypnagogic and Hypnopomic (pre-sleep and post-sleep)   "The drowsiness experienced as one falls asleep, and again as one wakes up, is often accompanied by pronounced imagery... The intermediate state between wakefulness and sleep is referred to as *hypnagogic*; that which precedes full wakefulness after sleep is termed *hypnopomic*..."[3]

Both types of dream images are vivid and realistic, and their content sometimes bizarre. Hypnagogic images are most often visual or auditory but they can occur in any sense modality.

"The most common type of hypnagogic imagery is probably 'faces in the dark' which often terrify children as they are falling asleep, and which are also reported by some adults. The 'faces' are often distorted in size and shape, and may be in bright but unnatural colors."[4]

A dream is the shadow of something real.

Aborigine aphorism

Just-Noticeable Differences (JNDs)   The threshold of sensory response, in which a very small increase in intensity is required to see or not see, hear or not hear something.

Lingam-Yoni   The lingam-yoni is a symbolic carved altar stone of the male and female genitalia. Joined together, the symbol is a spiritual representation of the integration of both sexes representing the generating power of the universe. It is commonly found in Hindu temples. In western countries it is often misinterpreted since many symbols are culturally defined. Edward Weston's photograph of the dancer Fay Fuqua[5] may suggest such a symbol.

The isomorphic commercial equivalent of the lingam-yoni, the joining of the sexes, can be found in western advertisements (see Figure A.1).

Mandala   The Sanskrit word *mandala* means "circle" in the literal sense, usually a concentric arrangement of geometric

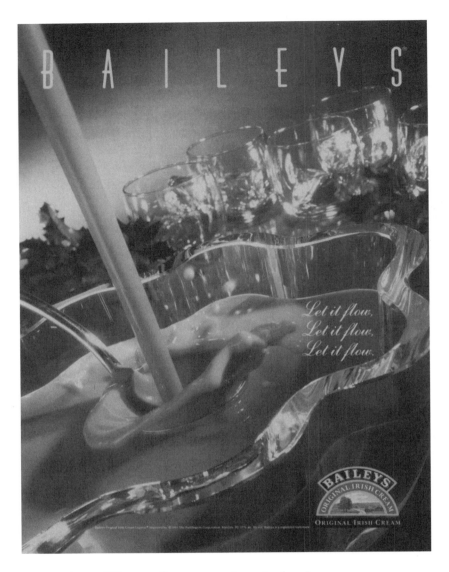

Figure A.1   Western lingam-yoni equivalent?

A Simple Mandala

shapes. As a religious symbol it represents wholeness as symbolized by any circular image that is painted, drawn, modeled, or danced. The lotus flower and stained glass rose windows found in churches are examples.

Mandalas can appear in dreams during periods of stress and conflict. Frequently they contain a multiple of four, in the form of a cross, a star, a square, and so on.

Mandorla   Two intersecting circles suggest a union of two worlds, the physical and the spiritual. Seen in a vertical position, the circles take on the shape of an almond, a symbol for the female genital, suggesting fertility and maternity.[6]

Maslow's Hierarchy   Abraham Maslow's hierarchy of needs proceeds from our very basic need for physical survival to our spiritual and psychological needs. Our basic needs must first be provided for before we can advance to other needs. Maslow's hierarchy, in order from the physical to the spiritual, are:

(1) Physiological needs (such as food and drink);
(2) Security and stability (shelter);
(3) Belongingness (love, affection, identification);
(4) Esteem (recognition and self-respect); and
(5) Self-fulfillment or self-actualization (being oneself).

Spiritual

Physical Needs

Maypole   A large erect pole decorated with ribbons around which May Day dances are performed. During the dance the ribbons become interwoven to represent the decking of the pole with colorful leaves, flowers, and fruit; all gifts from the moon goddess, giver of fertility.[7]

Metaphor   A figure of speech that provides an understanding of one thing in terms of another—having one thing represent another. For example, a feather can serve as a metaphor for lightness; a daisy for freshness. The term is from the Greek, *metapherein*, meaning "to transfer."

Misoneism   An unreasoning fear and hatred of new ideas.

Myth   "Any real or fictional story, recurring theme, or character type that appeals to the consciousness of people by embodying its cultural ideals or by giving expression to deep, commonly felt emotions."[8]

Negative Hallucination   "In ordinary visual hallucinations the subject 'sees' something which is not there; in negative hallucinations he apparently does not 'see' something that is."[10]

Oxymorons   A figure of speech that combines contradictory terms such as: holy war, paying guests, taped live, perfect mistake, plastic silverware. A visual oxymoron is one that includes contradictory elements in a picture such as a blatantly sexy model wearing a cross, a star of David, or other religious symbol.

Pareidolia   "Most people with strong visual imagery have seen pictures in the fire or in clouds. They would probably describe this activity as daydreaming or imagining. But strictly speaking it

The first function of a mythology... is to waken in the individual a sense of awe, wonder, and participation in the inscrutable mystery of being.[9]

Joseph Campbell

Myths and dreams are heroic struggles to comprehend the truth in the world.

Ansel Adams

involves misperception of an external stimulus, and so is classed as an illusion, the technical term for which is *pareidolia.*"[11] (See also Rorschach.)

Parks Effect   The perception of a complete image when a picture or word is passed behind a narrow slit aperture. If the picture is stationary and the slit is moved rapidly a complete undistorted image is seen. If, however, the slit aperture remains stationary and the picture is moved, the image is compressed. The reason for this is probably that the successive slit images are incident on the same part of the retina producing a masking effect. (See Figure A.2.)

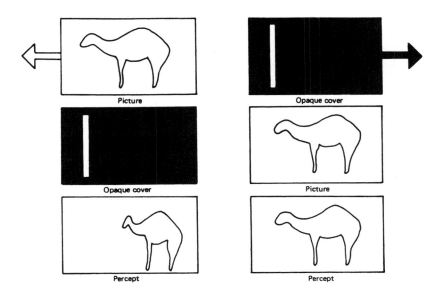

Figure A.2   *Moving a picture rapidly behind a stationary slit-aperture (left) produces the perception of a complete but compressed image. This has been called the Parks Effect. Moving the slit-aperture rapidly in front of a stationary picture (right) produces a complete and normal appearing image.*

Perception   A psychological process that includes sensation, memory, and thought and results in meaning such as recognition, identification, and understanding.

Perceptual Defense   A psychological process by which we use our perceptual system to avoid threatening stimuli. Perceptual defense is a form of repression, an attempt to prevent unpleasant situations from reaching conscious awareness.

Perceptual Dissonance "Dissonance is created whenever a person is confronted with information that is inconsistent with his expectations...[Imagers] by design introduce dissonance into their work to create visual tension. The viewer attracted by this, becomes involved, and finds pleasure in reducing tension."[12]

Persistent Image A visual image of high fidelity and short duration that is seen immediately after the stimulus has been removed. (See also Afterimage and Aftereffect.)

Phi Phenomenon The appearance of motion when two similar visual stimuli, somewhat displaced in position, are observed briefly with a short time interval between them.

Pulfrich Effect If an oscillating pendulum is viewed with one eye covered by a dark sun glass or filter, it will appear to trace an elliptical path, giving the sensation of depth. The information received by the brain through the filtered eye, being of less intensity, is delayed causing a spatial displacement. (During a Super Bowl football game some years back a TV commercial was specially designed to give a 3-D effect when viewed with one eye filtered.)

Art is a lie that makes us realize the truth.

Pablo Picasso

REMs Rapid eye movements during sleep signify a person is in a dream state.

Rhetoric The study and application of the artful, effective, and persuasive use of verbal or visual language.

Rorschach "The 'inkblot' test devised by the Swiss psychiatrist Hermann Rorschach. The shape of the blot can serve as a stimulus for free-association; in fact almost any irregular free shape can spark off the associative process. Leonardo da Vinci wrote in his *Notebooks,* "It should not be hard for you to stop sometimes and look into the stains of walls, or ashes of a fire, or clouds, or mud or like places, in which...you may find really marvelous ideas."[13] (See also Pareidolia.)

I cannot see or write or hear—I have nothing left but the will—and that I have in abundance.

Francisco de Goya

Sensory Deprivation A severe reduction in the variety and intensity of environmental information received through our sense receptors. In extreme prolonged cases, a person will become disoriented and begin to hallucinate. We are part of, connected to, and dependent upon our environment.

Stroop Effect Perceptual interference caused when a person is given a series of color names such as red, green, blue, yellow, and brown that are printed in contradictory colors, and asked to name the color, *not* the word. For example, the word red is in green, the

word green is in brown, and so on. The person seeing the word
must not name the word but rather the color of the word. This is
a difficult task at first but with practice, a person learns how to
filter out the word and respond to the color. The Stroop effect calls
attention to the fact that it takes time to learn new things,
particularly when they interfere with our established habits.

Applied to pictures, the Stroop effect suggests that it takes time
to accept the representation of objects in colors that are not
common to the object. For example, a green sky, purple grass, a
red lemon, a blue apple. Look at some of the paintings of Paul
Gauguin.

We see, hear, smell, and taste many things without noticing them at the time....

Carl Jung

Subliminal Perception   A response to a stimulus that is below the
level required for conscious perception. The hypothesis that visual
and auditory information can be processed without ever having
conscious representation. Subjective experiences, neurophysi-
ological and behavioral research support this hypothesis. Early
philosophers such as Aristotle, Democritus, Socrates, and Leibniz
were aware of this phenomenon and took it for granted.

Synchronicity   A term introduced by Carl Jung to describe meaningful coincidences in which an unconscious inner event such as a
dream is realized in a physical outer event concurrently or at a
later time. Jung referred to synchronicity as an acausal connecting
principle.

Here are two examples of synchronicity:

1. A person vacationing in Boston has a dream or envi-
    sions that someone has just broken into her apartment
    in San Francisco. Later it is confirmed that the event
    did occur, and at the time it was envisioned.
2. A person has a premonition that while traveling on a
    cruise ship two weeks hence, a fire will occur. Two
    weeks later, while on the ship, the event actually takes
    place as imagined.

These events, according to Jung, are not just mere coincidences
but rather *synchronistic* events—dreams or premonitions that
somehow connect to an outer event and are noncausal, that is, not
cause and effect. The inner event (the dream or premonition) did
not cause the outer physical event (the robbery or fire).

When I hear Bach in my photographs, I know I've succeeded.

Edward Weston

Synesthesia   The ability of one sensory input to affect another is
called *synesthesia*. In a 1993 article in *Wired* magazine, Nicholas
Negroponti wrote, "One of the most frequently cited studies
conducted by the [MIT] Media Lab was authored by Professor

Russ Neuman, who proved that people saw a better picture when sound quality was improved. This observation extends to all our senses as they work cooperatively."[14]

The Three Graces "The conventional image of the three naked Graces (Charites), the center one with her back to the observer, occurs again and again throughout Greek and Roman art, and similar figures are even found carved on Hindu temples. It was apparently one of the most popular pictures of the Triple Goddess, all three of her aspects seen as beautiful, joined together as one, like all divine trinities."[15]

Verbal Imagery The ability of words and phrases to arouse visual or other sensory images. A sampling of such words is here listed:

Seeing: colorful, bright, dim, dark, hazy, smoky, milky, clear, glaring, murky, blinding, dull.

Hearing: loud, soft, dulcet, piercing, melodious, raucous, cacophonous, dissonant, shrill, reverberating, throbbing, rhythmic, hollow, dull.

Feeling: sore, soft, warm, cold, moist, dry, hot, sticky, throbbing, texture, dull, excruciating.

Tasting: sweet, sour, bitter, salty, foxy, smoky, tart, spicy, hot, moist, dry, sharp, stringent, citric, musty.

Smelling: acrid, pungent, mephitic, putrid, sweet, spicy smoky, musty, fetid, rotten, fragrant, flowery.

And what is word knowledge but a shadow of wordless knowledge.

Kahlil Gibran

Visual Masking "When pictures or other images are presented in quick succession, the alteration or even elimination of the perception of one image by an immediately preceding or following image."[16] In a moving image such as a film or video, a single frame, preceded or followed by quite a different image can alter or eliminate the information on the other frame.

Visual Thinking "Visual thinking is problem solving with visual imagery, and involves the receiving, storing, retrieval and processing of pictorial information. These operations can be carried out consciously or subconsciously, voluntarily or involuntarily."[17]

To see means to see in relation…

Rudolf Arnheim

Waterfall Effect "In 1934 a Mr. R. Adams wrote in a British philosophy journal about an optical effect known as the waterfall illusion. The effect is evoked by staring steadily at a rapidly moving object—a waterfall is ideal—and then quickly glancing at a stationary object such as a tree. For a brief period of time the tree will appear to surge skyward, in a direction opposite to the flow

The waterfall illusion was first described by Aristotle

The essence of symbolic language is that inner experiences... are expressed as if they were sensory experiences.

Erich Fromm

of water."[18] If one looks at concentric rings spinning and expanding outward and then shifts his or her gaze, the rings will appear to reverse directions and move inward.

The human perceptual system strives to establish equilibrium by creating aftereffects that are opposite to the physical stimuli. This perceptual phenomenon seems akin to the biological phenomenon called homeostasis, which monitors the body to maintain equilibrium.

Word Imagery, Concreteness, and Meaningfulness   In an article by Allan Paivio and others an extended study was conducted to classify and quantify 925 nouns in terms of their imagery, concreteness, and meaningfulness.[19] Following are some examples:

IMAGERY

> *High*: acrobat, boy, car, dawn, elephant, fire, girl, honeycomb, ink, jelly, kiss.
> *Low*: adage, banality, chance, context, ego, fallacy, greed, hindrance, idea, jeopardy, knowledge.

CONCRETENESS

> *High*: lawn, mountain, nun, ocean, painter, queen.
> *Low*: love, malice, necessity, opinion, panic, quality.

MEANINGFULNESS

> *High*: research, season, tempest, university, valley, warmth.
> *Low*: rosin, savant, temerity, unreality, vanity, wench.

In captioning a photograph, choice of words is important since words serve to cue the intentions of the photograph. Ansel Adam's famous "Moonrise Over Hernandez" would probably elicit a different emotion if it were titled, "Moonrise Over Graveyard." A caption becomes part of the photograph. The name given to products can influence purchasers.

Words are symbolic and are associated with meaning, and trigger emotions, particularly high-imagery words. When the Eastman Kodak Company changed the name (not the product) of one of their films to "Royal Gold" there was a substantial increase in sales and customer satisfaction. Naming is important to perception. The Shakespearean question, "What's in a name?" can be answered, "Quite a lot!" A rose named "Pretty Pink" would not be as popular as one named, "Paradise Pink," nor would it "smell as sweet." Naming is part of the gestalt in everything we choose to produce or purchase.

Zoetrope ("Wheel of Life")   The zoetrope was the forerunner to movies and animation. It consisted of a series of narrow apertures arranged as a wheel. When the wheel was spun slightly, different pictures could be seen through consecutive slits, which gave the perception of movement. It was invented in the 1830s by William Horner, an English mathematician. Motion pictures were first shown in Paris, in 1895, by Louis and Auguste Lumière (see also Phi phenomenon).

Notes

1. Calvin S. Hall and Vernon J. Nordby, *A Primer of Jungian Psychology*, New York: New American Library, 1973, p. 46.

2. Graham Reed, *The Psychology of Anomalous Experience*, Boston: Houghton Mifflin, 1974, p. 53.

3. Ibid., p.37.

4. Ibid., p.38.

5. Amy Conger, *Edward Weston Photographs*, Tucson, AZ: Center for Creative Photography, University of Arizona, 1992 (Figure 555).

6. J. E. Cirlot, *A Dictionary of Symbols*, New York: Philosophical Library, 1983, p. 203.

7. M. Ester Harding, *Woman's Mysteries Ancient and Modern*, New York: Harper and Row, 1975, p. 45.

8. William Morris (ed.), *American Heritage Dictionary*, Boston: Houghton Mifflin, 1980, p. 869.

9. Alexander Eliot (ed.), *Myths*, New York: McGraw-Hill, 1976, p. 10.

10. Graham Reed, *Psychology of Anomalous Experience*, p. 52.

11. Ibid., p. 43.

12. Les Stroebel, Hollis Todd, and Richard Zakia, *Visual Concepts for Photographers*, London: Focal Press, 1980, p. 64.

13. Carl Jung, *Man and His Symbols*, Garden City, NY: 1983, p. 27.

14. Nicholas Negroponti, "Virtual Reality: Oxymoron or Pleonasm?" *Wired*, December 1993, p. 136.

15. Barbara Walker, *The Woman's Dictionary of Symbols and Sacred Objects*, San Francisco: Harper and Row, 1988, p. 256.

16. Les Stroebel, et al., *Visual Concepts*, p. 156.

17. Ibid., p. 44.

18. "The Waterfall Illusion," *Scientific American*, July 1995, p. 18.

19. Allan Paivio, John C. Yuille, and Stephen A. Madigan, "Concreteness, Imagery, and Meaningfulness Values for 925 Nouns," *Journal of Experimental Psychology* Monograph Supplement, Vol. 76, No. 1, Part 2, January 1968.

Appendix B
Answers to Selected Exercises

What is material, tangible and permanent to most people is ephemeral to me. Change is what I believe in. It is the essence of learning, growth and creativity.

Wynn Bullock

Phoenix (mixed media) © Andrew Davidhazy.

CHAPTER 1: SELECTION

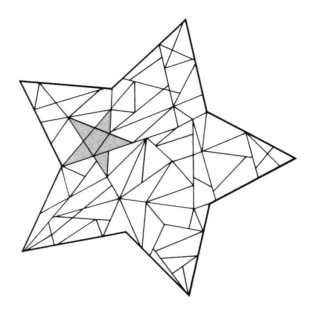

Figure B.1   Answer to the Star visual search.

CHAPTER 2: GESTALT GROUPING

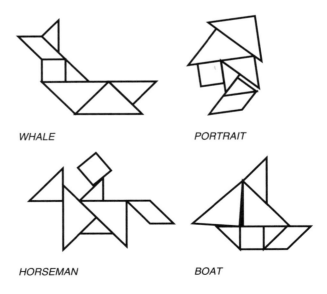

WHALE   PORTRAIT

HORSEMAN   BOAT

Figure B.2   Answer to Tangrams.

Answers to "Don't Be a Square"

Most people see the dot array as forming a square. This is predictable based on the Gestalt laws of similarity, proximity, continuity, and closure. Unconsciously, then, one assumes that the problem must be solved within the confines of that imaginary square. The moment this position is taken, the person is trapped and the problem is not solvable. Force yourself to think and see things in different ways, and by doing so you will produce new and exciting pictures. Look around at images you find interesting and creative and ask yourself why you find them so.

I have always been impressed with the plastic qualities of American Indian art....Their vision has the basic universal of all real art.

Jackson Pollock

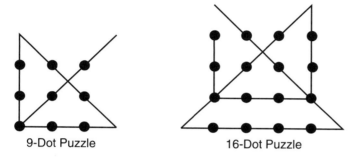

9-Dot Puzzle   16-Dot Puzzle

Figure B.3   An important perceptual lesson can be learned from these simple puzzles. Do not impose limitations or constraints upon yourself. Be imaginative, organize things differently, avoid habit. Sharpen things instead of leveling them and you will see and experience more.

CHAPTER 7: MORPHICS

Answer to "Swedish Gate" problem

If you tried to form a word out of the anamorphic letters on the gate in Stockholm, Sweden, you experienced the same problem I did at first. The letters do not spell out a word or words but rather they display the alphabet.

Bibliography

Art is a conventionally accepted reality in which, thanks to artistic illusion, symbols and substitutes are able to provoke real emotion.

Sigmund Freud

The Courtyard, Paris   © Dawn Tower-DuBois

269

Arnheim, Rudolf. *To the Rescue of Art: Twenty-Six Essays*. Berkeley, CA: University of California Press, 1992.

Arnheim, Rudolf. *The Power of the Center*. Berkeley, CA: University of California Press, 1982.

Arnheim, Rudolf. *Art and Visual Perception*. Berkeley, CA: University of California Press, 1974.

Berger, Arthur. *Seeing Is Believing*. Mountain Valley, CA: Mayfield, 1989.

Bloomer, Carolyn. *Principles of Visual Perception*. New York: Design Press, 1990.

Campbell, Joseph. *The Inner Reaches of Outer Space*. New York: Harper Perennial, 1988.

Cohen, David. *The Secret language of the Mind*. San Francisco, CA: Chronicle Books, 1996

Conger, Amy. *Edward Weston Photographs*. Tuscon, AZ: Center for Creative Photography, University of Arizona, 1992.

Dixon, N.F. *Subliminal Perception: The Nature of the Controversy*. New York: McGraw-Hill, 1971.

Ehrenzweig, Anton. *The Hidden Order of Art*. Berkeley, CA: University of California Press, 1971.

Eliot, Alexander. *Myths*. New York: McGraw-Hill, 1976.

Escher, M.C. *Escher on Escher: Exploring the Infinite*. New York: Abrams, 1989.

Fontana, David. *The Secret Language of Dreams*. San Francisco, CA: Chronicle Books, 1994.

Fontana, David. *The Secret Language of Symbols*. San Francisco, CA: Chronicle Books, 1994.

Green, Johnathan. *The Garden of Earthly Delights: Weston and Mapplethorpe*. Riverside, CA: California Museum of Photography, 1995.

Gregory, Richard, ed. *The Oxford Companion to the Mind*. New York: Oxford University Press, 1991.

Hulten, Pontus, et al. *The Arcimboldo Effect: Transformations of the Face from the 16th Century to the 20th Century*. New York: Abbeville Press, 1987.

Image, Object and Illusion. San Francisco: W.H. Freeman, 1974 (Readings from *Scientific American*).

Jung, Carl. *Man and His Symbols*. Garden City, NY: 1983.

Kohl, Herbert. *From Archetype to Zeitgeist*. Boston: Little Brown, 1992.

Leppert, Richard. *Art and the Committed Eye: The Cultural Function of Imagery*. Boulder, CO: Westview Press, 1996.

Marx, Kathryn. *Right and Left Brain Photography*. New York: Amphoto, 1994.

McCloud, Scott. *Understanding Comics*. New York: Harper-Collins, 1994.

Morris, Desmond. *Manwatching*. New York: Abrams, 1977.

Nadin, Mihai and Richard Zakia. *Creating Effective Advertising Using Semiotics*. New York: The Consultant Press, 1994.

Noth, Winfried. *Handbook of Semiotics*. Bloomingdale, IN: Indiana University Press, 1990.

Rand, Paul. *Design Form and Chaos*. New Haven, CT: Yale University Press, 1993.

Robin, Harry. *The Scientific Image*. San Francisco: W.H. Freeman, l993.

Shepard, Roger. *Mind Sights*. New York: W.H. Freeman and Co., 1990.

Solso, Robert. *Cognition and the Visual Arts*. Cambridge: MIT Press, 1995.

Sontag, Susan. *On Photography*. New York: Farrar, Straus and Giroux, 1977.

Stafford, Barbara Maria. *Good Looking*. Cambridge, MA: The MIT Press, 1996

Steiner, Ralph. *In Pursuit of Clouds*. Albuquerque, NM: University of New Mexico Press, 1985.

Stroebel, Leslie, Hollis Todd, and Richard Zakia. *Visual Concepts for Photographers*. London: Focal Press, 1980.

Stroebel, Leslie, and Richard Zakia. *Focal Encyclopedia of Photography*. Boston: Focal Press, 1993.

Twitchell, James. *Acult USA*. New York: Columbia University Press, 1996.

Walker, Barbara. *The Woman's Dictionary of Symbols and Sacred Objects*. San Francisco: Harper and Row, 1988.

What you are is God's gift to you. What you become is your gift to God.

An African-American mother to her son, long before he became a star athlete.

Williams, Robin. *Non-Designers Design Book*. Berkeley, CA: Peachpit Press, 1994.

Zettl, Herbert. *Sight, Sound, Motion: Applied Media Aesthetics*. Belmont, CA: Wadsworth Publishing, 1990.

Index